What rea

When Bluebirds Fly:

Ameri can Institute of Health Care Professionals: *Grief Counseling involves dealing with some of the most painful moments in life. The most painful moment is a loss of a parent's child. Deveny, in her book When Bluebirds Fly, examines the post-loss period. Taking from her own painful loss, she creates a story of how loss can cripple a family and drive them down paths of guilt, drugs, and possible divorce.*

~ ~ ~ ~ ~

Ed Huyck, Lakeshore Weekly News: *Audiences, in general, will find a gripping story as the family struggles with the aftermath of the death, which included marital problems, alcohol and gambling abuse, and bankruptcy.*

~ ~ ~ ~ ~

This book is well written and very lyrical in its style. Easy to read and hard to put down. A good primer for anyone who wants to do the right thing for someone in this situation. It's not easy to know how to treat someone who has experienced a loss and this book gives one insight into the intimate feelings of the ones grieving for their loss. Do not pass this one up. (Amazon.com 5-star review)

~ ~ ~ ~ ~

When Bluebirds Fly: Losing a Child, Living with Hope is such a touching story and experience and so beautifully written. This book was given to me as I had just lost a friend. Nothing could be harder than losing a child but JoAnn opens her heart and her family to us to understand how loss effects each of us differently. Most important is that eventually there is hope in life again. This book is good for the heart and soul. (Amazon.com 5-star review)

~ ~ ~ ~ ~

When Bluebirds Fly by JoAnn Deveny is a heart-warming read about the loss of a child and how it affects parents, grandparents, and so many close to the child and family. When Bluebirds Fly takes the reader on the journey of the author's grief after the loss of her child. I feel this book has the power to help so many people in similar situations — to let them know they are not alone in their grief and pain. I highly recommend this book for anyone who has dealt with the loss of a child. (Amazon.com 5-star review)

~ ~ ~ ~ ~

I shed many, many, tears as I read this book—yet I couldn't put it down. I knew the author years ago and the story about her tragic loss...I even knew the ending. But I now realize I didn't know a thing. Not really. I didn't have the slightest idea of the depth of her paralyzing grief, that she was in a place so unbearably low that even breathing became difficult. JoAnn writes with incredible honesty, holding nothing back from her readers. She takes us through every gut-wrenching minute of the horrible day

Billy died—when she basically died along with him—and then takes us through a detailed account of her long and painful journey of healing.

Page after page we find ourselves cheering Dick, Danny, and JoAnn on—we so badly want them to find happiness again. And, by the grace of God, they do heal. And along the way, we learn to be more compassionate, more empathetic, more appreciative, more faithful, more faith-filled. We come out of this book a better (if not at least a different) person for having read it. (Amazon.com 5-star review)

~ ~ ~ ~ ~

I could not put this book down. It was very powerful and real. The way Joann wrote this book was a way that you really felt like you gained an appreciation for the pain people go through when losing a loved one. Especially a child. Thank you Joann for taking time to write this and I am certain it will touch many lives in the future and give people light in their darkness. (Amazon.com 5-star review)

~ ~ ~ ~ ~

I couldn't put this book down! Not only do you learn how deep the grief is of losing a child traumatically, but how to be sensitive to those that have and how the entire family unit is effected. JoAnn is not only a talented writer but has amazing strength, insight, and faith. Great book for those who have lost a loved one, book clubs, emergency personnel, pastors and hospital chaplains,---for EVERYONE! (Amazon.com 5-star review)

~ ~ ~ ~ ~

It usually takes me several weeks to read a book. JoAnn's book took me only 1 week. I could not put it down. JoAnn & Dick's journey from beginning to end was not only heart-wrenching but amazing. I can't begin to imagine the pain and sorrow they experienced. I would highly recommend this book to anyone who has lost a child, no matter at what age. JoAnn, you are an amazing woman and an inspiration to us all. Thank you so much for the willingness to share your life and the life of Dick, Danny, and most importantly, your precious baby boy Billy. (Amazon.com 5-star review)

~ ~ ~ ~ ~

When I did put it down, it was all I could think about. If you have ever lost someone or know someone who has lost a loved one, you need to read this book. It is heart-wrenching. It is heart-warming. It is enlightening...I don't have the words. JoAnn lets us see everything her family went through with a talent that I obviously don't have. I love this book. What a strong woman you are, JoAnn. (Amazon.com 5-star review)

WHEN BLUEBIRDS *Fly*

LOSING A CHILD, LIVING WITH HOPE

Other books by JoAnn Kuzma Deveny

99 Ways to Make a Flight Attendant Fly—Off the Handle:
A Guide for the Novice or Oblivious Air Traveler
www.99ways.net

WHEN BLUEBIRDS *Fly*

LOSING A CHILD, LIVING WITH HOPE

JoAnn Kuzma Deveny

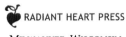 RADIANT HEART PRESS

MILWAUKEE, WISCONSIN

Over the Rainbow (from "The Wizard of Oz"): Music by Harold Arlen. Lyrics by E.Y. Harburg, Copyright © 1938 (renewed) Metro-Goldwyn-Mayer, Inc., © 1939 (renewed) EMI Feist Catalog, Inc. , All rights controlled and administered by EMI Feist Catalog, Inc. (publishing), All rights reserved. Used by Permission.

Everything Grows: Words & Music by Raffi Cavoukian & Debi Pike, © Copyright 1987 Homeland Publishing. Nettwerk One Music Limited, All Rights Reserved. International Copyright Secured. Used by permission of Music Sales Limited.

Six Little Ducks: Words & Music by Raffi Cavoukian, © Copyright 1977 Homeland Publishing, Nettwerk One Music Limited. All Rights Reserved. International Copyright Secured. Used by permission of Music Sales Limited.

Tears in Heaven: Words and Music by Eric Clapton and Will Jennings. Copyright © 1992 by E.C. Music Ltd. and Blue Sky Rider Songs. All rights for E.C. Music Ltd. Administered by Unichappell Music, Inc. All rights for Blue Sky Rider Songs Administered by Irving Music, Inc. International copyright secured. All rights reserved. Reprinted by Permission of Hal Leonard Corporation.

Billy's Song: Music by Jennifer Kuzma Adamczeski, text by Jennifer Kuzma Adamczeski & JoAnn Kuzma Deveny

Published by Radiant Heart Press, an imprint of HenschelHAUS Publishing, Inc.
2625 S. Greeley Street, Suite 201, Milwaukee, WI 53207
www.HenschelHAUSbooks.com
Please contact the publisher for quantity discounts and permissions.

Publisher's Cataloging-In-Publication Data
(Prepared by The Donohue Group, Inc.)

Deveny, JoAnn Kuzma.
When bluebirds fly : losing a child, living with hope / JoAnn Kuzma Deveny.
p. : ill. ; cm.
Includes bibliographical references.
Issued also as an ebook.
ISBN: 978-1-59598-195-0
ISBN: 978-1-59598-196-7 (ebook)

1. Children--Death--Psychological aspects. 2. Parental grief. 3. Bereavement--Psychological aspects.
4. Brothers and sisters--Psychology. 5. Spiritualism. I. Title.
BF575.G7 D48 2012
155.9/37   2012948535

Cover design by EM Graphics, LLC
Author photograph by Momento Images

Printed in the United States of America

Dedicated to my son, Danny — my reason to live

In memory of my son, Billy — my anticipation for the next life

Foreword

*L*ife is a gift that provides many joys and innumerable pleasures. But life also delivers unwelcome surprises. Occasionally, it even hurls us abruptly into horrific realities. Like the death of a son during a routine family weekend.

As an emergency physician, I chose a profession that is intimately involved with many similar scenarios. While treating people with acute injuries or illness, we often see lives that change—literally—in a heartbeat. We make a significant difference for many, but some events have gone beyond our abilities. Yet life goes on, for better or worse.

More than twenty years ago, during the final stages of my medical training, I was resting in a little boat on a local lake when life delivered an abrupt, jolting reality. There was a call for help, and consistent with my training, I responded. Many others responded as well and we did everything possible, but an eighteen-month old boy ultimately died. A precious life was lost.

With that, we lost hopes, dreams, and aspirations, and we dealt with many sobering issues. Worse than that, there were no answers to the most compelling questions: "Why? Why now? Why us? What if...? Why Billy?"

We knew that parents and family would be left with a lifetime of grieving and recovery. Their choices and adjustments would pave the way for their future, for better or worse. What path would they take? Would they find healing and hope again?

When Bluebirds Fly is about a courageous journey—a journey that connects us to memories, experiences, questions, and even pain that is inherent in any loss. In a unique way, this book gives a bold and authentic voice to feelings and experiences that are often unspeakable or worse yet, never spoken. It encourages us to find a voice of our own and eventually, find resolution. The journey is difficult, but if navigated well, it leads to genuine healing.

For me, a fateful day on a little boat resulted in an unexpected, yet remarkable deepening of my professional commitment to patients and families. I had already chosen to focus on medical emergencies, helping to impact people's lives when the very worst was happening to them. However, this experience gave me a much more meaningful connection to those who experience unexpected losses, and I'm more convinced than ever that our most enduring gift is not just our knowledge and skills, but our compassion and our willingness to stand beside others in times of greatest need. For as long as it takes.

This book stands in the name of hope and healing. It is a gift that will embolden all of us.

Thanks, Billy. And thanks to your wonderful family.

Randy Pilgrim MD, FACEP, FAAFP;
CEO and Chief Medical Officer,
The Schumacher Group

Prologue

*I*t was the brightness that drew me to him. While the beacon of light inebriated me with its warmth, I tried to move closer to its source. Even though I felt detached from an earthly existence, I thought of my family left behind. But I chose to stay there in the brightness, because somehow I knew they'd be fine without me. I never wanted to leave that place or the comfort of his presence at the end of that tunnel of light. It was difficult to articulate a physical description of him, but I knew without a doubt whose presence I was in.

Then He spoke. "There is a better place," a strong, but gentle, voice whispered. The words didn't seem to originate from his lips or travel on sound waves to my ears, but I heard them clearly.

My eyes flew open and I woke up. Even though the ceiling above me and weight of the blanket over me were familiar, I knew that it had been more than a dream. The experience was like no other before. The warmth of the light was still there.

For a moment, I lay basking in its comfort until my vision cleared. I glanced at the incompetent alarm clock on the miniature refrigerator next to the bed...five minutes to get ready for my first class. Despite my tardiness, there was a lingering feeling of complacency as I rolled out of the narrow twin bed and placed my feet on the cold tile floor. While navigating through the clothing tossed about the small dorm room, I couldn't shake the surreal feeling that my dream had left behind. How odd.

With the sleeve of my sweatshirt that served as pajamas, I wiped the smudges and dust from the tiny mirror inside the closet door and examined my face for blemishes or mascara smears, finding it acceptable for a casual collegiate occasion. There was no time for primping.

Knowing it wouldn't be difficult to play incognito in that morning's class of five hundred students, I merely hid my long blonde hair under a bandana, fashionable for the '70s. Thrown over the desk chair only hours before were my timeworn blue jeans, which I stumbled into while simultaneously searching through my overstuffed dresser drawer for a pair of clean crew socks.

Attending a college that was larger than my entire hometown had not been an easy transition. Suddenly finding myself an unknown among a multitude of students had left me feeling insignificant. But I had persevered and by the end of my freshman year, I felt comfortably at home in my new surroundings. And then in an untimely manner, my high school boyfriend dumped me, which sent me into a deep abyss of loss and rejection.

But, that morning, the strange dream seemed to ladle me from that quagmire and set me out to dry in the glow of its light. Things already appeared brighter.

The dream portrayed two things to me: there was something better than my present life and there was indeed a loving God. At that moment, I believed this completely, because I had been there in the light and He had told me so.

An urgent pounding at the door brutally snapped
reverie.

"Jo, are you awake!" Katie, my dorm-mate yelled throu
"Are you going to Psych' class this morning, I'm heading out!"

"Hold on, let me grab my backpack...wait for me, I'm
moved forward and left my dream behind.

William Joseph Deveny,
Welcome on your first day in this world! You're beautiful, innocent, fragile. Welcome to a world that may break you and your shell will not protect. I want to shelter you and hold you tightly in my arms forever. But I can't, neither can your mother or father.

  I love you, hope for you — thank you, little child.

Oh, the joy that you brought us
The gifts that you gave
The light of your presence
Will shine in your name
Will shine every day
—Billy's Song

Chapter 1

The world was still a friend to her. Nothing seemed out of place that morning, so the day started as any other while hiding its monumental secret. There was no warning that a blanket of darkness would smother the sun on that bright, summer day, leaving behind a wretched chill. It was a day of brightness and a day of darkness. Her eyelids flew open as she suddenly awoke at 5:30 a.m.

"Mamaa...Mamaaa...," your voice cried from across the hall, not a desperate call, but instead, a playful beckoning. It was always that way, because you knew that she would spring from her bed and appear through the door before the third summons left your lips. This routine had become a game for you and a necessity for her. Being that experience is always the teacher, your past attempts to scale the boundaries of your crib were etched in her mind. She knew that time was of essence once our youngest son woke up in the morning.

Your determination was great; even a few head dives to the floor and entrapment within the four-inch space alongside the dresser didn't stop you. You had become quite a spunky adventurer at the tender age of eighteen months.

I, on the other hand, was a rare contender in your game. As much as she was trained to leap from our bed, I was conditioned to sleep through your calls when she was there. Even you knew that, Billy. Consequently, if the onset of your cries didn't produce a mother at your bedroom door, you deduced that she was not within the vicinity of your little world. Then you would call for me, your "Dahdee."

Though I usually woke at the fourth—possibly fifth—cry, I'll never forget the morning when I pushed my luck and delayed beyond the boundaries of a toddler's patience. The moment I opened my eyes, your face was positioned a few inches from mine, sheepishly displaying an eight-toothed grin. As you giggled, your smile burst with the pride of accomplishment. Needless to say, that's when I started shutting your door at night when your mother was away. I had no need to discover where your explorations would take you while I was unaware in my sleep.

Remember that one morning, Billy, (I'm not quite sure what you remember now) when I surprised you in turn. Slowly responding to your cries, I crawled from my bed and haphazardly swung open the door to your room, thoroughly expecting you to be waiting within the boundaries of your crib. My action sent your tiny frame sailing through the air on the other side of the door. We were fortunate that you weren't hurt and you cried for only a moment from the surprise of the impact.

You would often fuss with those painful ear infections, but were durable when it came to head-on collisions. At least it seemed that your head took the lesser of the beating when ours met by accident. But no matter how attentive your mom and I were, you received cuts and bruises quite frequently. Consequently, your pediatrician had suspicions of abuse.

It angered me at first when the doctor insinuated this during an office visit because, of course, I was the suspect. After my first knee-jerk reaction to the accusation, I later appreciated his motives; he had dared to go beyond the basics of his job to protect my son.

Your mother was home as much as her job would allow her. But because she was a flight attendant, her travels left me shouldering the solitary duties of fatherhood three days a week while she was enjoying herself on overnights with her flight attendant friends. Although she would have chosen to be home if her seniority at the airline allowed her — and she wasn't enjoying herself, she would contend. And so our petty argument went. Even though we did love each other, I wish I could say that we were always in agreement. But then I'd be describing a hypothetical relationship. Ours was fairly standard as far as married-with-children goes.

So feeling unjustly burdened, I exclusively left her with the childrearing duties when she was home. Even though, I would never proclaim the title of "Mr. Mom" in your mother's presence. This would definitely test her intolerance for stereotyping.

"You're not acting as a mother in my absence any more than I'm a Mrs. Dad when you're gone," she would adamantly insist. When she was away on her trips, I was merely being a good dad.

Your mother tolerated more than some wives would have, so sometimes I allowed her an occasional explosive moment. Yet, I can't deny that they created some tense disagreements between us, to put it mildly. I'm usually a patient man in my sobriety. But that's another subject—this is her story, not mine.

A day of brightness and a day of darkness.

Half asleep, she sprang from our bed and stumbled through your bedroom door before the third call left your lips. As a reward, she was greeted by your smiling face peering over the bars of the crib in the corner of the room. Nothing could bring more instant gratification than those genuine, innocent smiles from her children.

When she leaned over your crib, you simultaneously wrapped your little hands around her neck and pulled yourself over the railing into her waiting arms. She placed your squirming torso down, and the legs attached sprang into action as though they had a life of their own. Like a battery-operated toy without an "off" switch, you scurried directly to your older brother's bedroom door. You were either "on" or asleep; there was no in-between. Trying to arouse your favorite playmate, you pounded your tiny fists against the hollow veneer door and bellowed his name before your mother could stop you.

"Dah-nee...Dah-nee!" You repeated your big brother's name until your mother swept you away from his bedroom door. Unless you needlessly woke your brother, it was just you and your mother in the early hours of the mornings. This was your bonding time as Danny and I slept unaware of the sunrise. And your mother's quality time with your big brother was in the evening once you were tucked in bed for the night.

After being redirected from your brother's room, your next stop would always be the kitchen. You were forever hungry and always eating. That day, a banana pacified your hunger while your mother nuked the usual frozen pancakes and sausage breakfast. A video of animated vegetables brightened the living room while you sat in front of the television in your toddler-friendly rocking chair. With a bottle dangling from your lips, you rocked to the beat of the singing asparagus on the screen.

As most parents of two children, we had adopted lazy parenting techniques with our second. So you were placated as our first never was. One could often find you in front of the television with either a pacifier or juice bottle quenching your oral needs.

At that time, the usual description of our modest home fell under the category of *disarray*. With no designated playroom for our boys, the living room became your battlefield, the bathroom acted as your munitions storage area, and the bedrooms housed your fortresses. In other words, our children ruled the kingdom.

Being "domestically challenged," your mother was inclined to overlook the cobwebs in the corner and scum layer on the baseboards. She was truly blessed with the ability to ignore dirt. Displaying her living quarters in *Better Homes and Gardens* was not one of her dreams and our meager monetary assets were spent on our kids instead of home décor. Cooking wasn't her passion either. She often claimed that she attempted to cook once a week just to make sure the smoke alarms worked.

"Women's allotment of household chores isn't due to any innate expertise," she would often say, "…and I'm living testimony that there's not an inborn desire in women to scrub slime from the floors only to have it return." Heaven forbid that I would ever buy her a vacuum cleaner for her birthday.

In your mother's defense, she wasn't raised to be a homemaker. During her upbringing, your Grandma Jen allowed her children after-school activities rather than designated chores around the house. However, your mother's older sisters claimed they were discriminatorily assigned some domestic responsibilities, which again portrays parenting differences between the firstborn and the ones who follow. Consequently, your mother's teenage years were filled with a multitude of after-school activities. Being raised as many boys were in those days, she would throw her dirty socks on the floor at night, knowing they would magically appear laundered in her dresser drawer the next day.

Grandma Jen and I didn't always agree on things, but I commend her for allowing her children to experience the boundless freedoms of youth. Uncomplaining, she tackled the majority of menial chores despite bearing five girls.

Even though your mother avoided any job that was domestic, she enjoyed any type of outside work, from painting the window sills to teaking our boat. So the interior was neglected, but our exterior was maintained. I loved her because she was different from other women, although I wouldn't have complained if I could have had it all: a strong, thrifty, sexy, comrade of outside chores (all of which she was) *and* a Stepford wife (which she was not). The dream of every man.

So your mother was never by any means lazy. Maybe this is one of the reasons I ended my expansive years of bachelorhood and married her...or maybe it was the pregnancy. Anyway, she was different from most of the girls I had dated. We shared a joke that I often repeated to others; I married her for her patio furniture and flight benefits, not her culinary skills. The flight benefits are still active and the furniture held up for many years, becoming a little tattered through the seasons. It persevered, much like our marriage.

Despite your mother's general disinterest in housework that morning, there was an apparent need to gather shrapnel from the floor before your brother awoke and a new battle began. But when she saw you rocking in that miniature chair, Billy, a diversion was found. She squatted beside you on our harvest-gold shag carpet, which harbored raisins and other small trinkets in its camouflage, forever lost in the pile forest. You jumped from the chair to snuggle into the security of her lap and you both shared a special moment together.

Being a minority gender in her home, your mother accepted the responsibility of leaving the toilet seat *up* after use. The chaotic lifestyle of raising two rambunctious boys felt natural to her after being raised in a small house among a family of six children. Consequently, she felt a certain sense of comfort with the activity level of our home and, masochistically, had dreams of bringing another child into our family. Her hopes were set on a passive girl.

At that time, your mother and I were in disagreement on the number of children we wanted. I did not want a third. We were, however, in total agreement that the number of bodies in our lakeside home outnumbered the maximum capacity of its 1,300 square feet. In the winter, we were figuratively—and you boys were literally—climbing the walls. Your Aunt Jeanne would often call you the "Vertical Boy," Billy, because you were always scaling some piece of furniture.

So a *For Sale* sign was posted in our front yard, and the search was on to find more living space for our growing children. Our real estate quest reluctantly led us to the inland areas of the Minneapolis suburbs, even though our real hope was to chance upon a larger lake home that would not deplete our children's college funds.

It really wasn't surprising that your mother had always gravitated to water. She had been raised in Hibbing, a small northern town in the heart of the Iron Range, where the Great Ice Glacier had left its pockmarks to form a majority of Minnesota's 10,000 lakes. So her love for the water grew along with her. When she and her young friends failed to hitch a ride to the nearest lake, they would set their sights within bike-pedaling perimeters. The nearest water source was a retired, open-pit mine, rain-filled with scarlet water and bottomed with layers of iron ore droppings. An old mine tower was perched in its center, which lent itself to perfecting their amateur diving techniques. To Grandma Jen's dismay, your mother would arrive home at the end of each day a bit more crimson than when she left, and not from sunburn.

There were many avenues to liquid playgrounds as she entered her teenage years. By thirteen, she joined the water ballet team, and by her fifteenth birthday, she was active on a woman's competitive swim team, which left her fingers raisin-textured through the rest of her high school years.

Brainwashed by her father, your mother knew that college was not an option, but a given. Due to the fact that there were three siblings in college ahead of her, it was necessary for her to work a few menial jobs during and after her high school education.

Being an iron ore miner's daughter, she was part of the first group of women hired to work manual labor in a mine of Northern Minnesota the summer of 1974. You could say it was nepotism that landed her a job at the Minntac Mine in Mt. Iron, Minnesota. It was a means to an end for the company—to financially assist the lifetime employees with their children's college expenses.

Though assigned to the dreariest and filthiest building on the mine site, she took on the challenge to earn union-elevated hourly pay of $12 an hour, wages which were quite high for 1974. Even though this could be why many plants went out of business, I can't deny that the long-term effects of breathing the dusty air required some financial retribution.

During her initiation, your mother needed to use every punch card minute shoveling the droppings of dirt and rock that fell off the conveyor belts. In the beginning, the women were an enigma in the dark, filthy, five-story structure and found it hard to blend in with their male coworkers. Needless to say, the supervisors kept a vigilant watch over the five female workers during their first few weeks on the job until their work soon surpassed that of the men. Consequently, this brought praises from the managers and taunts from the male workers. So your mother would often find herself the recipient of red sludge mysteriously cascading through the tiers of grates onto her hardhat.

Following the lead of their male counterparts, she and the other four women eventually learned to blend in with their environment. They hid inside the locker rooms and under the dark crevasses of the conveyor belts and slowed down their pace in order to not surpass the men. The women, in hard hats, safety goggles, and steel-tipped boots, soon became indistinguishable from the men, and side by side, they leisurely shoveled chunks of red debris in harmony. In that way, the genders learned how to *not* work together, and the men became cohorts to the women from then on. Two months after the end of that summer job, your mother was still blowing red dirt from her nostrils and reacquainting herself with the feminine skill of sitting with her knees together.

Working at the mine was the most interesting occupation your mother experienced. And it could be called educational, because she learned the skill of lifting large rocks without straining her back and how to nap without detection while balancing her weight against a pressurized hose. She also refined the art of spitting, and most importantly, she realized that a college education was necessary to escape the drudgery of those twelve-hour shifts.

To continue her higher education, your mother readily moved from the confines of her rural hometown to the metropolitan excitement of the University of Minnesota in Minneapolis. Once again, she gravitated to water by joining the women's diving team. This collegiate sport was quite a change from her belly flops off the iron ore tower into the tailings pond, but was similarly "abandoned" after crushing her wrist on the five-meter board while attempting a reverse one-and-a-half full twisting pike. So she switched to the safer sport of cheerleading, which required less practice and brought her more social enjoyment.

She was a natural athlete but not a great star, mainly because the practice ethic was not part of her make-up. Your mother felt her goals should be accomplished with little effort. So she spread herself thin by participating in everything and excelling in nothing. As your Grandma Jen kindly boasted, it made her daughter well rounded.

Your mother's academic routine was handled in the same way as her sports endeavors, so college became an expensive entertainment academy. After five years of enjoying herself at the expense of her grade point average, she obtained the minimum requirements to graduate. With her time consisting mostly of wild parties and last-minute cramming sessions, she walked away from higher education with simply enough credits to obtain an obscure Liberal Arts degree defined by a psychology emphasis. She often joked that the university made up a degree just to get her and her roommates out of college, because the BES (Bachelor of Elected Studies) degree was devised the year she graduated and was discontinued a few years later. Anyway, her super-senior roommates and she took advantage of the situation while they could. Needless to say, this indistinct collegiate diploma merely landed her a job as a flight attendant with a small commuter airline.

Because your mother was never that little girl who dreamed of becoming a "stewardess," her intentions of keeping this job were temporary. The longevity of her employment was determined by the length of time it took to rid herself of a 300-pound football player whom she had acquired in college. On the first day of meeting this hulk, she had vowed not to continue the relationship. But she found that he apparently had a magnetic, dysfunctional hold over her, which she felt both the need to maintain and escape. So it wasn't until after eight years of relocating to seven different states that the relationship finally came to an end. Knowing your mother better than anyone, I'm amazed at how spineless she was in her youth, while showing no traits of these weaknesses now. But I guess it's the adversities in life that lead us to strength and growth.

By that time, she had enough seniority at the airline to understand that her BES degree would not get her any farther than her flying career. So she took advantage of her flight perks to experience the vast world outside the sheltered confines of her upbringing. In the same way she concealed her reckless single years from her parents in the past, I'll also exclude them here. Many times I've accused her of being too honest with me; there are some things I don't need to know. I'll only say that she experienced the '80s peace and love era without restraint. I guess you got that from her, Billy. Although, I must say my Irish blood also influences that wanton behavior.

She was in between cities, working in Minneapolis and living in New Jersey, when we met on the shores of Lake Minnetonka. I can honestly boast that our meeting was the impetus that freed her from her football player and brought her back from the East Coast to the Land of 10,000 Lakes.

On that first day we met, I took her for a boat ride that neither of us will ever forget. However, it was a couple of weeks later, when she protected my boat with her legs against a algae-coated cement wall along the Mississippi River locks, that I truly fell in love with her. In turn, she said she was attracted to me because she felt safe and comfortable when we were together. On that premise, we found ourselves riding the waves of our eighteen-year marital cruise.

My preferred sport as a teenager was horse showing, which I gave up after entering college. Even though I attended the same university as your mother, we never met during that time. This was probably a blessing, because we never would have dated—I wasn't her type. Don't get me wrong; she would have found me attractive, she's told me so. But I was not a jock. I'm thankful that her athlete criterion became less important as she matured.

After I completed college, the horses were replaced by the mechanical steeds of the surf, so on the water of Lake Minnetonka I rode. You see, our lake was not only known for its aesthetic qualities, but also for its lively social atmosphere. It was, in other words, a party lake. I've often imagined sharing my "male tales" with you and Danny once you both reached an age when you wouldn't be affected by my bad example.

I enjoyed the water differently than your mother, but with as much intensity. As much as she loved the weightlessness of her body under the water, I enjoyed riding over the waves from the vantage point of a helm. But we equally felt a sense of solitude when we would gaze at that blue expanse from our chairs on the deck. Even though the windows of our neighbor's homes were a mere fifteen feet from ours, we always felt secluded while listening to the waves gently slapping against the lake-shore. I would savor a cold Bud and your mother would sip her chilled wine, both of us sharing our dreams of life, career, and children. My most cherished memories of our marriage are these shared moments and what I miss most about her.

It seemed that our attraction to the water was handed down to you, Billy. And any body of H_2O would do. You delighted in the bubbly water of our small bathtub to the mud puddle on the dirt road in front of our house. You thoroughly enjoyed, more than your mother, that fifty-yard sprint to that rain-filled pot hole after being released from our front door. Your little feet would seem to fly above the ground as you outdistanced both Danny and her during the chase.

But, like your mother, your real passion was swimming in our lake, which was only ten feet from our back screen door and five stairs down a rock retaining wall. Your body was like a compass with its magnet pointing to the wet surf instead of the North Pole. You would often climb onto our dock and race to its end, with one of us always in close pursuit. While you ran and giggled, your baggy swim trunks would inevitably slide down to reveal your tan line and a trace of your little white butt. It seemed as if you could never fill your desire for the cool lake on a hot summer day. Or did you, Billy?

I remember how every day that summer you, Danny, and your mother spent countless hours sharing the pleasures of your sandy playground. You must wonder now, Billy, if she ever learned again to love that murderous body of water beyond our back door.

JoAnn
A MOTHER JOURNALING THROUGH GRIEF

The sun crept over the horizon while you sat in the bowl of my lap, and I sang along with the video to you. "You are my beautiful baby, my beautiful baby I love." Why didn't I forget everything on my schedule that day and rock you longer? That way I could have safely held you in my arms until the sun set over the lake and that horrible day was past.

Even though the events of that afternoon seem to slowly surface in a dense fog through my thoughts, specific details of that morning are vivid. When I close my eyes at night, I see your face peeking over the shower door as you did that day. You cried when I disappeared behind the opaque door, and so Daddy lifted you up to show that I was still near. At first when seeing me, you grinned, and then you showed a puzzled expression while contemplating my comical face framed in wet, dripping hair.

Do you wonder where I am now, Honey? Does God lift you up to sneak a peek? Please know that I would never leave you. No one asked me, Precious. Momma had no choice.

Shakespeare once said, "All the world's a stage and the men and women are merely players." But when I replay the events of that day, I feel as if my world is a movie on a screen far away from my seat in the audience. I'm sitting as an observer at the edge of my chair, viewing a gut-wrenching horror flick. The characters in the movie are untroubled, and the day is routine—but the suspenseful music, scarcely evident in the background, grows more audible with each passing moment. Because of the ambience of the scene, the audience knows that some horrid event is about to occur, but the actors are oblivious.

The anxiety and suspense are so painful at times that I feel the need to leave the auditorium. Though sometimes I stay. Then I'll jump up from my seat in the audience and plead, "Don't go out. Don't leave your baby! Hug him once more!

Warn the sitter!" But the actors don't heed my warning, because they can't hear me, no matter how hard I plead.

Before viewing the movie, I anticipate the swelling lump in my throat and empty knot in the pit of my stomach, which will unfailingly appear. Still, I feel a masochistic urge to relive the scene over and over in efforts to rearrange its unacceptable ending. But everything goes according to script, no matter how many times I venture into that auditorium and watch my life unfold.

Chapter 2

DICK

*T*he curtain rose as the sky gradually brightened. The silence of the early morning was gone and the reality of a new day began.

Soon after Danny and I shuffled from our bedrooms, the Deveny family started one of our many rituals in efforts to keep you occupied, Billy. Our little marching band's instruments consisted of tot-sized Playskool horns and a few odd utensils from the kitchen that would make as much noise as possible when struck together. The parade path led us from the front door, through the living room, kitchen, dining room, and back again with the tempo accelerating with each stanza. Being the dad, I would lead, an honor even my feminist wife allowed me. My family of musicians was always in close ranks as I would methodically clap the steel pan lids together and march to the beat of the clamor. And you, Billy, would watch my every move to mimic me to the best of a toddler's capability. Your pudgy, bare legs would kick stiff and high in time with the beat, trying to reach the height of my long legs.

"Mo…Mo!" you would exclaim if we stopped for even a moment.

Our showers that morning were diligently planned as usual. While one bathed, the other guarded you. If only one of us was home, you would need to be locked in the bathroom with the bather during the process.

Although, I discovered, there was no foolproof method of keeping you safe. One morning, I pulled back the shower curtain to find you doing a perfect "Rocky" imitation on top of the commode tank—all you needed was the music.

Even before your first step at eight months, we learned that there was no protective haven for you in our allegedly child-proofed house. You could scale child gates, turn the safety covers on the door knobs, climb on top of couch backs to reach drape strings, and rattle the cupboard doors until those plastic child locks broke in two. You weren't an angry child, just impish and determined. I imagine once you saw that light at the end of the tunnel, your only motivation was to reach it no matter how many heartstrings you broke.

After our showers, I lounged on the couch and scanned the *Minneapolis Star Tribune* for the classified ads I had placed that weekend. After seven years in business, my small car leasing company was flourishing. I had ten automobiles for sale and more coming up for lease. DevCom Leasing thrived on word-of-mouth advertising, offering personalized delivery of each car by myself, the sole employee-slash-owner. My customers were pleased with my truthful, low-pressure sales tactics and competitive pricing, and so the leases were growing by leaps and bounds.

Reviewing the ads and finding them appropriate, I considered the prospect of adding an employee to DevCom Leasing's ranks. Life was good in the car leasing industry. Sprawled comfortably across the living room couch and immersed in thought, I was oblivious to Danny's battle cries and your mother's attempts to corral you for a grocery store excursion.

"I wanna go, too! I wanna go!" Danny wailed.

The weekly trips to the grocery store were always an undertaking for your mother. At that time, modern restraints were not available in the shopping carts to discourage two active boys under the age of four. While

Danny would grab any colorful item from the shelves to digitally investigate, you would scan the product orally.

Danny and your mom often chuckled when recalling your attempts to steal a juicy tomato from the produce shelf one day, only to be apprehended by a spray of mist to your bewildered face. Your fingers stopped somewhere between the broccoli and beans while you turned to look at your family with disbelief. Your lips trembled with indecision between a laugh and a cry as you shook your head to shed the droplets of water from your face. Upon hearing Danny giggle and viewing your mom's amused expression, you grinned and shared the humor of that moment with them.

So your mother usually took advantage of my presence on weekends and left one of you behind for the grocery run. Actually, I won the coin toss that Saturday. Keeping an eye on your brother was a much easier feat than keeping up with you, our eighteen-month-old Tom Sawyer.

So when Danny begged at the door to be included that morning, I didn't feel rejected. Despite a typical jealousy-lined sibling relationship, Danny felt more complete with his other half. Even when I would tease him that your two-year warranty from the hospital hadn't expired and an exchange was possible, Danny opted to keep you. A chancy game to play, but it never backfired.

"Honey, we'll be back in a little while. Daddy will read you a book...I don't know how you do it." Her attention was on me now. "How can you totally block everything out on demand?"

There was some tension in her words while she sarcastically smirked and shook her head. "You're truly blessed with a gift."

I didn't feel the need to reply. What would have been the point? I merely glanced around my paper to watch as you grabbed your mother's purse from the floor and scampered toward the front door with anticipation.

"Bah-bah!" you proclaimed good-bye to Danny and me in your little Southern accent. Being raised by Yankees and never in your life crossing south of the Mason-Dixon Line, we were forever puzzled by the slight flavor to your words.

Being diligent with practice, your throwing techniques were perfected at an early age. Beside pitching balls in the yard, you threw spoons across the kitchen, rocks down the retaining wall to our lakeshore, your pacifiers at the imaginary bull's-eye on the wall across from your crib, your toothbrush through the drain in the sink, and your mother's sewing kit down the stairs from our foyer, which you especially enjoyed because the lid would fly open and make a wonderful mess.

"Uh oh!" You would always exclaim, as though it were an accident. Your mother always reprimanded you, but was seldom harsh—excluding the time you skillfully tossed your bottle into the seal tank at the Minnesota Zoo that summer.

At the grocery store that day, you helped the cashier unload the cart with only one fatality. The squirt gun your mother picked out for Danny did a near miss at the foot of the elderly woman in line behind them. Keeping you in the cart was the priority; keeping the merchandise intact was secondary. But if she couldn't accomplish the former, the latter was nearly impossible. Your mother scolded you, which turned your grin into a pout. She remembered that with regret later. Grief bursts with regrets; that was just one of many.

At home, I paged to the weather report and then glanced over it at Danny, who was in front of the TV enraptured by a video. Guiltily, I had often used that video to babysit my eldest. Though probably not the most appropriate for a three-year-old, *The Wizard of Oz* was Danny's favorite. And even though the witch frightened him, she equally mesmerized him.

But mostly, he loved to sing along to *Somewhere Over the Rainbow,* because he knew all the words from his mother.

Returning from the store, your mother struggled through the front door, carrying you and a bag of groceries in opposite arms. You had a broken, green squirt gun in hand and one cheek was stretched into the outline of a round lollipop—its stick protruding from your bright orange lips. She harshly dropped the bag as you tried to wiggle off her hip. She shook her left hand and grimaced.

"Man, that hurts. I just slammed my finger in the car door…. I see you're right where I left you," Although she feigned teasing, I sensed a hidden rancor. Even though my relaxed nature was a product of your mother's absence during the week and the reprieve I allowed myself on her days off, I took the hint and left my spot on the couch. I approached her with a kiss and light squeeze of my hand around her waist.

"Take care of your finger, Babe. I'll get the groceries." Her demeanor warmed as she returned a brief peck to my lips.

"Man, Billy was a little hellion in the store today." She stooped to set you down. No sooner than your feet touched the ground, you scurried through the dining room to the back screen door for escape.

"Out! Out!" you demanded, while pushing against the mesh barrier with the full weight of your body.

"No, Billy. Don't push on that, Honey!" your mother scolded, trailing after you and leaving me with the groceries.

It was quite odd that you couldn't, or maybe didn't feel the necessity to say the usual toddler words like *baby* or *bottle*. Yet when your mother would come across a broken vase or a messy room, she would place her hands on her hips and inquire sternly, "Who did this?" And in turn, you would always proudly exclaim, "*Ah* did it!" Because, of course, you usually had.

Even though you weren't very vocal, your face often showed the consternation of deep meditation, as if continually planning your next endeavor. Your daycare provider often called you "Bam-Bam Billy," because you would repeatedly outsmart her. You would toss her twelve-pound cat across your shoulders and scale any obstacle that got in your way in her country blue home. For fear you might injure yourself under her supervision, she eventually felt the need to expel you from her daycare at the delinquent age of fifteen months.

So your mother and I had to frantically search for and eventually found a more Billy-proof setting in a structured daycare center — where the large room's walls kept you contained and floor mats kept you safe. A musty odor emanating from the basement of the old church permeated the first floor hallways and rooms above. After spending a day rolling on the carpeted floor, your hair and clothes became saturated with the essence of mildew. So it was never the scent of baby products that returned your memory to your mother; but when she held your musty daycare blanket next to her nose, the aroma intensified her grief.

The daycare had an enormous playground and, barring adverse weather conditions, I would find Danny and you there at the end of my workday. The moment I entered the playground, you would immediately notice me, as if your eyes had been glued to that spot throughout the day waiting for my arrival. Then you would instantly drop whatever pail, shovel, or truck you were holding and race down the wooded hill with your arms outstretched. While your little legs seemed to fly over the ground, your smile beamed and your eyes sparkled with anticipation. After jumping into my arms, you would immediately wrap both arms around my neck and turn to face your daycare providers, ensuring them of your intentions.

"Bah-bah!" While saying good-bye, your little hands squeezed my neck like a vise for fear that I would leave you behind. I'm confident that they didn't mistreat you, only that you wanted to be with me more. I would wave and smile at your caretakers, amused and proud of your precociousness.

Your mother was proud of your intelligence and physical coordination as well. Yet she would silently listen when other mothers boasted about their children, because she knew that wasn't necessary for her. She knew that you and Danny would famously accomplish great things one day, and those women would eventually find out how magnificent her boys were. Understanding that the future can't be presumed, she now brags endlessly.

~ ~ ~ ~ ~

As I retrieved the groceries from the car, I could feel the early warmth of a sunny day. On the sidewalk, up the hill from our easement, a couple with their white schnauzer walked by and waved. Even though I didn't know them, I waved back and reflected on the benefits of small-town life. In their wake, a group of preteens raced by on their bicycles, leaving shouts of laughter that blended with a whippoorwill's chirp from our neighbor's white poplar. The day was already alive with activity. While entering the house and setting down the last load of bags, I made a mental note to move up the sitter's time so we could have an extended boating day.

"Ha-woh! Ha-woh!" My trance broke, and I turned from my thoughts toward the sound of your voice. You were standing on the couch, holding the phone in one hand, while proclaiming your unique "Hello" into the receiver. While you randomly fingered the buttons on the handset, I pried the receiver from your determined hands and moved the phone from your reach.

"No, Billy, no...don't play with that!" I harshly scolded, as I had many times before for this same reason. You gave me a forced frown and stared with your wide, unblinking eyes. I couldn't help but smirk and shake my head. Your frown instantly turned to a sheepish grin, and then giggles trailed behind you as you shimmied off the couch and scurried away—enticing me to follow in pursuit. I couldn't help but remember this replay of antics.

The Saturday before, a policeman had appeared at our door to tell us that a 911 call had been made from our phone number. Your mother and I both turned around from the officer at the door to find you standing by the end table adjacent to the couch. You had the phone in hand and were babbling incoherently to the emergency operator on the other end. You were quite bright, Billy, but I can't pretend that you knew your numbers or how to dial 911 in an emergency. But somehow, you had dialed those three in sequence exactly one week before they were needed.

I continued to pile the food items on top of each other in their allotted place in our cramped kitchen cabinets. Because I had bought the house as a confirmed bachelor, the "galley kitchen" was not a deterrent to the real estate deal. Luckily, it was not a problem for your mother either; it was another excuse for her to avoid the kitchen.

After cramming the last can of corn into the stuffed cupboard, I returned to my spot on the couch and the newspaper. The Twins, led by Kirby Puckett, were on a winning streak, the Senate Crime Bill was up for vote, used-home sales were down in the Twin Cities, and the country was $3 trillion dollars in debt. Business as usual.

That summer of '91 brought us the rare visibility of Jupiter, Mars, and Venus in a triangle formation in the darkened skies at night and record-breaking temperatures on sunny afternoons. But that day, the wind blew softly, cooling the heat from the sun, motivating us to turn off the air conditioner and slide open the glass door to let in the fresh, lake air through the mesh screen.

JoAnn
A MOTHER JOURNALING THROUGH GRIEF

When I lie in bed at night, I sometimes see you through the reflection of the bathroom mirror as I did that day. The overhead lights flickered on and off while I dried my hair at the sink. This was your usual prank when I got ready every morning—to cut off my light source by flipping the finger-smudged switch on the wall across from the mirror. Even in the darkened room, your expansive grin beamed like the Cheshire cat in the mirror's reflection.

"Off!" you exclaimed. I gave your image a contrived, chastising glance just before your sticky fingers triggered the switch back into the "on" position.

"On!" Your face simultaneously lit up with the room. To reach the switch you had to shimmy onto our wicker laundry basket. The basket weave in the bathroom is indented with the imprint of a child's size-eight shoe, confirming your life and your absence.

When I force my eyes shut in efforts to sleep at night, I sometimes see you in the reflection of my car mirror, as I did that day on the way home from the grocery store. Through the reflection in the mirror, your eyes narrowed mischievously and your eight-toothed grin appeared. You began to kick your feet with unleashed excitement. An intense love was exchanged between us, and I knew that you felt the same powerful connection as I did. I saw it in your eyes.

"Oh, Ma...Maaa...," you taunted through the image in my mirror.

"Oh, Bill...eee...," I responded right on cue as we had rehearsed many times before.

"Oh, Ma...Maa...."

We played our little game until I tired of it, because you never did.

Then the air filled with deafening screams of sirens, and I slowed the car to determine their direction. As we neared our neighborhood, they grew increasingly louder.

Our neighborhood is often the recipient of fire truck traffic, being that the fire station is two blocks north of our home and our driveway abuts the only entry to the southern residential area of Phelps Island. Whenever we would hear sirens, I would lead you and Danny to the window, cover your ears, and show you the source of the noise. Things seem less frightening when they're recognized. But being unable to shield your sensitive ears with my hands from the front seat of the car that morning, I could only placate you with words.

"It's okay, Honey. Mommy's here." You disliked loud noises, possibly due to your many ear infections. You had nearly ingested equivalent amounts of Amoxicillin to milk in your eighteen months. Danny was free from ear infections, which might have been because he was breast-fed for three months and you for only one.

I'll never forget the first time you latched onto my breast, searching for comfort and nourishment—I never wanted it to end. The experience bound my love to you at that moment, and I felt as if you belonged to me. Was I wrong? Your exuberance for suckling made me feel as if you would continue to seek nourishment from my breasts and excitement from life until there was no more to experience. But, you were the one to ultimately choose the conclusion of our bottleless dining experience. I imagine this was because you were unable to examine your new world while attached to an immobile milk source. Nevertheless, I blame myself for putting you on the bottle. I've always possessed a predisposition to blame myself for my children's ailments. Now I wish I were more like your father, who doesn't have that tendency.

When we neared our block that day, the flashing lights from police cars drew my attention. Their brightness was diminished by the flames covering the entirety of our neighbor's home across the street from ours. It was evident that there would be no hope for salvage. Flames were licking the upstairs window sills, the front door was blackened and splintered, and the street-side walls were toppled; reminiscent of the cross section of a miniature doll house. Seeming a total intrusion of privacy, the bedroom beds and dresser drawers were exposed to all.

Unknown to me at that time, there would be two more three-alarm emergencies for the small city of Mound that day. July 13th—a triangle of tragedies. Jupiter, Mars, and Venus.

Chapter 3

DICK

*A*s your naptime grew nearer that morning, your temperament wavered. Your mother hurriedly prepared your lunch, and we all ate our last meal together.

We were often entertained by watching you eat, Billy. We found it interesting how you would dip your French fries in ketchup, only to suck the sauce off until the soggy potato stick disintegrated from kid spit. At the conclusion of each meal, you would unfailingly announce it by draining your milk cup over the highchair tray. Though it should have been quite predictable, we could never stop you in time.

Most of your meal ended up in your hair, nose, ears, or on the adjacent china cabinet, even though you could skillfully maneuver the miniature eating utensil with either hand. You were naturally right-handed from birth, but became ambidextrous after your dominant hand received third-degree burns a few months earlier. In our defense, I must say that you were extremely quick.

We could only conclude that your arm must have grown overnight, because you could never reach the full expanse of the bathroom counter before that incident. But on that St. Patrick's Day, your mother belatedly pried the curling iron from your hand seconds before the pain was acknowledged by your brain and after the heat permeated the palm of your hand. She watched in horror as your face morphed from a smile, to surprise, to shock, and then anguish. The piercing screams sent me tearing from bedroom to bathroom, to find your mother in her evening attire holding your body over the sink while forcing your hand under the flow of cold streaming water.

"It's okay, Honey. Mommy's here. Everything's all right." Even though I could barely hear her words through your shrieks, the edge of panic in her voice was clear. Our little leprechaun had been surprised by his own mischief that St. Paddy's Day.

All the Deveny boys, big and small, were part Irish. However, your mother's clan, the Kuzmas, was purebred Yugoslavian. At this time, the Croatia and Slovenia heritage was still considered a part of that empire, and your mother was half of each. Like most non-Irish unfortunates, your mother always wanted to claim the Irish blood on March 17th—which, in fact, she was truthfully allowed in 1987. When Danny was a two-month old fetus inside her womb on that particular St. Paddy's Day, she liked to declare that she had a "wee bit 'o Irish" in her.

To your Grandma Deveny's dismay, your mother and I were not yet married on that St. Paddy's Day of 1987. Actually, we were not even speaking to each other. But I must tell you, Billy, we were very much in love.

Being the eternal bachelor, I had not quite reached the maturity level that my thirty-four years should have produced. Even your mother would admit that her responsible, maternal instincts only kicked in after experiencing your brother's kicks to her womb. I wasn't afforded that sensation, so continued to ignore her pregnancy to the best of my ability. Yet she inflicted no guilt or pressure toward me as she determinedly planned her future as a single mother. She had come quite a distance since her spineless, fugitive years of the 1970s.

Well, I've always been stubborn, but never stupid. I was totally in love with the woman. No sooner than she became independent from me, I realized I couldn't afford to lose her or the baby. From that Mother's Day of 1987 on which we were engaged, and forward, I never looked back nor regretted my decision.

Amazing both your mom and myself, once the decision was made, I jumped feet-first into marriage and fatherhood. So we were married in July, took our Honeymoon in August, and had your brother Danny in September. For me, fatherhood came as love at first sight and with very little prodding from your mother, I agreed to a second child.

Even as a fetus, Billy, you would cause turmoil within your cramped quarters. As with Danny's powerful kicks to her ribs, she also complained about your aerial somersaults and the nausea that followed. During her pregnancy with you, your mother received an interesting contraption from a friend. It was a cloth sash with a speaker woven inside its seams, and it, supposedly, transmitted her voice through the womb. After running sodas to the masses at 30,000 feet, at the end of her work day, your mother would often kick up her swollen feet, don her audio belt, and serenade you with the help of the attached cassette player. All the songs on the cassette tape were soothing instrumental pieces, but your mother knew all the words to only one—*Somewhere Over the Rainbow*. That was the lullaby she sang to Danny every night.

"Somewhere over the rainbow, way up high, there's a land that I heard of once in a lullaby…" she would sing through the wires attached to the belt on her swollen belly and rock her chair in time to the beat. Being a skeptic at heart, I didn't believe that you could hear as a fetus. But then I was like that about most things back then. Now I've found that validation is not always tactical.

Immediately after entering the world at 3:51 p.m., January 16th, 1990, your stomach and lungs were suctioned by the medical staff in response to a condition known as meconium staining of the uterus. As explained to me in layman's terms by the doctor, this merely meant that you had defecated before birth. You were even impatient as a fetus.

As soon as I cut your lifeline to your mother, you were stolen away through the doors of the birthing room with an urgent silence trailing your departure. I was allowed to follow and anxiously observed as the professionals stuck tubes down your stomach and lungs to remove the excrement. Because of chafing to your throat, I returned you to your mother with your desperate, muffled squeals. Failing to placate you, I readily laid you in her arms. For the first time, your mother cuddled your blanketed body into the crevasse of her body and nestled your rounded head under the protection of her cheek. Your muffled cries determinedly continued until the familiar voice that had echoed through the walls of your solitary home returned.

"It's okay, Honey. Everything's all right. Momma loves you." The determined beseeching of our newborn abruptly halted while she whispered her first words to you outside the womb; her theory was proven.

I leaned over your mother to watch as your lips eagerly latched onto her breast. You sucked heartily, as though you had done it many times before. My thoughts drifted to another miraculous moment two years and four months before when your brother was born. When examining his wrinkled, slight forehead, and widespread eyes for the first time, I had the sensation of always knowing him; Danny definitely resembled your mother's side, mostly Grandpa Joe due to his baldness.

It was different with you, Billy; more like gazing into a mirror. You were a miniature Dick Deveny, so much like me. A familiarity washed over me as I studied your high forehead, sloping nose, and sculptured chin while you sucked from your mother's breast for the first time. My second child, another boy. Though I was disappointed, for a moment, that fleeting thought haunted me later. How could I have been dissatisfied, even for a second, on the day of your birth when the pain of your death ended up defining me?

The abrasions in your throat left us with a newborn whose cries were no more audible than a raspy squeak of a mouse. That worked for me, because it took more than that to wake me. Even your mother imagined one heavenly night of undisturbed sleep—if only the baby monitor could be set to *off*. Yet she continued to station the receiver next to your crib and its speakers on the night stand next to her pillow so your slight shrieks could be heard every two hours throughout those first sleepless, nighttime marathons.

~ ~ ~ ~ ~

"Time for your medicine!" Your mother positioned herself in the kitchen with a dropper of pink, gooey liquid in hand. Right on cue, you raced through the door with your head tilted back and mouth opened. Aiming the dropper about three feet from the ground, she squeezed the dosage out of the tube—chancing to hit her moving target. Weeks later, that half-empty bottle of Amoxicillin would taunt her from the refrigerator every time she opened the door. It seemed to be in suspension—waiting for you to run back through that kitchen again. She couldn't force herself to dispose of it; every parent knows not to throw antibiotics away before the dosage is finished.

Because you were becoming slightly irritable, we anticipated an early nap for you. A book always preceded a nap, so your mother read to you from your favorite, *Where's That Puppy?*— a birthday present from your babysitter. Her chin rested atop your curls while you settled into her lap, and mother and son sleuthed out that little critter on the juice-stained pages.

Denise was your favorite sitter. She was 17, responsible and caring, and above all, she loved you and Danny immensely. She was to arrive at the house soon, allowing your mother and me time alone. On occasion, we liked to discuss other topics besides diapers and Big Bird. We felt confident with Denise as your bodyguard, having *sat* for you (an oxymoron when used in the same sentence with the word *Billy*) on several occasions over the past eighteen months.

The need for a new diaper became evident as your mother felt the warmth in her lap. She placed you on the floor and positioned herself for the difficult mission. You squirmed like a captive worm, while your mother wished she had a third hand to complete the task. So my thoughts returned to the day Danny was first brought home from the hospital.

Instructions, noting the importance of covering the work area with a rag at all times, were not included with our bundle of baby boy. Consequently, there were still urine stains on the blinds of your brother's room where the changing table once stood. Danny's facial expression was always one of surprise when receiving that warm, yellow shower to his face. I'm sure he's mortified having this revealed, but Danny must now know that his mother doesn't have exclusive rights to embarrass our son.

Your mother always included goodnight kisses—I wonder if I ever thanked her? She leaned your face toward your brother's so you could plant a sloppy smacker on his cheek. Danny returned the gesture.

And this I'll always remember. After setting you down at her feet, she asked if you would like to say goodnight to Daddy, or your *Dahdee*, as you would say. I leaned forward on the timeworn couch with my arms awaiting your embrace. While absorbing the image of my healthy, spirited son, I couldn't stop a spontaneous smile from spreading across my face. You always made me chuckle.

Though you quickly ran toward me that day, your actions eventually became a sequence of frozen frames. I've managed to hold back that moment from the passage of time and encapsulate it through repetition. You see, I never wanted it to end, so I replay it over and over.

"Dahdee!" you squeal and run across the room with your arms reaching forward. I can still see you waddling across the room nearing my embrace. And I can't help but to be fascinated by the sparkle in your eyes and the radiant smile meant just for me. The similarities of your features and mine never cease to amaze and bind me to you. As you collide into my chest, I feel your little arms wrap around my neck as I stoop to wholeheartedly receive them.

"Night-night, Bud." I still whisper into your golden curls and embrace your small frame between my arms and chest. The warmth of our bodies blend together, and we hug each other one last time...again and again. Oh, how you love your Dahdee.

And I love you, son.

JoAnn

A MOTHER JOURNALING THROUGH GRIEF

After changing your diaper, I scooped you up off the carpet and felt the familiar weight of your twenty-eight-pound body. I imagine that most mothers, even while blindfolded, can distinguish their child from another just by holding them. That's why I can still feel you in my arms, Billy.

I balanced your bottom on my right hip and your left arm spontaneously wrapped around my neck. Then your right hand reached inside the collar of my shirt to rest on my left breast. This is something you always did with the special women in your life. Three to be exact: Grandma Jen, my friend Jeri, and myself. Maybe this was because of the warmth there or that you found tactile comfort in a past nutrition source.

With you on my hip, I climbed the steps toward the upstairs bedrooms. Then I was suddenly jerked backward when you grabbed the stair railing as we passed it. I should have known better, you always loved playing that game.

Unlike adults, toddlers are comfortable with shows of affection; embarrassment at the expression of love must be a learned emotion. So you and I gazed into each other's eyes without hesitation, Billy. Your bright, blue eyes sparkled, and an enchanting gut-giggle escaped your lips warming the core of my heart. One more trick on your Momma to make me smile—and how you could make me laugh. Why can't I laugh when I think of you now?

The darkness of that summer day
Was hidden in sunlight,
When you smiled at me the last time
And we both sang your goodnight.
You didn't want to leave me –
I thought you never would.
A voice said, "Let it be."
I wish I could.
—Billy's Song

Chapter 4

DICK

As the movie of life is being filmed, events don't always happen as intended by the actors. The direction of the story line can be unintentionally modified by a forgotten word, inflections in the voice or a changed facial expression by a character. But the director can rearrange the plot at will. And once the plot is performed for an audience, it can't be altered. There were a few scenes that deviated from the original script on the sunny day that cast a shadow on our lives forever.

That weekend, we were invited to a friend's cabin "up north," as Minnesotans call the densely wooded area of the northern state. Your Grandma Jen would have watched both Danny and you at her house had we decided to go. Because your mother had worked three days that week and was gone overnight for two of those, she had no interest in leaving you and Danny for the weekend. At my reluctance, we declined the offer and planned a weekend at home. So the story line changed.

In the first draft, an old college roommate of your mother's was scheduled to visit our home with her family. Your mother's alumni friend called to cancel, so a line was crossed off the script.

The neighbors to our left were on vacation and had placed their daughter in charge of the house. When she was house-sitting, she would spend the entire day basking in the sun on the dock adjacent to ours. That morning, she went out on an impromptu lunch date with a friend, and an actor was deleted.

Early that morning, Danny was scheduled for what parents call a "play date" at a little friend's house, which would have left Denise's undivided attention on you, Billy. The friend canceled and the plot took a new course.

Three young men, our neighbors to the right, were fishing and exercising their dog on their dock that late afternoon, but their lines and attention were cast westward instead of eastward toward our lakeshore. Also, your mother and I would normally wait until evening to leave the house. But on that clear sunny day, I choose to hire the sitter earlier. So the cast was changed.

The lakeside screen door had been replaced a month earlier, because the original had become warped with age and would not easily slide open. And so, a prop was added.

The wind blew gently, cooling the humid air, prompting us to turn the air conditioner off and slide open the glass door facing the shoreline — which left only the screen as your barrier to the outside. Beyond that door, the lake water temperature continued its deadly climb due to the record heat wave of that northern summer.

The stage was set and the dark music commenced.

As the melting ice exposed the water's edge that April of '91, your mother had felt an undefined apprehension. Subconsciously deciphering it as a lurking omen, she connected it to herself and me. After we married and had children, your mother had a tendency to worry over small matters, in my opinion, unlike the girl I had dated. So I wasn't concerned about her fretting as she continued to take action. She scheduled doctor's appointments for herself—even attempting to do the same for me, unsuccessfully. I had always been adverse to doctors, except on a social level.

She determinedly priced life insurance for us both. Though we had been "married with children" for four years and long overdue for this action, I couldn't understand her sudden urgency. Furthermore, I was an eternal procrastinator. To my relief, her compulsion subsided and the anxiety she felt that spring abated—but returned on the day you left, Billy.

After Denise arrived at the house, your mother neurotically dictated instructions to her. I was in the kitchen loading the cooler with Budweiser and ice while your mother was prancing from one room to the next, rapidly melding her words together into one long sentence.

"There are snacks in the freezer and Billy needs his medicine at about 3:00…Oh, and the monitor is on and he went down at about 1:00. You can take Danny swimming, but bring the monitor with you, and make sure he wears water wings, and keep Billy away from that screen door, he keeps pushing at it, I swear he is going to break through it someday…." And so she went on.

I always left the hiring of, and instructions to, the sitter up to your mother. Even though I was very self-reliant when she was overnight on her trips, she had a tendency to be a bit more detailed than I. Although, with Denise as our sitter, it was unusual for your mother to be as thorough as she was that day. This very mature seventeen year-old girl had watched our boys weekly for the previous four years; she knew our house and our children well.

While your mother was reviewing her list, Denise sat on the couch smiling and nodding, acting somewhat like a mother to her.

"Go on and don't worry." Denise was amused at your mother's atypical fretting and easily scooped Danny into her arms after he ran to her with excitement upon seeing her.

Your sitter had the large frame of an athletic girl. Her hair was layered above her ears, surrounding a very pleasant face. She was one of those people who could win another's trust by just smiling at them.

"Everything will be fine. Run along, have fun!" she reassured your mother.

After loading the boat with provisions for the day, I backed the vibrating vessel away from the dock. Danny and a kneeling Denise were both waist-high in the shallow waters of the shore, and they stopped their play to wave. When we left the house by water, Danny always felt the need to continuously wave good-bye until we were but a dot on the horizon. The baby monitor was perched atop the deck railing, and the static became inaudible as the boat backed away from the slip. When I look back on that moment, the darkness of that day is evident. Why couldn't I have seen it then and protected my family?

Your mother was silently preoccupied in thought as the majestic homes on shore appeared to move by our Sea Ray. I studied her silhouette for a moment and couldn't help but marvel at the fact that I only met this woman seven years before. In that whirlwind of change, she had become so much a part of me. We were a piece of each other, incomplete without the other. Despite the years gone by, her weight had remained the same as when we met—though had shifted ever so slightly to accommodate the two pregnancies. She had the body of a woman now, slightly larger at the hips.

That day, she was wearing her skimpiest bikini, purchased after discarding her baby fat from your nine-month incubation, Billy. This swimsuit was still a bright peach in color, yet to be faded from the sun. Because most of her swim time was spent with her "little boys," she usually sported a less revealing tank suit for those water activities. The peach suit was reserved specifically for my enjoyment; it was my favorite and she knew it. I had always been attracted to her, even during her pregnancies and the plump months that followed your birth. And a part of that attraction was because she was the mother of my children.

Despite the lack of your mother's culinary skills, I had added a few much-needed pounds to my tall, thin frame over the past few years. The gray in my hair gradually overtook the brown, making it the dominant color. Some would have said I looked *distinguished,* although that didn't fit my persona as a whole. Your mother would have possibly described me as often cordial, usually ethical, at times meditative, too often stubborn, and playful when I drank. Our love for the drink had given us a common ground when we first met and oddly, became the wedge that divided us later.

I glanced at my wristwatch. It was 3:30 p.m. Soon we would start arranging our dinner plans with friends at the local lakeside bars. I was looking forward to setting aside my parenting hat for an evening of unbridled enjoyment. What else was happening then? Were you running out that screen door, Billy—laughing with that mischievous gleam in your eyes? Then did you turn around to close the screen door behind you like we had taught you?

JoAnn

A MOTHER JOURNALING THROUGH GRIEF

Unlike your brother, your bedtime routine didn't consist of lullabies. If anyone was in your room at bedtime, you would always conclude that it was time for play. But that day was different.

As I leaned over the crib to place you down, you unexpectedly squirmed in my grasp. Your left arm clasped stubbornly around my neck to avoid being lowered in your crib, and your right hand determinedly pointed to the old bentwood rocking chair in the corner of the room. You had never done this before — you wanted me to rock you that day.

The teddy bear night-light softly broke the darkness as you lay in my arms and gazed serenely into my eyes. I kissed your curly, blonde hair and rested my cheek on top of your head to smell your innocent aroma. Remember how you hummed along as I softly sang to you?

> *"Somewhere over the rainbow, way up high,*
> *There's a land that I heard of once in a lullaby....*
> *Where troubles melt like lemon drops,*
> *Away above the chimney tops,*
> *That's where you'll find me..."*

If happy little bluebirds fly beyond the rainbow, Why, oh, why can't I, Lord?

When our song was over, I carried you across the room to your crib and caught a glimpse of us in the mirror on the dresser. The image of your body almost encompassed mine. I noticed how your lanky legs dangled to my thighs, so I contemplated on how tall you had grown. You weren't my baby anymore. You were a little person — my little boy. I laid you down next to your blue blanket, five strategically placed pacifiers, and your brown bunny that had its sharp, fish line whiskers lobbed off to create a suitable sleeping companion. I brushed a soft wisp of hair from your forehead and looked into your eyes.

"*Time to go night-night, Honey,*" *I whispered.*

Even though your mouth was hidden behind the pacifier, I could still see the corners of your smile as I backed away. Your vivid, blue eyes stared at me through the bars of your crib, seeming to penetrate all the way to my soul; almost a prophetic look. I gazed back lovingly.

"*Momma loves you,*" *I whispered my last words to you.*

I've cried those words a thousand times since that day, but I don't know if you can hear me now, Baby. Why was I in such a hurry to leave you?

Then I quietly backed my way toward the door, and you continued to stare into my eyes as I crept out of your vision.

DENISE
THE SITTER

Even though your mother told me I was your favorite sitter, you would usually whine a bit whenever she left. But that day was different in many ways.

After your nap, I opened the door to your room and your grin appeared over the side of the crib to light up the room. And when I lifted you from the crib, you wrapped your little arms around me in a tight hug. In the next two hours that we were together, I received several unexpected hugs from you. Did you know then that I would feel immense guilt after your death, Billy?

Because you were very dear to me, I'll never forget the loss we all endured that day. As much as I enjoyed the sweet personality of your three-year old brother, Billy, I also enjoyed your mischievous spirit. Having known you both since birth, I can honestly say that I came to care deeply for you and Danny. As a parent would, I hurt when you cried and shared your happiness when you were elated.

That's why I grieve.

Chapter 5

DICK

As we entered Excelsior Bay, the harbor furthest from our home, your mother went below to mix cocktails for the two of us. When returning to the deck with drinks in her hand, the VHF radio was buzzing with boaters' conversations seeking comrades to join in their festivities. Though I owned a cell phone for my business, many people did not at that time. So the mode of communication on the lake was always through our marine radios.

Whitecaps formed before our bow and the water came alive with an assembly of watercraft as we neared the Park Tavern, a popular lake establishment. We searched the piers for a coveted docking space. This is the last memory of my life as it was.

".... and JoAnn Deveny..." Then came static. Your mother sat up rigidly in the swivel seat next to me when she heard her name.

"....Dick and JoAnn Deveny..." The radio crackled. When paging other boats on the lake, it was customary to summon a boat by its name — ours was the *Incognito*. A person's name was rarely spoken over the radio. The official voice didn't have the casual tone of an acquaintance calling to discuss dinner plans. Instinctively moving my hand toward the mike, I answered the call.

"This is Dick Deveny on the *Incognito*."

"This is the Lake Minnetonka Water Patrol..." I can still hear the words. We were tuned to channel 16, which was a calling station for all boats. Once a party is reached, both callers must switch to another channel to converse. Only the water patrol had the frequency to interrupt dialogue among boaters on the communal channel of 16, and only in the event of an urgent situation.

Then the words were spoken. "There's a family emergency at home. You need to return home immediately."

My father, it must be my father. I immediate reverted to my constant worry, my 83 year-old father's health.

"Do you want a patrol car to meet you in Excelsior?" the water patrol queried.

"No, we'll head home by boat—it will be faster" I heard myself speak too calmly, imagining that everything was right in my world—denying any other option. Later, your mother questioned my tranquil demeanor on that day. I never told her that I had, in essence, removed myself from the situation; it was happening to someone else from that moment on.

Now I wonder how the story would have unfolded had I choose to go by land. Did I make the right decision? Probably not. But then I ask myself, would it have made things easier for us had I chosen differently? Definitely not. Nothing could have made our nightmare any less terrifying.

"We'll send a patrol boat to escort you. Go to channel 68 and stay there," the water patrol instructed. I immediately gunned the engine and turned the helm's wheel around toward Big Island and Lafayette Bay.

Adverse to my reaction, terror surged through your mother's body, seeming to permeate her every extremity. Feeling powerless over her own emotions, her body shook violently in the seat next to me while she tried to stifle her sobs. The guttural sound was alien me, and I found it hard to believe that it originated from my wife.

"I...I'm sorry Dick; I can't stop," she stuttered, while staring at the expense of water in front of our bow. *Oh please, not my babies!* She thought of her most prized possessions. "It could just be something like a broken leg," her voice stammered with reasoning.

"Honey, it could be one of our parents—something happened to one of our parents." And so I wished it on my father.

"Yes, it must be." Your mother's sobs abated as she placed her concern elsewhere, because nothing could happen to her boys.

You see, our children were immune from harm, because we had always been strangers to tragedy. We often worried about them, but at the same time, we never allowed ourselves to venture to that worst-case scenario. So in our minds, tragedies only happened to other people. Even though we believed that no parent deserved one, we could only concur that an unintentional mistake was made by them to allow it. If we were protective parents, nothing grievous could ever happen to our children— that would be the only fair way. As arrogant as it sounds, we used to feel that way.

Your mother reached over the helm in front of me for my cell phone on the steering panel. I watched her faultily attempt to push the numbers etched in her memory. Although our phone at that time was gigantically prehistoric compared to current devices, I watched as her shaking fingers repetitively missed the desired keys. With each attempt, a small green light rhythmically blinked through the phone's glass window—taunting her like an evil green eye. The wind of our momentum blew her hair from her face as she grew more frantic with each failure to select the desired buttons. When finally succeeding to reach our parents' phones, the endless ringing at the other end confirmed that they were not home.

Boats were lined up in front of ours, blocking our path and mandating me to reduce our speed while entering through a channel called The

Narrows. Ironically, this inappropriately named channel was one of the widest on Lake Minnetonka, allowing cabin cruisers an ample two-way portage and anglers a safe haven for their lines along the cemented tiers at each side. Compared to our high speed of moments before, we seemed to be at a standstill.

After we exited the channel, the boats in front ours sped into the open water and disappeared from view. Similarly, I gunned the engine as soon as we reached the channel markers. Like a bucking bronco, our bow took a leap into the air into Carman's Bay.

Above the roar of our own engines, wailing sirens filled the air and flashing blue and red lights became visible across the expanse of Upper Lake. The illumination of the water patrol's boat became visible, close enough to define the silhouette of the driver's arm waving in a motion to follow.

With polished expertise, the emergency vessel seemed to spin on an invisible turntable below the surface of the water to reverse its direction and clear a path through the crowded whitecaps before us. The vibration of our engines shook the deck, and a deafening roar kept time with the ear-piercing sirens.

As we rounded Casco Point, your mother silently shuffled down the three teak stairs into the galley of our boat. Her shoulders were stooped as her feet measured each step for fear of falling. By the time she appeared back from the V berth with clothes covering her swim suit, I can honestly say that my mind was devoid of any emotion. It was as if I had grabbed my fear and threw it far away in the depths of the lake before me.

"Grrr....rrr..Grrrr...rrr....BANG!!"

The engine sputtered just before a metallic explosion silenced the roar of the engines. The vibration beneath our feet stopped and the sudden forward momentum of the boat threw your mother a step backward into the cabin from where she came. There was an unnerving stillness as our boat became a rocking cradle in the rolling waves—a useless shell. I forcefully turned the key in the ignition.

"Grrrrrrrr…" Nothing. "Grrr…rrr…" Again, nothing.

Your mother regained her balance and groped for the railing of the deck, seeming to simultaneously lean toward and hold herself back from the water. Horrible visions appeared in her mind—her children's mouths open in a scream, calling out her name. She felt a compelling urge to dive into the waves and swim the distance to you. In timely fashion, the water patrol boat suddenly appeared at our port side.

"I'm going with them." She faced me with conviction; there was no hesitation in her voice. "We can leave the boat here if you want to come, but I have to go with them."

"You go, Babe. I'll stay with the boat," I said while assisting her over the teak railing onto the catwalk of our boat.

Making her way onto the rocking bow of the sheriff's boat, her legs shook while balancing along its edge. As I stretched my hand to support your mother's left arm, the female sheriff was reaching out to grab your mother's right hand, urging her to step carefully but quickly. A male sheriff was at the helm trying to keep their craft in place beside ours against the force of the rolling waves. While their eyes focused on hers, their faces portrayed grave consternation. Like a slap across my face, the gravity of their countenance attacked my denial.

Your mother leaned against the passenger seat to brace herself for the rough ride while the female sheriff threw a life vest over her shoulders. I released the edge of their boat just as the sheriff gunned the engine. The sirens screamed and the red lights pulsated above your mother's head as she prayed out loud, beseeching the only person who knew the horror of her circumstance.

It's ironic how the most important decisions in our lives must be made in a split second. Normally very good at judgment calls, I now question mine on that day. But then, I have learned that hindsight is always disputable and often regretful. This I know is true—my concern for our boat's fate was trivial compared to that of my children. The love for my sons was intense. Never in my life have I ever experienced a more passionate emotion.

Yet, I believe that the denial of the circumstances coupled with my instincts as a captain made me choose to stay behind. I refused to assist in making the emergency a reality. So stranded and isolated in my disabled hull, I merely stood frozen and gaped at the patrol boat as it sped away with my wife. A powerless urgency engulfed me.

~ ~ ~ ~ ~

"Hail Mary, full of grace, the Lord is with thee. Blessed are thou amongst women, and blessed is the fruit of thy womb, Jesus. Holy Mary, mother of God, pray for us sinners now and at the hour of our death. Amen. Hail Mary, full of grace…," an unforgotten prayer from your mother's Catholic upbringing repetitively spewed from her lips in a fervent whisper as the female sheriff held your mother's shoulders in a gentle embrace. While humbly beseeching the Madonna's help, she cradled her imaginary babies to her chest and rocked back and forth to the cadence of her own words.

Even though she desperately needed information, she didn't question her escorts. The dreaded details of the events waiting at home were feared by her. An awareness of them would have made her ineffective to journey to her babies' sides. It was imperative that she get there, because she believed that she was the only one capable of saving them.

"It's okay, Honey. Everything's all right. Momma loves you," she would whisper. Then you and Danny would stop crying, the doctor would splint the broken leg and everything would be "all right." Healed by the magic of your Momma's words.

JoAnn

A mother journaling through grief

Despite Denise's reassurances, I took the water wings out of the shed and laid them on the porch in full view so she wouldn't forget to use them when you and Danny went swimming. The upstairs windows could be opened no more than a crack to prevent a fall from the second story, I warned her, while actually showing her the distance with the tips of my fingers. I reminded her to leave the baby monitor on while you were asleep and she was outside. While explaining your dosage of medicine, I wrote down lengthy instructions and a phone contact on the tablet lying on the dining room table. Feeling more apprehensive than usual, I searched my imagination for worst-case scenarios and directions to prevent them...continually asking myself, "What am I forgetting?"

The bright props of the lake scene camouflaged the future events of that day. As our boat slowly cruised at what your father and I would call "cocktail cruising" speed, Willie Nelson's "You Were Always on my Mind" mingled with the hum of the engines. Willie's music was our personal favorite during our dating years. You see, Dick Deveny wasn't a perfect boyfriend, so you could say it was his theme song. Though he had become a wonderful husband and father, and at that moment, I was feeling so in love with the person he had become.

I gazed absently at the shoreline as it moved by. My thoughts were devoid of pain and worry but, at the same time, they weren't filled with happiness as they should have been. I should have been ecstatic, merely in knowing that my two boys were at home waiting for me. But life's habitual routine distracted me, made me preoccupied and heedless. Although I would thank God for the blessing of you and Danny in my prayers, I assumed the entitlement. So while watching the preten-tious mansions pass by, I was looking into the future and wanting more, unaware that in that future, I would look back and long for what I had.

The words of the water patrol and my next thoughts still echo through my mind. Please, don't let it be my babies!

While my heart raced, our boat moved torturously and slowly behind a line of boats. We seemed to merely bob up and down through the turbulent waves of the channel. My uncontrollable sobs alerted the anglers on shore, because they stopped baiting their hooks and casting their lines to gawk at me as we moved by them. The teasing green eye continued to taunt me as my fingers stumbled over the black buttons of the phone and we crawled toward the open water of the next bay. I wanted to scream at them, pleading for their help. But I couldn't say the words, so my inner voice remained silent.

Brrrinnnng...Brrrringgg....brrringgg. The consecutive rings resonated in my head as I dialed our home phone. The click of a recorder finally broke its sequence, and my own voice answered. While impatiently waiting for the conclusion of my own cheery message, I knew that person had already become a stranger to me.

"Denise! Denise! Please, pick up the phone!" I heard my own trembling voice speak into the uncaring machine. Where are you, Denise? Are my babies all right? I wanted to let go of my contrived composure and release all my anxiety into a deafening scream. But the fear of not coming back from hysteria was greater.

In the darkness of the V-berth cabin, I attempted to cover my peach swimsuit with a tank top and shorts. Then while being tossed about the cramped galley, I grasped the counter top for stability and mechanically poured my untouched Bloody Mary down the sink. More than ever, a clear mind was needed—at that moment, my head felt like a hive full of riled bees. My eyes transfixed on the thick liquid slowly flowing down the drain, leaving a red stain in its place.

Denise...What had I forgotten, what did I leave out? We talked about your meals and about keeping you away from the screen door. Did I ever tell her you were able to slide that door open, Billy?

"Lock the screen door, Denise!" I now yell, while jumping up from my seat in that theater. The nearby observers in the audience avert their eyes and shake their heads because they know. They know that no matter how loud I cry out, the movie will proceed as filmed.

DENISE
THE SITTER

Your disposition that day was tranquil, a very odd term to describe any behavior displayed by Billy Deveny.

After your nap, you calmly played with your toys by yourself in the corner of the living room as your brother watched television nearby. I took notice when you silently walked over to the couch and placed your diapered bottom next to Danny on the cushion. I remember thinking you were acting quite unusual. You would normally divert his attention from the television by striking him over the head with the wooden spoon from the kitchen or any other convenient solid object. But you weren't yourself that day; your demeanor was serene.

You gazed up at your older brother with admiration while sitting leg to leg on the couch. Your feet dangled in the air while you intently gazed at Danny's profile. He stared at the television screen, oblivious to your presence—or was he aware and merely comforted by your closeness?

With the image of Danny and you still in my mind, I turned to grab two fruit snacks from the kitchen. The memory of what came next is still there, despite the efforts I've made to forget.

The distance from the living room to that cabinet was only three feet. But in the seconds it took for this small task, your smiling face next to Danny vanished—gone forever.

Chapter 6

*A*fter racing through the no-wake zone of Zimmerman Pass, the water patrol's boat rounded Cedar Point into Cook's Bay, giving your mother a full view of our harvest-gold house. A halo of lights pulsated over the emergency vessels hovering around our dock. Surrounding them was an entourage of drifting civilian boats.

As the sheriff patrol boat neared the shoreline, gawking interlopers could be seen lined up on both property lines. They boldly invaded our neighbors' yards, yet stopped short of that imaginary border into ours—as though the yard were communicable. Only toys lay inside that boundary, scattered around in a pattern where they had earlier been dropped during play. The water slide, inflatable pool, and two sand pails were eerily idle, waiting for Danny and you to animate them.

During the daylight hours of summer, our family would only be inside the house during thunderstorms, naptime, or meal times. Our winters seemed endless, so once the temperature hit above freezing, we were free to enjoy the beautiful Minnesota ambience until the snow fell again— leaving our playground covered for five out of twelve months.

Our outside time was limited during the winter, and not only because of the sub-zero temperatures. True Minnesotans are quite thick-blooded if dressed appropriately, but you, Billy, refused to be confined in your hat, mittens, and scarf. You would peel off these wind-chill deterrents one by one and hurl them into the nearest snow bank within seconds after leaving the house. So summertime was an exodus from the confines of our snowbound prison, and we spent countless hours outside in the lakeside elements.

It's late afternoon, she thought while scanning the vacant yard. *It isn't naptime or mealtime—it's peak playtime.* Though the neighbors' yards were alive with activity, the expanse of our yard looked unusually still. *Why aren't my children outside playing?* Searching, she scanned our home's shoreline as the sheriff's boat neared the slip.

A uniformed man suddenly appeared around the corner of our house. Though racing up the dock, he seemed to move in slow motion toward her. Each of his shoes met the dock in a rhythmic beat, the metal dock poles vibrating with urgency. *He has the answers. He knows what happened.* Your mother's apprehension heightened while watching the distance shorten between them. There were so many questions she needed to ask to stop the chaotic buzzing in her head. But she feared him and the secrets he knew.

He simultaneously arrived at the Water Patrol boat as it abruptly rammed the dock's end section. Shaking, your mother climbed over the gunwales to gain a solid raceway to her children. She looked up into the man's eyes as he held out his hand to assist her to the dock. As soon as her inquiring eyes met his, he spoke before she could formulate one of the many questions running through her mind.

"What's your son's birth date?" The urgency in his voice hung in the air.

At that moment, she thought of the numerous times she had been asked that question. And she had always eagerly recited those dates— September 17, 1987 and January 16th, 1990—to admiring strangers. She thought of all the times she had proudly written down those numbers on doctor's forms, birth certificates, and daycare applications. But on that dock with exigency in the air, she had to ask a pivotal question before she could respond—a question to which she didn't want an answer. Either response would make the nightmare more real.

"Which son?" She heard the words escape from her mouth as if hearing them from someone else.

There was a slight hesitation, and then he answered, "Your little one."

A powerful vise seemed to crush her chest and a searing bolt of heat radiated into her throat, leaving a choking sensation. *Of course...Billy. He's too little to understand. He won't know why I'm not there to help him. Oh, Billy, Momma's coming, Baby!*

After reciting your birth date to her escort, she followed the man around our house to the puddle-mottled road in front.

A sheriff's van waited there for her, and without direction, she climbed into the back seat, not knowing its destination, but trusting that the driver would lead her to you. As they moved out of our driveway and onto the street, the eyes of gawking spectators tried to peer through the tinted windows.

Your mother's thoughts brought her back to junior high, an adolescent year filled with whispered secrets and cruel taunts from her fellow classmates. The same insecure feeling washed over her. It's funny how shock works—allowing escape from the present, bringing one back in time to the familiar. *They're talking about me,* she thought. She wanted to read their thoughts, shake them until they revealed the fate of her son.

The sirens surrounded her like a thousand screaming demons, taunting her in the expansive back seat of the van. *Oh, Billy, don't be afraid. It's just a loud noise. It won't hurt you.* She felt you near.

The vehicle quickly transported her down the main road away from our house. Wilshire Boulevard, definitely not to be confused with Hollywood's, was a familiar street in which you, Danny, and your mother routinely used for daily walks. Your mother would chauffeur you in your milk-stained stroller. And Danny would walk by her side, often stopping to pick up a special stone or a unique leaf to fill his treasure (shoe) box buried beneath the bed at home. The excursion usually led to the playground adjacent to Shirley Hill Elementary School. There you would spend countless hours pretending to be pirates on the metal play gyms that served as your ships.

Now the soccer field next to the playground was filled with a cluster of staring onlookers. Dirt and leaves flew through the air on a gust of wind while a loud chop and a clanking sputter overcame the sirens. When the sheriff's van took a sharp right around the corner onto Bartlett Boulevard, there came into vision the flashing lights of three police cars and an ambulance parked in the center of the field. Past those lights was a mechanical monster, a helicopter, spinning aimlessly while leaving its earthly foundation. The thumping rotation of its blades pulsated throughout your mother's body as she stepped out of the van. All she could see were the bottom runners hovering overhead.

She imagined you in that enormous metallic shell with strangers, and hoped you weren't awake and frightened because she wasn't there. She hoped that the deafening sound of the helicopter blades wouldn't hurt your sensitive ears. Above all, she prayed that you weren't in there at all, that it was just a dream.

Nearby, three-year-old Kendra was standing with her mother in the crowd on the soccer field. Her mother squinted through the sunlight at the helicopter while the little girl persistently pulled at her sleeve to break her trance.

"Mommy."

"Yes, Honey."

"I've got a friend Jesus, and He's with that baby."

Wait for me! Please come back. He needs me! I'm his mother! Your mother ran through the crowd toward the helicopter. Every nerve of her body reached out to what resembled a dragonfly disappearing over the branch tops of the maple trees lining the road—stealing her son away. While the whirling of the blades abated, the screaming of the sirens became more apparent. But she had no interest in what was transpiring around her on ground level; her sights were set on that expanse of the skies in which you disappeared.

Gentle hands grasped her arms and led her away from the soccer field. The sheriff placed her back into his van—I say *placed* because, at that time, she couldn't feel her legs move beneath her or remember any intent to enter there. But she instinctively knew that her guardians would bring her to the only plausible destination, wherever that helicopter was heading.

The woman sheriff from the boat ride was sitting next to her in the backseat, a mesh screen separating them from the driver. The driver was quietly conversing on the radio in indecipherable tones as they sped down the street, seeming to part the sea of people and leaving them scattered in the car's wake.

She was on the final leg to her destination. Now that she trusted her chaperons to take her there, she had to know what was waiting for her. While trying to formulate one question through intentions of many, the words came tumbling from her lips.

"What happened?" *That's it, I said it. Just ask and you'll know what horrifying direction your life will take,* she thought.

"Your son had a cardiac arrest."

Was he talking about, Billy? Billy's heart was fine.

"Right now he's not breathing on his own, but has a slight heart rate of 20 beats per minute. He was found in the water, twenty feet from shore."

A flashing vision of your tiny body floating in the water appeared.

Your mother heard her own words as if coming from somewhere else, "How long was he in the water?"

The driver placed the radio transmitter to his lips and repeated her question into it. The information came from a static-filled speaker to the driver, and in turn, he spoke them aloud to her. The words came with a whisper through the dry conditioned air of the back seat.

"Five to ten minutes." Though gently spoken, the words set off a clamorous explosion in her head. *He'll never be the same.*

You see, Billy, she had made your body. You were nourished in her womb with every morsel of food and every prenatal vitamin consumed. Then, like a painter, she lovingly cleaned and pampered her creation stroke by stroke for eighteen months. Painstakingly, she worked on your mind and body to create an intelligent, happy, beautiful masterpiece. And then when she turned away for only a moment, someone walked by to smudge the magnificent colors on her easel. And when looking back, she would only find an ugly quagmire of browns.

Would she want a painting that was a mutilated, contrasting re-minder of the beauty that once was there? Did she want you alive like that— unable to recognize or to understand her? Would you be happy that way, Billy? And was she capable of raising a handicapped child? These questions played through her mind in a nanosecond before, she utterly dismissed them. *You're not a painting, Baby. Yes, I want you alive, Honey, if only to hold you.*

~ ~ ~ ~ ~

While your mother was abruptly discarding her misgivings, at the same moment and not so far away, seven-year-old Brian Dodds was riding his bike. Then this boy, whom Denise had also babysat on occasion, flew from his bike, and his head hit a cement wall.

~ ~ ~ ~ ~

"What time did he go into the water?" she heard herself calmly question her escorts, still wondering how this could possibly be her own voice.

"The 911 call was at 3:38 p.m."

Unaware if it was five minutes or five hours since her life was altered, she asked, "What time is it now?"

"It's 4:20."

Forty-two minutes without your Mommy, Billy. She longed to move back the hands of time but, being unable to, she deleted the information as if swiping a large eraser through the pages of her mind.

Though the woman sheriff wrapped her arm around her, your mother couldn't return the embrace because she had her arms full of you, Billy. Holding your head over her shoulders, she could actually feel your back on her cheek. She rocked and whispered her prayer.

"Hail Mary, full of grace the Lord is with thee. Blessed are thou amongst women and blessed is the fruit of thy womb, Jesus ..." She could feel your weight in her arms as she moved back and forth. Anguished sobs came from the depths of her soul, while she rocked—praying and pleading over and over. *Breathe, Baby, breathe!* And then she would breathe deeply in and out—showing you how, Billy, while cradling your imaginary body in her arms. Blowing air into your lungs for you; breathing for her baby.

As soon as they came to a stop in front of North Memorial Hospital, your mother tore out the door of the vehicle with her escorts trailing behind. While dashing through the parking lot toward the large glass doors of the brick building, the rocky pavement cut into the soles of her shoeless feet. Like a shaman walking over hot coals, she would not have felt the pain if her heels had been torn to bloody pulps.

The automatic doors opened in front of her and a rush of cool air hit her face as she entered the building. A nurse behind the desk absently stared over her reading glasses at her, while another merely glanced up and then back to the chart in front of her. With bated breath, her escorts reached your mother's side and led her by the arm through a door labeled the "Family Room." *A misnomer,* she thought as she entered the room, which contained only rows of empty chairs.

She found herself sitting in one of those cushioned chairs and vacantly staring at the wall across the room. The woman sheriff was seated next to her. Her purpose as your mother's protector was accepted without introduction. And so she remained at her side with no name. The wall moved closer.

"Where is he? Can I see him?" your mother asked as though this woman had control of her path to you.

"The doctors are working on him" the woman words sounded as if you were an engine with defective pistons. *Didn't they know that I'm the only one who can fix you?* The wall in front of her moved closer.

Though leaving her shoes behind, your mother had instinctively remembered, like most women would, to bring her purse. She groped for the phone book in its confines. Being that her family was often her lifeline, she paged through the miniature pages for the phone numbers of her five siblings.

Childhood memories of a close relationship with her four sisters and one brother were nonexistent because their ages spanned twenty-one years—a full generation. Just as her older sisters were preoccupied with peddle-pushers and the Supremes, your mother had been too busy with bell-bottoms and Carol King to play with her younger sisters. One of them grew up in the disco era of the late '70s and the other through the new wave years of the '80s. Your uncle, the oldest and only boy, merely used the house for sleep and nourishment. So eventually he felt the need to escape their one-bathroom, six-female household out of necessity. When he left home at eighteen, your mother's older sisters were in the last years of high school, your mother was leaving elementary school, a younger sister was leaving kindergarten, and the youngest was but a whim in her parents' minds. Despite their chronological age differences, the passing years moved the Kuzma siblings into adulthood, and they bonded as a family—always assured they could rely on each other in a crisis.

"Something's wrong with Billy, Jeanne...I don't know what" Your mother spoke into the answering machine to her eldest sister. "We're at North Memorial Hospital." She couldn't embellish further; saying the words out loud would only condone the event. While she placed the receiver back in its cradle, the wall in front of her moved closer. *Please, God, save my baby!*

Theresa, six years her junior, was her next lifeline. *Brrrinnnng.....* *Brrrinnnnng....* She heard the rings through the receiver. *Please, answer the phone Theresa!*

"Hello!" Theresa spoke cheerfully, without pause, because life was still the same for her.

"It's me, Theresa. Something has happened to Billy!" Your mother's voice escalated. Even though she couldn't go into detail, this time she wasn't able to conceal her panic. While replacing the receiver, she looked up to find the white walls surrounding her from all four sides as if she could reach out and touch their coldness.

JoAnn

A mother journaling through grief

Though the door opened slowly at the opposite side of that large room, I remember flinching for fear of it knocking me over. A doctor entered. He was wearing a white, sterile jacket and exuding a strange mixture of timid resolve. Even though the door from which he appeared seemed to be but two feet from my chair, it seemed an eternity for him to reach me. He sat down by my side and looked into my eyes. I gazed back and tried to look deep inside his mind, seeking any information about my son.

Then he gently placed his hand on mine.

No! He's okay! I just saw him a few hours ago! Billy's fine! I screamed my thoughts through my eyes.

"We've been trying to get his heart rate up and his breathing started for about twenty minutes..." The words were spoken gently and slowly, while I detected a trace of sadness in his eyes. That's why I couldn't let him finish.

"Can I see him?" I interrupted. Once more, my mind's eraser obliterated the chalk marks of reality.

"That's what I came here for."

As a last desperate measure, I grasped onto my mission. He's finally come for my help, I thought. So I tore out the door of that family room, leaving that doctor and his sentiments behind me.

There were people at my side trying to direct and keep up with me at the same time. My body was numb. Even though I couldn't feel my own movements, the walls rapidly passed by and steel doors opened in front of me. The room was offensively bright and eternally long, and at the far end, I could see the backs of five people in scrubs surrounding an elevated bed.

Their arms were in continuous motion, and the area was filled with a nervous energy. The abrupt, raised voices abated as I neared the bed. While penetrating the human barrier, a vision of your slender legs and bloated stomach emerged.

Oh, Billy, you must have a terrible tummy ache, Honey, I thought. The people turned around to stare and moved aside as I forcefully shimmied between them to reach you.

Being that my sole mission was to help you breathe, I supported my body with my arms on each side of your shoulders and positioned my mouth close to yours. While stroking your soft cheek I spewed desperate, whispered pleas and audibly breathed in and out to show you how.

"Billy, breathe. Baby, breathe ... You can do it, Honey. It's okay, Momma's here. Everything's all right." I coached. Then I looked into your eyes.

At that moment, whatever I had seen as good in this world turned evil. Whatever positive thought I had ever envisioned, turned negative. Every word that had been spoken became a deceiving lie. What was aesthetically beautiful in my life suddenly turned grotesquely ugly. Because what was once innocent and pure had been desecrated and violated.

The irises of your eyes were rolled upward and partially hidden by the drooping of your lids, as if searching for something unreachable. Those saucer-shaped orbs, which always elicited compliments from other parents, were still the same blue in color, but without sparkle of life. They reminded me of the inert plastic marbles that could be bought at a cheap corner store.

Your little nose was invaded by a clear tube, which let out a hideous gurgling noise like the slurping of juice through a straw. Blood was moving through it —a crimson life fluid oozing in and out of your body. Your mouth gaped open to allow another tube entrance. In and out, the deep-red fluid flowed in syncopation with the incessant gurgling. Through your flaccid lips, I recognized the familiar space between your two front teeth and the minute chips that edged their surface due to numerous falls you had taken. It was you. The earth seemed to open up beneath my feet, and I found myself in hell.

"Oh, my beautiful baby. I love you, Honey!" I placed my face on your skin and gently kissed your entire body to honor its innocence—to make it clean and whole again. I kissed your soft curls, which still shone a rainbow of gold, cream, and auburn beneath the offensive florescent lighting.

Ignoring the tubes, my lips continued to that little point on your right ear, then kissed the light brown birthmark beneath your right shoulder. I kissed your rounded tummy to your navel, remembering the cord once attached and severed. I kissed the soft skin of your pelvis next to your little penis, which you loved so much to fondle—never to understand why. While moving my lips down the length of your bruised legs, I cursed the place they took you. Then my lips gently caressed your feet all the way to the ingrown toenail of your left big toe, which I had often soaked in warm water to soften the pain. Your toe would be a healthy pink when emerging from the tub at home, but now it was blue. The whiteness of the room surreally swirled around me.

"Do you want to hold him?" The question broke the silence, seeming oddly phrased. As if I needed permission; as if you weren't mine anymore.

I instinctively reached one arm under your shoulder and one under your knees, while others busily attempted to disconnect the tubes and wrap your body in a heated white hospital blanket. Ironically, that soft, pediatric wrap brought me back to another time. So I allowed my thoughts to move from death to new life and momentarily relived our first minutes together.

With your face buried on your own pallid chest, I could only see the top of your head and down the bridge of your upturned nose. And I could pretend that your face looked no different than it had through the glow of the night light in your bedroom a few hours before.

While stroking your beautiful curls, I rested my nose within them to smell your distinctive aroma once more. Noticing the contrast of both, I moved my tanned, aged hand down to your pale, smooth legs that hung limply over mine.

You have feet like your dad's. A thought formed through my trance. Instinctively, the nape of my neck tensed, waiting for your little arms to encircle it as you had earlier that day. I anticipated one of your "face hugs," an intimate caressing of your face with mine. I imagined you turning toward me to pinch my nose with your dimpled fingers. Then your eyes would open with a sparkle after hearing the horn sounds I would make.

But my thoughts could only deceive the tangibles for a moment. Your body felt limp like a ragdoll's—such an odd sensation. Your face remained expressionless while your head flopped backwards like a newborn's, and I needed to raise my elbow to support it. Just a few days ago, I had discovered your ninth tooth peeking its way through the gum tissue. It couldn't possibly stop halfway, could it?

He's still growing and he's not done yet, damn it! I screamed with silent vehemence to a God who had turned into a stranger. *I can't save my baby by myself...I need help! Please, somebody help us!*

Around the curtain, which hung across the bed from us, appeared a slight man with a beard and mustache wearing a white gown. He reminded me of an image from a child's illustrated Bible. You see, this man was staring into my soul with the eyes of Jesus.

While gazing passionately at us, he moved quickly around the foot of the bed and sat down on a chair next to ours. Through the haze of my tears, my bewildered stare held his compassionate eyes. I felt as if I had always known him.

His voice had the warmth of a kitten's purr as he held his arm around me and placed his face close to mine. His own pain bore through my heart as he gasped in a whisper, "Oh, no!" as if he was suddenly moved by the sight of us. But his empathy was lost on me, because I couldn't fully comprehend the reason for his pity.

I offered a gift and pleaded for one in return. "Do you want to see my baby?" *I wanted to show you off one last time, Billy.*

"Yes...yes, I would," he whispered convincingly while trying to peer under your limp, drooping head.

"He's beautiful, isn't he? Isn't he beautiful?" I needed to hear it once more.

"Yes," he whispered with rich emotion and looked at me, his soft brown eyes brimming with tears. "He is so beautiful." And I knew he meant it.

With his left arm around my shoulder and his right hand gently resting on your leg, his compassion embraced us. Though rhythmically rocking together like the ticking of a clock, time stood still. Pain tore from the dark corners of my soul, surged through him, then back again to me again—surrounding us both as we rocked you, Billy. It was as though this man was absorbing my pain, protecting me from its full force. I don't recall how long we rocked and cried together—you, me, and the man with Jesus eyes.

Chapter 7

I don't remember seeing him there when I arrived, though she insisted that I must have. It was confirmed a few years later, through your Uncle Dave's mother, that there was a man who rocked with you both. Arlene knew him through his involvement at Minnehaha Academy in Minneapolis, but he was also North Memorial Hospital's chaplain and a fire marshal and trauma minister for the Robbinsdale Fire Department. Arlene said he described the exact sequence of events of that day in detail to her, even though the physical description of him was unfamiliar to your mother. He was actually a large man with no facial hair. He was wearing a plaid, cotton shirt and jeans, not a white robe—a much different picture than the one your mother described.

It could have been her own private delusion, but the experience was very real to her. And even though I was a man of tangibles, I believed that the man sent by the hospital staff was not the same man who walked into that room.

My journey to your mother's side, Billy, was the most excruciating physical distance I had ever traveled in my life. The details will never leave me. But as I've said, this is her story, not mine.

Through much distress, I finally arrived at the curtain that would reveal my family to me and tore it open with one sweeping motion. She was sitting in a chair beside the bed with a backdrop of white seeming to illuminate the area around her, giving off a halo effect. Her long hair hid her face and arms, barely exposing your lanky legs hanging from her lap. It was an angelic image of my wife rocking our child, like the Madonna in tranquil repose—until she lifted her head and her face was revealed. Her round, vacant eyes stabbed through my heart portraying bottomless horror.

"He's dead, Dick! He's dead!" The words struck me from across the room with a forceful blow. My body snapped back from the impact and my face became distorted with anguish. Then I heard a wretched wail. My weakened, hunched body, now shrunken from its six-two stature, fell to the bed rail, making it necessary to catch my fall with my arms. With both hands I steadied myself while navigating to her side.

We sat together rocking you, our baby; a part of her, a part of me. She cradled your body while I put my arms around you both. We moved as one—crying with disregard for the world around us. It was just your mother, you, and I as time stood still in our own corner of pain. So it seemed as if our onlookers were miles away in another dimension. They were of no concern to us.

This was your mother's and my most intimate moment ever, more so than our vow of marriage, our sexual consummation, or the miraculous birth of our children. Though the term *intimate,* in this case, was a negative concept. But, I can't find a better word to describe it, because that horrifying moment could not possibly be shared with anyone—no one else could feel the entirety of our pain. We owned it; it was ours to keep.

I stared without focus beyond your mother's shoulder at a sterile, white shelf where numerous multi-colored medicine bottles idly rested. Couldn't one of them cure you? Why couldn't I save my son?

Coldness permeated through the blanket, gradually chilling your mother's thighs and arms as though she was holding a wrapped block of ice. The weight of you in her arms and the curvature of your body in her lap felt so natural that she had been fooled. It took her cloudy mind a few minutes to accept that her once warm, soft child was the source of this unnatural, chilling sensation.

Reluctantly, your mother relinquished your cold body to the arms of a stranger. Though moving gently, this man seemed to tear you from her grasp. Your legs and arms dangled loosely from the shelf of his elbow. Your head hung limply, seeming to unnaturally pull at your neck.

Be careful of his head! Hold him closer, damn it! I silently yelled and watched in horror as our child was carried away. Just another fatality in the hospital record book. Tag him up, haul him out.

Your mother sat motionless next to me in her chair at the side of the empty hospital bed, still experiencing the lingering chill of your body. Even though she sensed movement and voices, she had no peripheral vision, and the view ahead was hazy as she tried to focus on a future filled with nothing. The condition of my mind was much the same. I was able to convince myself that I had just witnessed your death. But the repercussions of this event were peripheral, and I couldn't thoroughly comprehend it; I couldn't look beyond the moment.

"I know this is a difficult time, Mr. and Mrs. Deveny, but in order to save what we need for organ donation, I must ask you at this time. Only his corneas can be used because of the circumstances of his death."

We were back in the family room with the doctor and a strange woman holding a clipboard seated in front of us. As in the previous hours (or was it minutes?), the most pivotal questions were asked during our time of duress: Questions about funeral homes, churches, autopsies, and burial plots. We couldn't understand what any of it had to do with us. We only wanted to go home and be reunited with our children.

Did we want to donate your corneas from your beautiful blue eyes, Billy? For us, your ninth tooth was still inching its way over the gum line, and they wanted to take you apart. Your mother slowly shook her head and rose from her chair, mumbling something about needing to use the bathroom. So she left me with their pathetic stares and difficult questions. When she returned, it took me a moment to recognize the aged face of my young wife.

Like a dress rehearsal for the funeral procession, our families came one by one to the hospital in disbelief. And with each entrance, your mother would fly from her chair and her trance to shockingly greet each newcomer with the same repetitive exclamation.

"Billy's dead! Billy's dead!" she shouted as she met each guest with a desperate hug. Sometimes she would say it twice, sometimes several times, but those were the only words she was capable of uttering. I'm not sure if she was trying to clarify her confusion or to will her family to share the same incredible pain. Either way, the greeting seemed appropriate at that time.

When finally leaving that sterile room, your mother and I walked down the white narrow hallway, clinging to each other for support. Every step took a concentrated effort as we tried to place one foot in front of the other. We passed through the doors of the hospital and stepped into the formidable outside. And I remember carrying with me that unsettled feeling we all get from time to time; that feeling of leaving something very important behind.

JoAnn

A MOTHER JOURNALING THROUGH GRIEF

PLEASE DON'T LEAVE HIM ALONE! I remember silently pleading to no one as your body disappeared from my sight. My head seemed to float above my shoulders like a helium balloon, while a heavy emptiness crushed my heart. Then I remembered the lyrics to a song by the Beatles and heard the answer to my Hail Mary's of only moments before. "Let it be."

The impression of your weight still remains here in my arms as I write on these pages. But at the same time, I can feel the tearing of my soul after you were taken from me, leaving a twenty-eight-pound void that can never be filled.

There's much confusion about the sequence of events that followed after they took you from my arms, Billy, though I can clearly see the bathroom mirror at the hospital. I remember glancing in it after entering through the door marked "Women," only to find a tear-streaked face staring back. It was as if I had known her once, but just couldn't place her. I turned from the stranger in the mirror and hid from her behind a stall door. Feeling the walls close in around me, I physically relieved myself while abstractly reflecting that you should need a diaper change by now. I remember thinking that my old world would come back after leaving that stall, as if stepping out of the looking glass with Alice.

But when I opened that door, my new world closed in on me like the boundaries of the stall had, and the strange, stupefied reflection accusingly stared back from the mirror on the bathroom wall. The image was me: that guilty mother who had committed the most grievous sin and had been punished by its conse-quences. How could I have let my baby die?

My father's face looked much like mine had in the mirror when he entered the family room. Because he was a man who usually didn't reveal his emotions, his expression was foreign to me. I had only seen this demeanor from him once; so I willingly moved to the past. I found myself climbing into the packed Chevy Vega, my means of escape from Minnesota to California in the fall of 1978. I could see my father through my rear view mirror, standing motionless with that same powerless, confused look on his face. I continued to wave good-bye out my window without looking back, bound for the California coast. In that hospital room, I tried to look down that road and drive off. But I couldn't run away this time.

"Daddy, Daddy! Billy's dead! Billy's dead!" I screamed, reverting to my childhood name for him. I was that little girl again. As my father neared me, I turned that Chevy around and ran out of the car to embrace him.

Because I relive that day as a spectator in the audience, I vividly see the clothes I was wearing. Now I judge myself for wearing that skimpy bikini, short shorts, and tiny tank top, forgetting my responsibilities as a mother while my child was in danger. And so the guilt returns every time I see the small blood stain on that pink-striped top, which is still in my dresser drawer. Sometimes the urge to throw away that reminder is strong, but not as powerful as the need keep a memento of the last time you were cradled next to my body. So I hold on to both. The memory and the guilt.

Chapter 8

After leaving the hospital, I found myself in the expansive backseat of your Aunt Jeanne's and Uncle Dave's car with your mother at my side. If I spoke, I can't remember. I had my arm around her shoulders and sat motionless, because every movement required too much energy. Your mother's eyes fixedly gazed out the window like a carp washed to shore.

We're going home. Billy and Danny will be waiting for us. And as we walk into the doorway, they'll both run to us. That's when I'll wake up, she thought.

Our vehicle pulled to the curb in front of Denise's brown-shingled house, and I shuffled up to her doorway to retrieve my oldest son. The few hours that had passed since I last laid eyes on Danny seemed like an eternity, and I felt my heart suddenly warm at the sight of my child emerging from the house.

"Daddy!" he yelled with a welcoming smile and threw his chubby arms around my knees. I stooped down to embrace him and felt the warmth of his body. I kissed him on the cheek and looked into his eyes, returning his smile.

"Let's go home, hey, Bud?"

I grabbed his little hand as he skipped happily down the steps at my side. I remember thinking that he looked incomplete without your little legs trying to keep up at double-time to his, Billy.

Danny sandwiched himself between your mother and me in the back seat of the car. One strand of his white-blonde hair fell between his blue eyes, which were wrinkled at the corners from the expanse of his grin. I gently put my arm around his shoulders while studying his perfectly formed hands, admiring his flushed, dimpled cheeks and his thick eyelashes. He seemed more animated than ever, so alive. At that moment I understood the precious gift in my unique child—never again to take him for granted.

While we walked through the front door of our home, Danny chatted nonstop without taking a breath between sentences, narrating the events of his exciting day. For the first time in his almost four-year old life, I blocked out his words.

The vision of toys scattered throughout the living room broke my stupor. Upon seeing the freckles of raisins dispersed throughout the carpet, an image of you appeared—shaking that small red box like a maraca until its contents were spewed. Your little fingers could never reach the corners of that cardboard container to free the sticky fruit from its insides. Your mother also scanned the room, but she couldn't focus on any one thing, because every detail was a reminder of you.

One little Mickey Mouse sandal sat in the middle of the living room as if it had just been kicked from your foot. A half-eaten pretzel lay underneath the coffee table as though it had just touched your lips moments before. Your favorite squeaky toy looked as if it was recently thrown into a corner, and the highchair was yet to be wiped of the food from your early lunch. A used diaper sat on an end table, still warm from the heat of your body's urine. Near it was a half-filled juice bottle, tipped over and dripping onto the carpet as if it had just fallen from your mouth. Your energy was everywhere, but we couldn't find you anywhere. A vise seemed to slowly tighten around my throat, making it hard to breathe.

"Mommy, are you staying home now? Do you know what happened today? Billy went way too deep in the water, and his tummy was too full of water. We couldn't lift him. Then he went to the hospital. When is Billy coming home, Mommy?" Danny excitedly rambled on, while looking up at his mother with round, questioning eyes. I held my breath for her reply.

Even in that moment, I knew that there would never be a more difficult question asked of her again—and Danny's life would be changed forever by her response. I couldn't help but remember him, only days before, skipping around that very same room and chanting, "I'm a lucky boy, lucky boy, lucky boy!" The room was different, the child would be different.

"Honey...," she whispered, while stooping down to the floor so she could look directly into Danny's trusting eyes. Her hands gently held his slight shoulders. "Billy will never come back. He'll stay in Heaven with God now, Honey." Your mother's voice hesitated while she momentarily choked on the words. "...Billy died... and the angels came to help bring him to a big playground in the sky." Your mother immediately questioned her response to your brother as the sparkle in his eyes vanished and the horror of reality took its place.

Looking into his mother's eyes and finding nothing but pain, for the first time in his speaking life, Danny had no more questions. A wet tear flowed from his reddening eyes, and a sob escaped from his lips. Although he couldn't thoroughly understand the ramifications of what she said, he believed her. You see, she had never lied to him.

I joined my diminished family. By wrapping our arms around Danny, we both tried to protect him from the truth—and by mixing our tears together, we started to mourn with him.

JoAnn

A MOTHER JOURNALING THROUGH GRIEF

Time had stopped, so it seemed as if the car were stationary while the scenery rapidly moved toward me. The houses at the side of the road raced forward, closing in at a menacing speed, while the panes of their windows glared down on me. The trees lining the roadside reached their hideous, sharp talons over my head as if trying to tear apart the protective refuge I had in the roof of our vehicle. Lamp posts craned their necks into my pathway, and road signs were filled with indecipherable words. As the signs moved toward me, the E's turned into sneering, gaping mouths with sharp teeth and the O's seemed to open their black lips to suck me into their endless throats. All the colors were too vivid, too bright—they hurt my eyes and invaded my numbness. Like a pack of deadly predators, the approaching cars seemed to attack my protective bubble on wheels, trying to find an entrance. Evil lined that winding road around our lake, though it had once been kind.

I had driven down that road many times with my two boys strapped securely in the back seat, either screaming from reciprocated punches or laughing from a shared joke only two young brothers could understand. Often times, Danny would urge me to sing a song, which would inevitably put you both to sleep. But there was an eerie silence in the car as we drove down that mutant road on that horrible day.

At 4:50 p.m. July 13, 1991, you were proclaimed dead in the eyes of the legal system. One year, five months, twenty-seven days, and one hour from the time you were born. One year and three days from your Catholic baptism. Three days short of your eighteen-month check-up, which was scheduled on the same day you were measured for a coffin.

The obituary in the newspaper on the table bears your name in bold, harsh print. Your death certificate displays the cause of death in bold scrawling handwriting—drowned. Staring at the word in front of me, I have an obsessive urge to use stenographer's whiteout over the ink. The newspapers and local television news report the circumstances of that day with innuendoes of exaggeration, misconception, and blame, as if speaking of another script of life.

But in my mind you're not dead, because in my world there's no such thing as the passage of time and no meaning to the phrase "forever gone." Life's lessons haven't prepared me for this, because there are so many things that stay the same and so few events that are final. How can I understand the finite definition of your death, Billy? However, my previous life, as I knew it, has definitely ended. The earth has stopped rotating, the days and nights are one, and the seasons have been put on hold. Act II will never come; I'm stuck in the first scene.

I insist that Dick draw the blinds in the living room to block out the American flag flying at half-mast on the shoreline and the body of water beyond it. But despite the barriers I place between the lake and myself, I can't block out the continual sound of slapping water. With each lap of a wave, I imagine your lifeless body floating in it.

You were too quick for me when you ran behind Danny's swing last May. Back and forth, back and forth...wham! The impact sent you flying through the air while I watched in shock. And you were too quick for Denise; that's why I can't blame her. Back and forth, back and forth...wham! The waves took your body as I eternally look on in horror.

How is it that I can't feel or taste anything, as if my body was shot with Novocain, but at the same time, every waking moment is intensely painful? For hours (or has it been days?) I've sat curled on the couch, clutching your blue blanket to my nose, breathing in your smell. And when I hold that blanket over my shoulder, I can feel your weight while I rock back and forth. But sometimes, I lie on the couch motionless, staring at a framed picture of your smiling face in my hand. In that snapshot, a bruise is evident on your cheekbone, and when I gently kiss it, I'm able to feel the smooth texture of your skin on my lips.

Frightened that I'm slipping away from him, Danny often leans his head down to mine and gazes into my vacant eyes. Then he smiles lovingly, and says, "I love you, Mommy." He knows that this is the only time my mouth will invert into a semblance of a smile. A profound devotion flows from him to me when he gazes into my eyes and utters those phenomenal words, which make me feel such a rich love for him. But at the same time, my heart skips a beat in knowing that I'll never hear those words from you, Billy.

Sleep is my only respite from the pain, but for it to come, I need Danny's body protectively cocooned into my curved frame. Looking from the top of his head and down the bridge of his nose, I'm able to see the silhouette of your face in his, Billy. Within that moment I can pretend that he's you. In this way, we'll wrap our arms around each other until our eyelids surrender to sleep.

I wake up throughout the night as Danny tosses in bed, cries out your name, and sometimes yells with his eyes opened in terror. Although we both find comfort in waking to find our bodies unconsciously intertwined, even in our sleep, I am afraid to let go—frightened of losing Danny as suddenly as I did you. Similarly, Danny has already lost the mother he once knew and desperately needs to cling to the physical fragments that remain. At those times, your brother always falls back asleep before I do. This leaves me alone, staring at the picture on my wall.

There's a rowboat in the foreground with trees framing a tranquil setting of a sunset over the lake. Though a cheap print from a department store reproduced in mass quantities—my picture is very different. In the last few nights since you left me, Billy, I find myself gazing at it from my bed. The longer I stare at the colored images, the further I become absorbed into the picture. Then the waves start rolling and the two-dimensional rowboat becomes three, rocking gently, up and down with the surf as it comes to life. I can actually hear the rustle of the leaves in the breeze and the waves lapping on the sandy beach depicted there—such a subtle, peaceful sound. Sometimes I can even smell the fresh, moist smell of the grass lining the shore. At that moment, I succeed in leaving my world and entering into another. Finally at peace in that serene setting, I want to remain in the picture on my wall forever, because I know I'll find you there.

PATTI
BRIAN'S MOTHER

Where are you, Brian? Ever since that horrible bike accident, I've been missing you so—even though your body is right in front of me, hooked up to those tubes and that breathing apparatus. Can you feel my hand when I hold yours or hear me when I talk to you and tell you how much I love you? I can deal with anything, Brian, as long as you live.

I sit by your hospital bed every day praying for you to get better. I pray that today is a good day with no more brain swelling and no more MRIs—please, dear God, help us get through this!

I mostly pray for you to open your eyes, Brian, so I can see the sparkle in them again. But in the meantime until that happens, I'll continue to watch you in this coma, hold your hand, and pretend that nothing has changed.

Chapter 9

DICK

"Mamaa ... Mama ... Mamaaa...!"

At 5:30 Sunday morning, her eyelids abruptly sprang open at the sound of your voice. Half asleep and without thought, she jumped out of bed and flew across the hallway to your room. Her movements were automatic, while she anticipated your beaming face as her welcome. But when she threw open the door to your room, the sight of your empty crib stopped her. While her mind woke to consciousness, her legs lost all feeling and she collapsed to the floor. As she buried her face into the carpet, the knife of reality stabbed her heart, splattering the blood of her grief to every nerve of her body.

The lower level of our home was filled with a jungle of potted flowers and plants, which emitted a blanket of aroma that permeated every room. At your mother's insistence, your toys were not stowed away in some box, but moved to the side walls of the dining area. Even after an informal search party combed the house and yard for its mate, your lone little Mickey Mouse sandal sat by itself in the closet—so your mother assumed you took the other one with you. Your miniature rocking chair in front of the television was idle, seeming to be waiting for your return.

Like a revolving door, the entrance to our house welcomed in and spit out numerous visitors who lined our couches and filled every folding chair. This stream of guests was needed by your mother, Billy. And I, too, appreciated the distraction by having a drink with them and pretending that nothing had changed since the last time we toasted. But if the atmosphere turned to tears, I would quickly retreat to my bedroom.

Nevertheless, your mother was the key player invading my denial. As each friend bravely ventured into our house, she would jump up from the couch and run toward them with open arms, exclaiming, "Billy's dead! Billy's dead!" Being unable to greet the guests with any other salutation, she repeated her shocking welcome with each new face. With each occurrence of this ritual, I would flinch. Then I would feel resentment toward her and overwhelmed by a death I wanted to deny. I didn't know, at that time, that she also fluctuated between comprehension and denial.

Your mother had never been very narcissistic, but she was still a woman and had always made some effort to take care of herself. After your death, Billy, there was no semblance of vanity left in her. She couldn't bring herself to look in the mirror to apply make-up or put in her contacts. The physical world didn't seem to concern her. And it was her guilt that made her feel unworthy of aesthetic attention when her son's body lay lifeless. So she left her hair unkempt, donned her glasses, and wore an unflattering, oversized black T-shirt over her shorts each day to hide from her imagined accusers and her own shame.

With best intentions, a friend, who was a nurse, provided your mother with a month's supply of sedatives. I once found her staring at the boxes of tiny white pills lying on the kitchen counter while contemplating the choices in front of her; to ingest them in their entirety to end the constant pain or finish raising her other son. Of course, it was a fleeting notion and she, reluctantly, chose life.

Afraid of losing control while under the influence, she refrained from medication or alcoholic beverages except for a sleeping pill at night. She knew that drugs would only postpone the reality of your death. I, on the other hand, often had a drink with our guests, trying to delay the inevitable.

Incapable of making high-level decisions, we relied on others to do so for us. When people asked how they could help, we could never state our needs, because we had no desire beyond wanting our child back. Try as they may, no one could take away the pain, but they somehow smoothed the harsh edges of everyday life. The helpful gestures from family members enabled us to cease functioning when needed. Each person gave a part of themselves as only he or she knew how, from assistance with thank-you notes to the offer of illegal drugs from one of your mother's uncles—the latter was graciously declined.

"I'm so sorry." Our parish priest stood on our doorstep on the eve of your death. He had married us four years earlier and had baptized both our children. *No. I'm* sorry, I wanted to say. *I'm sorry I wasn't there. I'm sorry my son died, and I didn't save him.* Your mother stood speechless next to me at the doorway, expectantly searching his face for news of your return. But he didn't bear any. If he couldn't answer her questions, who could? So while he stumbled over the appropriate condolences, she interrupted him.

"Can you pray for us?" She was hoping he had some influence or possibly an expedient, direct line to the one who could bring you home for dinner. As he bowed his head in beseeching prayer, I understood that he had no more power than I did to alter the events. *That's why he's sorry*, I thought.

"Our Father who art in Heaven, hallowed be Thy name...," I held my arms around your mother's shoulders and her head weighed heavily upon my chest as his voice droned beyond comprehension.

Although we were the only ones who could feel the other's anguish, your mother and I were seldom aware of the other's presence. It didn't really make much difference; neither of us had the ability to offer comfort as it was. We possessed the minimum energy to literally put one foot in front of the other. Even walking was a chore. If one of us stumbled, we absently picked the other up as a parent would to a child and turn away, reverting to our private battle of survival.

Since I couldn't give her the first or second thing she needed most, the first being your return, Billy, the second being some comfort for her pain, your mother was nurtured by her sisters. They held her close in their arms as she silently cried and diligently listened while she rambled on about you. At dusk, they read to her in bed, as a mother would to a child — to the child she was. Danny and your mother always retired to bed early, leaving me alone with my insomnia. Eventually, I would join them in the early hours of the morning, but only after intermittently pacing the floor and napping on the couch in the family room downstairs.

During the day, the phone rang incessantly, leaving your Aunt Jeanne to answer most of the calls, although your mother managed to answer two. Unaware of your death, a friend, who had cancelled a play date for her son and Danny that Saturday, called to reschedule. I listened with puzzlement at your mother's reserved calm while she spoke to his mother over the phone.

"No, I'm sorry, Karen, Danny can't play today because Billy died — but maybe he can play tomorrow. I'll call you when things are less hectic." Your mother believed you would be back, Billy, and things would soon return to normal. I marveled at her repose, quite a transformation from her hysterics of only moments before. It was like that in the first few days, panic followed by denial.

The second call she took was from her supervisor at work, wanting to know if she could contact any flight attendants for support. Being that her closest friends had already heard of your death, Billy, only one name came to her mind. Your mother had flown with this flight attendant only once, yet Jeanette had made an impression on her. Jeanette had spoken of The Lord as being a personal friend of hers. Having many questions and needing a direct contact to you, your mother asked her supervisor to only inform her. Your mother's request unnerved me at the time.

There were a few reasons I was threatened by your mother's search for God after your death, Billy—one being that I absolutely hated Him at that moment. Also, I wasn't comfortable with people who outwardly showed their compassion toward their faith. Maybe it was because the evangelists on television had always turned my stomach. I couldn't understand how someone could preach about a salvation beyond earthly treasures and then ask for money in the next breath. I didn't trust them and didn't want your mother transforming into one of them. I desperately wanted to hold on to what was familiar.

JoAnn

A MOTHER JOURNALING THROUGH GRIEF

Before we can sleep at night, Danny and I kneel on the bed and lean over the headboard to look out the bedroom window. We search the sunset for you, because we believe you must be somewhere in those beautiful pink clouds. We pray to God for a sign of your continued life, because the tangibles are not there for us. Do you hear us pray to you too, Billy?

Somehow praying to an eighteen-month-old doesn't seem odd, because I think of you as being omniscient after your death. You've gone where I've never been and know secrets that no adult on earth could fathom.

"Billy, don't talk to any strangers and never go in swimming without Mommy and Daddy. And don't you ever go off the deep end of the dock. It's very dangerous!" Danny scolds and shakes his finger out the window toward our imagined location of Heaven. When Danny continues to be the protective big brother, it reminds me of how he would remove small objects from the floor so you wouldn't choke or when he would chase you down the shoreline so you wouldn't go near the water.

How does a mother choose the clothes her son will wear for eternity? For eighteen months, I changed your clothes without much thought. My only goal was keeping you warm and dry. That's all that mattered at the time, because you would grow out of every little shirt, pant and shoe within a few months.

Your dad let me pick out your death clothes, Billy. He doesn't seem to care about the small things since you've left. On the other hand, I always need to be doing something for you. I even miss changing your diaper — that natural motion of lifting your legs and wiping your bottom. My hand possesses an ache for that repetitive stroke. I've done it for four years, including Danny before you. Usually a parent is gradually weaned from it; for me, the routine has abruptly ended. How do I just stop?

With much reflection, I chose a sweat suit that your Grandma Deveny had sewn for you nine months earlier. I immediately noticed it was too large for you when I opened the gift last October. I also knew that it would be too small for the cold of the next winter when you would near the age of two. Ironically, you never would have worn it had you lived. Multi-colored sailboats decorate the front and the background color is the same as your eyes. The material is a plush layer of warmth for the cold Minnesota months. A rational mother would never dress her child in this outfit in the heat of the summer, but I did, because it would keep you warm in the cool earth surrounding your casket and you'd never outgrow its protective sleeves.

DENISE
THE SITTER

Why did you run around the house, instead of through the kitchen, Billy? Of course, you knew that path was the only way to escape without my noticing. And if you hadn't closed that screen door behind you, I would have found you giggling and running down the beach with me in close pursuit. That way, I would have absently forgotten that incident by the next day. But now it will stay with me forever.

I've often relived the anxiety I felt while searching the house for you. Each time, the memory pulls me into its terror as if it were happening for the first time. Even though parents in the area have kindly hired me to sit for them, I find it very difficult. I must have sight of their children every second or my mind will replay the panic of that day.

Only a few minutes had passed before I opened that screen door and scanned the lake for you from the deck. But it must have been just enough time for you to hide behind the neighbor's dock. If I had only walked five feet to my left, I would have seen you playing in the water. I was only five feet from that alternate fork in the road.

Chapter 10

DICK

We rarely left the refuge of our home in those first few days after your death, Billy. However, we learned that with a sudden death, there are places one can't avoid, such as cemetery plots, funeral homes, and places of worship. Though we were coaxed unwillingly to these engagements, we readily chose to pay a visit to Denise. We wanted this to be her tragedy, not ours. Because of our denial, we actually felt more sympathy toward her than ourselves at the time. So we ventured out to comfort the seventeen-year old whose life would be scarred forever by your journey into the water.

As she listened to Denise relive our mutual horror story, your mother began her search for the precise sequence of events that had occurred on that tragic day. While accepting her need to know, I personally preferred to cling to a vague, medicated description of your death.

What songs should a father choose for his son's funeral? The examples given to us by the church were conservative, ancient melodies, reminding me of my grandmother's funeral several years ago. Were there any children's funeral tunes for our toddler? Where was Raffi when you needed him?

"Do you want me to say anything special about Billy?" The priest's voice broke through my thoughts. He sat across the long table from your mother and me as the birds flitted from tree to tree outside the window behind him. I stared vacantly into that unreachable, sunny world, trying to find the words to his question. Neither your mother nor I could formulate a sufficient way to describe your uniqueness, Billy. Knowing that a few sentences could never encapsulate the effect you had on our lives, we just shook our heads.

How does a father pick out a coffin for his son? Walking through the room of choices, your mother opted for a soft velvet lining on which to comfortably lay your tiny head. And I choose the model with a hard white exterior and a vault surrounding it to protect your body from the dirty parasites of the ground.

How does a father pick out a gravestone for his child? While we leafed through the catalogue of engravings, a picture seemed to jump from the page. It was clearly you—a little angel with curly hair embracing a lamb. Nevertheless, we had quite a difficult time choosing the words to engrave. How could we sum up your life in just one phrase? Your mother wanted "Our Sonshine and Brother." I wanted "The Only Little Devil in Heaven." But neither would fit across the expanse of the cold, hard stone. So we settled for "Our Little Angel," even though the phrase didn't quite suit you. I could only imagine a tilted halo over your head and a slingshot in the back pocket of your denim robe.

During our visit to the funeral home, your mother and I choose not to have your body prepared for a viewing. Neither of us felt we needed to subject ourselves to that. Besides, a mortician could never portray the essence of your spirit in an inert body. But no sooner than we arrived home from that day of choices, we received a call with pleas for a change of heart.

Your Aunt Kathy was an idealist by nature—sometimes I found her refreshing and other times overly optimistic. She called us that day with a suggestion that we have your body prepared for viewing; she believed that saying good-bye in this way was an essential part of healing, a type of closure. Being that neither your mother nor I could manage strong feelings about any matter except our grief, we called the mortician to request that your veins be filled with formaldehyde.

JOANN
A MOTHER JOURNALING THROUGH GRIEF

Last night when I wrote a letter for you, Billy, my thoughts easily flowed onto the paper. But when I finished, I was at a loss of what to do with it. The letter isn't meant as a good-bye, Honey. I'll never say good-bye. You'll come back, I'll die, or the world will come to an end, because my life can't possibly continue this way.

While I wrote the letter, Danny slept fitfully by my side in bed. As soon as I finished signing it with hearts, he abruptly stilled from fretful tossing of only moments before, and his verbal ramblings stopped. I turned from the page of my notebook to find his eyes opened wide in wonder, a smile on his face, and a peaceful glow radiating from his eyes. He didn't seem to be awake, but he spoke very clearly.

"Billy," he whispered while dreamingly staring past me. I turned around to find nothing there. Then his eyelids closed again, and he fell asleep with the grin still on his lips. His face showed a relaxed contentment, which I hadn't seen since your death. With that vision in mind, I allowed my eyes to close along with all conscious thought, and the sleeping pill took effect.

A LETTER TO MY SON

Billy,

My precious, wonderful little baby. Every day you brought so much joy to my life and someday I'll laugh when I think about you, instead of cry. I miss you so much.

Your hugs were so tight, I felt as if you would never let me go. Then all of a sudden you would—running and laughing to the next door to break into or next chair to climb onto. I don't understand this, Honey, but could it be that someday I will?

Danny loves you so much. He's your best buddy and talks to you every night before he goes to bed. I know you hear him. Please, help him understand this. Help him remember you forever.

My arms ache to hold you—to stroke your soft, curly blonde hair that I loved so much. I want to rock you forever and sing to you like the last time. I hope you're happy and comfortable. No more ear infections, Honey.

Please, Billy my love, don't run away.... Let God hold you safely in his arms until I get there,

I'll Love You Forever,
Momma

Chapter 11

DICK

*Y*our mother and I sat in our allotted places on the living room couch while waiting to leave for our appointment at the funeral home that Monday morning. We were surrounded by numerous family members, who had become such routine fixtures that I didn't notice them anymore. Danny appeared at the top of the stairs.

Oblivious to anything else but navigating down the next step, he sported an elated grin as though waking from a wonderful dream. He skipped light-heartedly from the last step and then looked up to see the dejected entourage of visitors. His smile and the spark in his eyes vanished, and then he buried his face into the carpet on the bottom stair. Your mother jumped up from her seat on the couch to embrace him just as a tear started down his cheek.

For the last two days, everyone had tried to rationalize your death and comfort us with fancy, well-meaning words. And in turn, your mother and I tried to formulate the many questions ricocheting through our minds. But it was our three-year old son who said all that I wanted to scream at an unhearing God. While he pressed his face into your mother's shoulder, he said something so simple it seemed profound. In only three little words, he described everything I felt.

Danny defiantly stated, "I want Billy."

"Yes, Danny," your mother mimicked him. "I do, too. I want Billy, too." I joined them, and we held each other—Danny, repeating a wish that would make him happy again, and myself, wishing I could grant it.

As suddenly as his dejection started, it abruptly took leave and his face brightened again. He backed away and looked up at his mother with eyes as round as saucers.

"I saw Billy, Mommy" He stood upright, waiting for a reaction.

"When did you see him, Honey?"

"Last night. I saw Billy just drop by. He walked right through that door! He was as big as the door, Daddy...and he had angel eyes!" he exclaimed with wonder while his eyes excitingly pranced from his mother's to mine.

"That's wonderful, Honey. Did you have a dream?" I gently insinuated.

"Nope. It wasn't a dream. He just came to visit," Danny avowed, setting me straight without hesitation.

Believing her oldest son and desperately looking for a sign from her youngest, your mother earnestly prompted, "Did he say anything?"

"Uh-huh. He said, 'I love you and I miss you.' Then he said 'Good-bye.' And then he left. He was talking like a big boy!" Danny exclaimed with animation. And then, "Mommy, how did Billy get back to Heaven?"

~ ~ ~ ~ ~

I maneuvered the car up the winding driveway past the towering funeral home sign. As we were the only invited guests, the lot was vacant. So I parked directly in front of the white majestic doors. Your mother marveled at my ability behind the wheel—she felt that she was incapable of even a small feat such as driving. Though not understanding the reason for entering there, she shadowed me like a duckling after its mother into the hallway of the foreboding building. And I was only able to lead the way by not allowing any thoughts of the past or the future.

We had been dreading that morning, when your mother and I would see your *old body*. That's what we called your corpse, Billy. In the first few hours after your death, Danny couldn't comprehend that you were alive somewhere, while not being able to see or play with you. So we referred to your *old body* as the one to be buried and your *new body* as the one given to you in Heaven. It was odd referring to you as an *old* anything, but your brother could more easily understand your death in these terms.

Danny was a bright three-year old, but had never been exposed to the definitions of death, God, Heaven, or the meaning of *forever*. Consequently, he had yet to understand any of these four abstract concepts, which is why we decided to leave Danny at home for the viewing. We also decided, with as much reflection as we could endeavor, that Danny was too young to understand the presence of an immobile Billy. It was a decision we regretted later.

I needed to hold the door to the funeral home open for your mother, Billy, because her arms were full of your memories. She clutched three nighttime necessities: your little brown bunny, your blue blanket, and your pacifier. The letter she had written to you was folded into an envelope, which she placed in her back pocket. She wrote *Billy* on the front of it, as if there were any question of who would receive it while intending to place it next to your body in your coffin.

The little, white casket sat by itself across the large, florescent-lit room. The pathway seemed endless as we walked by rows of vacant seats and neared the pedestal at its end. The profile of a small face stood out from the background of shining white satin, protruding from the confines of the brocade box. Even though we stepped gingerly, the sound of our footsteps echoed through the empty corners of the room.

The little boy in front of us seemed to be sleeping. *Who is that unfortunate child?* There were no curls—his hair was drastically combed backward from his smooth forehead with a shiny layer of greasy hair product. His mouth and chin were puffy, while his little lips were forced together in an effort to mimic the semblance of peaceful sleep. The skin of the boy's face had a dull finish; there was no luster of life on those rouge-painted cheeks. He wore an aqua sweat suit with sailboats stenciled on the front.

As we stood above him, your mother's hand moved without thought toward his forehead. While her fingers trembled over fine strands of hair, the cold hardness of his face touched her back. Then one lone golden lock sprang into a curl and fell naturally onto his face. That's when she noticed the pointed nodule on the top of his right ear and finally understood.

The truth hit her like an arrow through her heart. It was your body, Billy. Its vitality had charmed her only three days before. This is where you once lived, though she found no recognition of her spirited child in the cold shell left behind.

But if not there, where are you, Honey? This is the only place I knew you. You trusted me to take care of you and I failed. I'm here now—please come back. I'll never leave you again. She silently begged for atonement.

I urgently pulled your mother's hand from the grotesque creature that dared to mimic my son. Still slick from hair gel, her fingers groped the confines of her back pocket for the letter. She placed it, your bunny, and pacifier next to the aqua-blue sleeve of your garment, fully aware that it was within reach of your immobile hands. But she couldn't force herself to leave your blue blanket in the satin that surrounded your body. She held it tightly to her nose, breathing in the musty essence. Somehow she knew you had no need for it anymore. The flesh casing in that box wasn't you. So your blanket was hers to keep.

JoAnn
November, 1985

"That's just how I feel, Sheryl. I don't believe in that paranormal stuff, why do you think it's called that? PARA-normal....and he charges how much?"

I was riding in the passenger seat shotgun to Sheryl, while my other friend, Shirley, remained neutral and silent in the back seat. We were often a threesome, usually frequenting the popular singles bars. This outing was an unusual deviation from our party ways. Sheryl had made an appointment with a clairvoyant on a whim and in celebration of Shirley's birthday.

"Oh quit whining. It'll be fun. He only charges $30 for a palm reading, which is below standard, and I've heard he's very good."

In deference to Shirley, I refrained from further protest but silently thought, *Thirty dollars! We could have a good meal and a couple drinks.*

It was 1985. At that time, your father and I had been dating over a year. Although our romance was in full swing, we were still committed to our single life and held no intentions of marriage in the near future.

Despite my aversion to the psychic session, I found myself sitting at a kitchen table holding hands with a stranger. My palm was outstretched, showing every crease and wrinkle in full view of the alleged prophet.

"I see a little boy...."

Yeah, right, he's so off the mark—why did I let Sheryl talk me into this? I thought while discretely rolling my eyes away from the man.

"Does this mean anything to you?" *Why is he asking **me**? He's the clairvoyant.*

"Nope, doesn't mean a thing" I wasn't about to play into his little game. But he didn't react to my snippy reply and merely closed his eyes for what seemed like minutes.

"...and I see sailboats."

Well, okay, Dick is a boater, but not a sail boater or a "blow" boater, I thought. I had learned from your father that power boaters call sail boaters "blow boaters," as they call us "stink boaters," usually in a friendly, teasing exchange.

"Nope, sailboats don't mean a thing either," I tersely replied. *Lucky guess, but not on the mark, try again.* The clairvoyant continued this time with emotion in his voice.

"I see a little boy...he's sleeping ....and I see colorful sailboats....."

"No, that doesn't mean any...." I stopped in mid-sentence when seeing his eyes fly open with a panicked expression. Staring wide-eyed, the clairvoyant seemed to look right through me. Was it pity in his eyes, or did I depict a hint of fear?

He quickly regained his composure and turned his attention back to the wrinkles on my palm. *Strange man,* I thought.

"I see a check coming to you, I see the figure $5,000...." He changed the subject while his voice droned as if far away in thought.

Yeah, right, I mused.

Chapter 12

DICK

*A*bove all, decisions kept us busy after your death, Billy. The black suit waiting in the back of my closet was an easy choice. But what does a mother wear for her son's funeral? As we dressed ourselves for the funeral, your mother methodically pondered her options—even though she had no intentions to impress anyone.

Your Aunt Jeanne brought three outfits from her closet for your mother to choose from. One dress was a soft blue, reminding her of her baby boy, another was a conservative tan screaming of respectability, and the last was a red, black, and white garrulously patterned dress. Your mother tried to choose the outfit that would most symbolize her son's death.

Why she picked the red, black, and white patterned dress puzzles me to this day. Was it to deny that you had died—making it unnecessary to be dressed in subdued pastels or morbid black attire? Or did she identify the flamboyant print of the fabric as the chaotic pattern of her own mind?

The day of your funeral, Billy, was the day I saw your mother as she must have been as a small child—quite a contrast from the feisty young woman I had once known. She stood next to your coffin in the back of the church still clutching your blue blanket in her arms. By habit, your mother stationed herself next to her toddler's side. Though not intending to form a receiving line, that's exactly what happened.

One by one, consolers approached her in turn after viewing your pictures on the table in front of your casket. Along with your photos were one Mickey Mouse sandal, your bottle, your favorite books, your size-eight dock shoes, and the sticks and rocks you loved to gather from our yard.

We choose not to have strangers gawk over a freakish replica, so the casket was closed and in lieu, we displayed an 8 x 10 image of your smiling face atop its white brocade. Whenever your mother moved even slightly, your eyes in the picture seemed to follow her. So she would, periodically, experiment by walking a few feet to the left or right across the room, with her line of consolers in tow. I watched as the row of visitors smoothly moved in syncopation in front of her, waving back and forth like grass in the wind. Of course, her intention was not to amuse me at the expense of our guests, but to see the motion of life appear from your two-dimensional face, Billy. And she couldn't stop herself from smiling back at you.

One of the earliest guests at the church was the first firefighter at the scene of your drowning. To show his respect, he had come in full uniform. Not knowing you but recalling your face, he leaned toward each picture on the table as if trying to get a closer look, when in fact, he was really attempting to hide the tears brimming in his eyes.

Soon after his arrival came a flight attendant in uniform, whom your mother called her angel-with-metal-wings. Jeanette, the only co-worker who had been notified of your death by the airline, had a three-hour layover in Minneapolis that coincided with the time of your funeral. Any flight attendant would marvel at this miraculous coincidence because Jeanette's trip had been scheduled three weeks before you died.

The church started to burst with activity. There were friends and family dating back to grade school, high school, and college whom we hadn't seen for years; there were church and community acquaintances we had seen a few days before. Numerous extended family members of mine came from Texas, Canada, and even farther away—some your mother had never met at all.

Whispered conversations filled in the foreground and there was an indistinguishable distant drone in the background, like the hum of an electrical wire. She could hear sporadic words through the murmurs.

"I'm so sorry."

"He was a beautiful boy."

"If there's anything I can do."

When looking into the revolving faces before her, she could read raw emotions of fear, love, passion, and oddly, in a few she detected righteousness. Through the emotional boundaries that shock allowed her, her intuition was at an enhanced level. While some guests gave condolences, she could read accusation in their eyes. It was the absence of empathy in them that she saw as evil.

"Well, some people learn too late how dangerous the lake can be," the strange woman in front of her spewed. The woman frowned with her lips and laughed with her eyes while her words formed a wrecking-ball, crushing your mother's chest where her heart once was. This woman seemed to know your mother's guilt—that she had killed you by the hands of her own neglect.

On occasion, piercing laughter permeated the rumbling voices. Every semblance of levity taunted her, and she couldn't tune it out. Her only diversion from the invasive laughter was the people who valiantly approached her with words from their hearts. And it was their tears that ultimately embraced her. But she wasn't able to shed a tear of her own or express her appreciation for theirs.

"It was meant to be," the next woman in line stated while holding her own young toddler in her arms. *What gives you the right to defend my son's untimely death? How can you claim that my child wasn't meant to live, but yours was?* your mother wanted to ask her, but remained silent.

"God never gives us what we can't handle," the next man proclaimed as he held your mother's hand in his, attempting to console her. *But I can't handle this,* she wanted to yell at his ignorance, *and I would hate God if I believed He had caused this.*

The surrounding world was alive; she was not. Her isolation from the world was due to its vibrancy, and not from the fact that she was excluded. You see, she didn't want to occupy that lively place—she wanted to be with you, Billy. So when friends and relatives approached her with stuttered words of sympathy, she surreally watched them from a distance. Even though every corner and aisle of the church was filled with a mixture of strange and familiar faces, she wasn't a component of their world—she was alone with you. She watched your eyes in the picture follow her as she moved again with her receiving line in tow.

"Is there anything else I can do for you, Mrs. Deveny?" A questioning young man appeared at her side. It took a moment for her to identity his face—his dark hair was slicked backward at the temples as yours was in your coffin. She reasoned that he must be the coroner. Though she had never met him, he had called our home numerous times in the past few days with the same question.

Yes, you can bring my son back, she always wanted to say in response. Even within her insanity, she knew he wasn't capable of this, so she could never think of a single request. But at your funeral, she remembered that empty space in your baby book.

"Could you measure and weigh Billy for me?" she requested, because your eighteen-month pediatrician's appointment was scheduled for the same day the coroner measured you for a casket. "…and could you also cut me a lock of his hair?" she said while recalling our trip to the mortuary earlier that day. She wanted to wash the oil out of your curls.

Seeming to be the center of attention amid the numerous visitors, I was clueless of the reason for the gathering and my presence in church on a Tuesday. It was as if the guests were there for a party in my honor, though the event escaped me. So I left your mother at your casket, Billy, and blended in with the crowd. Ed Worley, Rick Mieneke, and Jim Fox came to my rescue in succession—friends who had been essential for my survival through the prior three days. It was friends like these who could truly share in my loss, unlike those who had not known you.

A very disheartening notion for me was that there were very few people at your funeral who could genuinely portray tears of grief while remembering you. You weren't school age or in any organized sports— although I often fantasized that you would have been an excellent athlete. Many would never get the chance to experience the delightful gift you brought to this world. But, I understood that these people were very much like me before your death—trusting in the future years, believing that your life would unfold for all to see.

Such a normal human fallacy; to assume a child's continued life. I also held the typical assumption that I'd be afforded another chance to say "I love you" or "I'm sorry" for my failings. And I assumed that I would merely be able to say "good-bye" one last time. So I felt no resentment for those who didn't know you, Billy, only empathy. What a loss for them.

The ones who knew you best, your daycare providers, were all there; Odessa, Teresa, Beth and her teenage daughter, Jessica, who wordlessly cried in your mother's arms.

"Calm down, Jessica," Beth whispered to her daughter, while your mother wanted to correct her.

Please, let her cry. I need her to cry for me, your mother silently pleaded. *Scream, pull out your hair…pray on your knees for my son to come back and curse the God who took him from me! I'm expected to put on a facade of stoicism while burying my true emotions so you can be comfortable and say that I'm "taking it well." Please, let her cry for me.*

It wasn't completely the barriers of social etiquette that stopped your mother from showing her true feelings, Billy—she just didn't have the energy to scream out as she wanted to. Also, she was afraid of never coming back from insanity once arriving there. *Please,* she wanted to say to each guest at the macabre party, *do it for me.*

So she continued to silently stand near your coffin as guests approached her. There was only one whom she approached herself—the bravest of all visitors, your babysitter, Denise. By wrapping her arms around the young woman, your mother embraced Denise's guilt and tried to take it as her own. But Denise refused to relinquish it and seized it back.

"I'm *so* sorry" Denise whispered almost inaudibly. She raised her tear-stained face from your mother's shoulder and looked deeply into her eyes. *No, I'm so sorry,* your mother wanted to say to her.

"This is for you." Denise handed your mother a red rose. And in one motion, your mother took her pardon from Denise and turned around to surrender it to the top of your coffin, Billy. And there it remained, dangling between the two of them.

The warmth of an embrace encircled her leg. Your mother looked down to see Danny's smiling eyes. His ankles were revealed under the outgrown pant legs of his navy blue suit that Grandma Jen had found in the back of his closet for the unexpected affair. His expression was genuinely pure; there was no sign of hidden emotions behind his innocent grin. She stooped down and held his goodness close to her body as a shield.

Danny skipped between the shuffling feet of his distant parents while we moved down the aisle toward our reserved front pew. As if our backs were frozen in place on the hard wood, we were unable to participate in the sequence of physical calisthenics that Catholics endure. While the congregation around us kneeled, stood, and sign-of-the-crossed in congregational unison, we sat idle. The shiny white casket cast a foreboding presence in the aisle next to our seats. The banal hum of the organ filled the expansive room and the tenor from the choir loft belted out *On Eagle's Wings*. But we sat songless in the pew.

I remember staring vacantly from our front row pew, wondering why we weren't in our normal hiding place in the back row. The six innocent faces of your cousins, ranging from ages twelve to six, transported the symbolic gifts of Christ's body down the aisle to the altar, and so I thought of the companionship these relatives could have brought had you lived.

One niece was missing, little Michelle. She was the same age as you, Billy. To avoid comparison and in deference to your mother, your Aunt Theresa left her at home. Your mother's sister thought Michele's presence might be a painful reminder. But Michelle was nothing like you, Billy. Nobody could come close. Besides, there seemed to be a knife twisting back and forth in your mother's heart already; nothing could make the situation more painful. So like a tourniquet for a wound, she clutched your soft blanket against her chest.

We left our seat in the pew to follow behind your six uncles, who firmly grasped the handles of your casket in their hands. Audible sobs could be heard from my brother-in-laws as they effortlessly carried your body down that endless aisle. As these grown men cried, I silently thanked them for putting down their shields of male pride to mourn for my son. The casket, they said later, was too light.

"I'm so sorry."

"You have all my sympathy."

"It was meant to be."

"God wanted him in Heaven."

"You're so lucky you have Danny."

"If there's anything I can do...."

Your mother's glasses slid down her nose on a lubricant of sweat, so she pushed them back in place to view the accumulation of people satiating the small confines of the parish cafeteria. Members of the Women's Guild busily dished out casseroles and carefully poured liquid from silver pitchers for the crowd. Gentle, well-meaning words were accompanied by a rumbling drone of voices. Still, the prattle was diminished by the laughter from well-wishers of only moments before.

What are you laughing about! she wanted to scream, but had no energy.

"I'm so sorry."

"It was God's plan."

"Something good will come of it."

"You should eat something."

Your Aunt Jeanne appeared at her side. While gently placing a hand on your mother's shoulder, she leaned down to her and asked, "Do you want to donate the flowers from the altar or bring them home, Honey?"

Drops of sweat rolled down her bangs and into her eyes. Your mother pushed the sliding glasses upon the bridge of her nose again. It was a constant struggle to keep her body upright in the hard, metal chair, and her eyelids struggled to remain opened. She found it hard to think above the noise of the laughter. *Stop it!* She silently shouted. *There is absolutely nothing to laugh about!*

"I don't care what we do with the flowers...I can't think. I have to get out of here. I have to go home," Her lungs grasped for breath as she took in the humid air that permeated the room. Seated next to her, I wrapped my arms around her while her body folded into me.

"Let's go," I whispered in her ear, even though I didn't know where we could possibly go from there. She nodded.

While I strapped Danny into the back seat of our car, your mother absently stared out the car window to watch her sisters load their cars with baskets of flower arrangements from the church. And in that manner, we prematurely drove away from our own party, your mom and I in the front seat, both aware of the void in back next to Danny.

When we walked through the door of our house, in unison, the three of us automatically scanned the room. But the miniature rocking chair in front of the television still sat empty.

JOANN

A MOTHER JOURNALING THROUGH GRIEF

Oddly enough, after seeing your corpse, my belief in the afterlife is more solid. When discovering that your spirit was gone from your body, I can only conclude that it had to have gone somewhere.

It makes me wonder how some people believe that a life could possibly end — especially scientists when they, above all people, know the proven law of energy. Energy never disappears or ceases to exist; it just changes form. Your energy, your spirit, your soul, or whatever man has named the core of your personality, couldn't possibly disappear or vanish. But in fact, it must have changed form and traveled beyond your earthly body. In that moment at the side of your coffin, I felt you inside my heart. It was a revelation — my child was not going to be buried as waste into the cold, dark earth after all. So I left that empty shell at the funeral home and carried your spirit home with me.

The coroner gave me a snip of your hair today, Billy. I imagine I'll keep it in that teddy bear frame I bought for your 18-month photo that will never be taken. I'll label it "authentic angel hair" — that would be appropriate, don't you think?

After removing the lock from the coroner's envelope, I gingerly rubbed it with the same baby shampoo I had always massaged into your scalp. I took such care not to lose one strand of my precious golden commodity while rinsing the shampoo from it. Then I placed the wet hair between two tissues, patted it gently, and held one end between two fingers. As the moisture gradually vaporized, it came alive in my hands. I wondered, at that moment, how the rest of you could be so completely dead.

And even though I know you exist somewhere, Honey, I couldn't help but question my God as the beautiful gold hues of your lock appeared and gradually curled into a question mark. Why? Why?

DENISE
THE SITTER

After not finding you at the lakeside, the dangers of the street behind the house occurred to me. Because as humans we are unable to peer through docks or predict the future, I left the waterfront to search the busy street in front. Was it five minutes or ten minutes? I know it wasn't any longer.

But it was just enough time for your little lungs to fill with water. When I returned to the lakeside (this is the last moment I vividly remember), your lifeless body was floating face down in the rolling waves.

I've been told that I screamed at that moment. I've been told that with Danny in one arm, I tried to lift your bloated body out of the water with the other. I've only been told that, because that part I've succeeded in forgetting to this very day.

Would you know my name,
If I saw you in heaven?
— Tears in Heaven

Chapter 13

DICK

Wink, wink, wink. The green light pulsated from the cell phone in front of us. It was Wednesday; we hadn't seen you since Saturday. Four eternal days. Your mother and I had only left you once for that length of time, and she had always blamed me.

I foolishly persuaded your mother to take a vacation to Tampa in the spring of 1990 when you were only four months old. We were gone for a week and, in retrospect, she didn't enjoy herself at all. Within a couple hours of leaving the house, she missed you. To make matters worse, you didn't recognize her when we picked you up from your Aunt Kathleen's and Uncle Tom's home after our vacation. Your mother vowed that she would never leave you for that long again and never did.

The green eye continued to wink on and off, on and off. I wondered if you would recognize us, Billy, if we spent a month, five years…or fifty years away—which could be the reality. Without a trace of cloud in the skies, the sun shone brightly down on us while the tinted windows of the car screened us from the brightness. I was driving, your mother was in the passenger seat, and Danny was seated between us. We knew he should have been safely strapped in the car seat, but that day we couldn't bear to see him alone in that expansive backseat designed for two. The tail end of a white Cadillac was our view as we followed the vehicle to the cemetery. We passed under a sign posted outside a local restaurant, *Billy's Lighthouse*. The large scripted words disappeared behind us as we paraded behind the corpse of our son.

Our destination was St. Mary's Cemetery in the heart of Minneapolis, your final resting place. As we drove beneath the archway and through the gates, they seemed to swallow us with their formidable welcome. Your mother wore a yellow and white polka-dotted dress, a likeness to the arrangement of daisies she had requested Aunt Theresa to order for your casket. She had selected daisies because they seemed to be the perfect proclamation of your innocence and the farthest extreme from the hard, ancient headstones towering over your gravesite. Odd that your final surroundings should be such a sharp contrast to your soft, pure life.

Your white casket stood on a lift over a cloth-covered hole near a withering elm tree, while the arrangement of daisies was positioned in front. A large stone read DEVENY in the midst of five existing gravesites; Your Great-grandpa and Great-grandma Deveny, great-uncle, great-aunt, and some relative thrice-removed—none who ever knew you. Nevertheless, I felt some comfort in knowing that your body was resting next to my Grandma Deveny, who in life had clearly shown a preference for little boys. The memories of fresh-baked cookies and warm hugs were still vivid in my mind.

At the time of your death, only one vacancy remained in the Deveny plot, Billy. Only a child could have occupied that space because the elm tree's roots had invaded it, diminishing the remaining plot by half. It seemed to have been waiting for your death.

Danny stood between your mother and me with two helium balloons grasped tightly in his fist—one for him and one, we told him, to release for you to catch in the heavens. But even with the wall of death separating the two of you, Danny refused to release the one designated for you, Billy. He felt, as we did, that you still existed.

The sun warmed our shoulders and the wind softly caressed our faces while the priest prayed in front of us. Family members and a few close friends surrounded our family of three, some in silent reverence and others with muffled sobs.

Empathy surrounded us. The air seemed to be filled with sadness for your mother, me, Danny and also for you, Billy. And there was a sense of fear—not for us, but for themselves. This event reminded everyone that the destiny of our bodies would be the darkness of the ground. This moment seemed to ultimately preach that life is short, some lives much shorter than others.

Your mother gave Danny a blue carnation and prodded him to place it on your casket. "Give this to Billy, Honey…it's okay, go on," she instructed him. Your mother and I clung to each other while looking on in silence. Danny needed to stretch his full body to reach the top of the casket with the carnation in hand. After doing so, he turned around toward us, beaming with accomplishment. Your mother reached out her arms to him, welcoming him back into our embrace.

It was over. No more rocking, no more diapers, no more tricks to make us chuckle, no more nose tweaks, no more face hugs, no more sparkle from those sky-blue eyes. Ended. Gone. Oh, so absolutely final—to give up everything in that moment and relinquish your pampered body into the cold ground.

One lone voice started to sing behind us, and then another joined in with a lullaby of yesterday. One by one, vocalists surrounded us until everyone was singing your song, Billy.

Somewhere over the rainbow, way up high.
There's a land that I heard of once in a lullaby.
If happy little bluebirds fly beyond the rainbow,
Why, oh, why can't I?

The clouds suddenly moved in and darkness enveloped the gravesite. And just as quickly, I imagined that our little bluebird flew to that place of no troubles. When your wings cleared that rainbow, the heavens broke loose with the rumbling of anger and a clap of anguish.

And God wept for those left behind.

JOANN

A MOTHER JOURNALING THROUGH GRIEF

It was odd how the weather seemed to suddenly come from nowhere; there hadn't been a cloud in the sky before the interment. But, when we reached Jeanne and Dave's house afterward, the rain poured down.

I wanted to cover my ears as the idle chatter surrounded me in their newly constructed kitchen. Hadn't you, Danny, and I been there just a few weeks before, Billy? Remember when I had to crawl after you through the dirt when you escaped under the newly-boarded steps?

It was a relief when your godfather, Uncle Dave, asked us to gather in the living room to say a prayer for you, because you were the only thing on my mind. As we took our places, the thunder roared and you patiently waited until the last person was seated before you turned all the lights off. The room became dark and silent; no one spoke. Only a few moments passed before the lights came back on, but it seemed much longer. When the room lit up, a release of tension was felt from all.

Was I the only one who could clearly hear your little voice say "Off!" as if you were standing next to me in the darkness? And when you said "On!", changing the solemn ambience of that room to a new brightness, did anyone else see your eight-tooth smile light up with it?

As suddenly as the hard rain started, every cloud vacated the sky. The rain then stopped and the thunder was silenced—leaving only the sun and the echo of your voice. "Off, On."

Am I losing my mind, or is it already gone and that's why I'm so numb? How can people continue their futile motions as if your death changed nothing at all? The common aspects of life disgust me. I struggle to survive through each endless minute during the day yet wake up at night to suddenly realize that it's already been a week since you breathed your last breath. The trees keep growing, the flowers keep blooming, and my lungs keep pumping life's air in and out when you're at a standstill in time.

This has left me with one foot planted on earth with my oldest son and one hand reaching into the skies for my youngest, finding myself in a land called Nowhere. And here I remain, a stranger in a vital environment—a ghostly apparition walking aimlessly through a living world. As I grasp onto the whispers of your soul, the world is leaving you behind—and I look on in horror as it forgets you.

ELLEN

A MOTHER JOURNALING THROUGH GRIEF

It's been said that if a major piece of news is relayed to a flight attendant, it will travel around the world by the next day. The day after it happened, I had just left the aircraft and entered the jetway when a flight attendant informed me about Billy's death. Even though I hadn't met JoAnn Deveny at that point, I could truly feel her pain. It seemed as if a smothering wave of unpleasant memories and buried feelings suddenly consumed me.

For three days after, even the simplest task ended up with a display of tears and embarrassment. Sheryl, a mutual friend of both JoAnn's and mine, tried to persuade me to contact her thinking I could be of help. But how could I, when just the thought of Billy transformed me into a blubbering idiot?

Had I not reconciled with my own grief? Or was I afraid that I'd cry in front of JoAnn and make her feel worse? Whatever the reason, something happened that made none of that matter anymore. I had never experienced anything like this before and never did again.

It was three days after Billy's death. I was at the kitchen sink, vacantly staring out the window in front of me while running warm water over the dinner dishes from the night before. My dinner guest was a five-year steady relationship, the only one since the death of my husband in Vietnam twenty years before.

By that time, I had left the longing for husband behind and had become a stronger woman. Some may have said I was a bit hardened in my attempts to mask the pain. But I know that it was really the guilt and grief from my own son's death that formed me and which I had yet to resolve.

Being raised by conservative parents in my homeland of Germany, I believed in their religious views: one God and skepticism toward ghostly apparitions on this earth. My upbringing gave me a sense of security through my adversities...and had also taught me how to successfully bury my feelings.

The warm water flowed over my hands as I reflected on JoAnn's loss, which brought back the fresh stab of my own. Joey had only been six. The questions surged through my mind. *Why didn't I see the car before it hit us?* I definitely remember seeing the green left turn arrow, its image is seared into my mind. Then why did the police issue me a ticket, and not the other driver? I know that I wasn't in any position to defend myself at that time. Why did I take that road to the car wash when I never had before? And why had God allowed Billy to run into the water unseen?

I held back my tears and turned to transfix on the condensation gradually forming on the window in front of me—and that's when I heard them. My hand stopped its movement while my whole body froze. Even though the water gushed noisily through the faucet, I could only hear their laughter. It was a blend of warm chuckles and gut giggles from young children. Even though I hadn't heard it for years, at once I recognized his laugh. For some reason, I turned toward the dining room on my right and saw the beaming face of my own child.

My heart warmed and I allowed the tears to flow down my cheeks, finally released.

"Joey...Oh, Joey, I love you, Honey," I whispered. The energy and mirth seemed to radiate from both children in a blinding halo of brightness. My son seemed amused by the golden-haired toddler running in front of him as he chased him through a rolling field of glorious colors, which I could never name. The younger boy seemed to fly through a light as he threw back a mischievous eight-toothed grin at his pursuer, my son. I felt my face relax and an unusual smile appeared on my lips.

Then too soon, the outline of their bodies gradually faded and the dull, beige dining room started to appear in the background. Trying to delay their departure, I blinked and squinted through my tears. The gush of running water became more audible, but I could still hear the children's abating laughter. Though they disappeared into the halo of light and I never saw them again, the warmth of their laughter never left me.

I called JoAnn that afternoon.

Somewhere a child has risen
Someday I will rise
To meet you gladly
My precious Billy,
My precious Billy.
—Billy's Song

Chapter 14

DICK

After July 13th, your mother and I learned that negative events in life don't wait for a tragedy to dispel. Only a few days after your funeral, we discovered that your godmother, my sister Susie, had surgery that week for advanced melanoma. Your Grandpa Deveny was diagnosed with prostate cancer that Thursday, and when I returned to my office on Friday, I found that an uninsured vehicle was stolen from my lot in my absence. It had undeniably been a formidable week.

I returned to work in order to escape your memory, Billy. I found the ambience of our home stagnant and the silence deafening. It seemed as if I were tiptoeing around a deep, dark hole that you had left behind.

But your mother couldn't stifle the sounds of your existence. She saw you running through the barren hallways and heard your voice beckon through the stillness. While walking aimlessly through the house still looking for your lost sandal, she would habitually close cupboards and push back chairs so you wouldn't harm yourself.

Even though she could sense your presence, it didn't stop her from placing your pictures where they comforted her the most—on each wall and table of every room. When visiting others' homes, she also expected your timeless image to be in clear view. Soon every family member eventually caught on and sensitively retrieved your picture from hiding before her arrival at their homes. Our families became quite knowledgeable in grief etiquette, and I appreciated them for it.

Your mother gathered your photos and included them with her thank-you notes, hoping that the recipients would come to know you through visual aids. I didn't complain as she spent her last paycheck on reprinting your pictures in an attempt to bring you back. This fruitless mission only left us with numerous manila envelopes stuffed with inert images and a diminished bank account.

Accumulating in an old shoebox was the memorabilia of your death: the sympathy cards, obituary, mass intentions, letters from your cousins, your death certificate, and a photo taken at your interment. She felt that the evidence of your death couldn't be thrown out because, regretfully, they were a part of your life. Had it been my way, they would have been discarded in the nearest trash can along with my grief. But your mother held on to them with hers.

These items seemed to have no place in your baby book or family photo album. So she was at a loss to their allotted place until the pastoral minister at our church gave her a binder to place them in. The front of the binder read, *There is a land of the living and a land of the dead, and the bridge is love.* So she collected her memorabilia in that binder and spanned the distance.

Every time she opened the refrigerator door, the bottle of amoxicillin for your ear infections was a painful reminder, but she couldn't bring herself to throw it away. When entering the downstairs bathroom, she would turn to look down the sink drain, knowing that the toothbrush you had thrown down that long dark tunnel still remained even though she couldn't see it. Just like you.

Wandering aimlessly through the house, she would climb stairs and walk into rooms only to forget her purpose for entering there. When she washed her hair in the small confines of our shower, a claustrophobic anxiety enveloped her. Without warrant, your likeness under the water would appear; unable to take a breath, crying out for help. She kept reliving your death scene with a different cast of characters and incessantly felt an urge to physically lift your body out of the water.

All the memories of rejections in her life replayed themselves in her dreams. The jilting of a high school boyfriend and the teasing by classmates during her gawky, adolescent years came back through unconscious thoughts, summoned by an inferior opinion of herself. The pride and self-confidence she had maintained through her lifetime was gone. How could she not be humbled? How could she feel above God after He raised His arm with one effortless motion and backhanded her to the ground?

She felt cast out and worthless. She still wore no make-up and recklessly lopped off her hair with sewing scissors when it blocked her sight of your pictures. Being imprisoned by her guilt, she wore shabby, black clothing suitable for an inmate. Pound after pound was shed from her dwindling frame. Her breaths became involuntary, incessant sighs, which irritated me like fingernails on a chalkboard.

The frivolous sitcoms Danny and I watched were offensive to your mother. We could tune you out for a while by turning up the volume, but she wasn't able to. While searching for answers, she would tune into the Christian radio stations. Trying to find your new companions, she would pour over the obituaries in the newspaper. While I read fictional books by authors like Michener and Clancy to divert my thoughts, your mother read books on death, religion, Heaven, after-life, and near-death experiences. She said she could only concentrate on your new home and new daycare providers.

Her favorite author was Elizabeth Kubler-Ross, because it was within the stages of grief where she learned about her fluctuating emotions: denial, anger, bargaining, depression, and acceptance. Your mother learned that these stages don't always come in sequence nor occur singularly through the grief process. The pattern is custom designed by the individual griever.

I found that your mother's and my grief pattern were mirror images of the other. We were never at the same stage together. Within a few months, your mother had experienced a touch of each stage, barring acceptance. This stage, she swore, she would never allow herself to reach. At that time, I seemed to be stuck in the anger stage.

"Death is like shedding a winter jacket in the spring," Kubler-Ross wrote in one of her grief books. Though your mother attempted to take on this fresh outlook as her own, the gaiety around her was offensive to her hypersensitive emotions. She felt that everyone was overly energetic and cheerful. Lacking passion for anything but having you back, she wanted to silence their laughter and endless chatter; she wanted them to only talk about you.

This was about the time that your mother started smoking again, Billy. Being a smoker myself, I was left without judgment and somehow understood how the addiction gave her something to anticipate.

Each morning, I would wake up to find her gone from our bed. After hearing your voice at 5:30 a.m. and finding your crib empty, your mother would make her way down to the kitchen table to write down her thoughts in your incomplete baby book. Sitting there under the light of the lamp, she would try to commemorate your memory so the world would stop for a moment to remember your life. Yet each day, the sun insisted on peeking its bright nodule over the pink horizon, announcing the beginning of a new day.

I removed the *For Sale* sign from our front yard, because the need for a larger living space vanished when you did. The drapes on our lakeside windows were finally opened. Even though I frequently entertained guests on our deck, it took your mother longer to venture to the lakeside of the house. Facing the backdrop to your death was a challenge for her, but she eventually forced herself to prevent her fears of the lake from permeating to Danny. Reluctantly, she journeyed to the water three weeks after it took your life.

When she opened that sliding door for the first time, you ran outside with her and she subconsciously relived your actions on that day. You followed her to the dock, and when she sat down on its edge, you ran into the water and disappeared.

"I don't want to wear a life jacket, Mommy. I want my water wings!" Danny begged from the water.

"No, Honey, not today." Her toes barely brushed the water as they dangled from the dock, the contact sent a chill through her body. She would normally be in the water, playing the role of a shark with Danny and you as her prey. There she would mimic the soundtrack from *Jaws* while skimming the top of the water, her eyes always on her boys. You and Danny would feign desperate screams, intermingled with giggles at the sight of your docile mother turned predator. Routinely, Danny wore water wings because she would be at his side at all times. But there was nothing normal or routine about the water anymore.

While staring at the sandy bottom of the lake before her, she imagined your desperate attempts to lift your little nose into the life-saving oxygen above. She tried to stop her mind from envisioning scaly sunfish nipping at your beautiful body as it buoyed among the schools. That once-sandy lakeshore appeared polluted as she selectively viewed the black rocks, slimy weeds, and foul dirt at its bottom where your last view of life must have occurred. Danny, clad in a life jacket, splashed happily at her feet.

"Help, help! I'm drowning!" Danny screamed, flailing his arms around his head, splashing the water into the air. Her thoughts broken, your mother stared at him with shock. "I'll save you, Billy! I'm coming!" Danny's words followed him as he dog-paddled deeper into the water. His little arms scooped up a handful of seaweed and brought it to shore. Your mother cringed.

"Danny! Don't say that unless you really are in trouble, please....and stay in the shallow water!" His head briefly disappeared under the surf while her words hung in the lake breeze unheard. She stared vacantly at the horrors of the past while Danny romped in the water and played lifeguard, saving you over and over with his repetitive game.

Your mother and Danny stayed for a couple hours at the water's edge that day, reacquainting themselves with the memories and the imaginings, coming to a truce somewhere in the middle.

JOANN

A MOTHER JOURNALING THROUGH GRIEF

Our lives aren't our own anymore. In knowing our loss, everyone in our small town also knows our address, our children's ages, our occupations; basically, the entirety of our lives. It's impossible to remain anonymous when I go to the local grocery or drug store. Most of the cashiers know our story, and for the few who don't, I often feel the need to explain the reason for my rude behavior.

But by far the hardest place for me is the grocery store, where there are shelves of items reminding me of you: diapers, squirt guns, and the produce section with the automated mist spray. I had to force myself to drive there to return the diapers I had purchased the day you died. Complete, unbroken families were everywhere. Even Danny noticed and commented, "Everyone has a brother but me."

The cashier who had always teased you was there. But she didn't ask me where you were as if you never existed. Did I only imagine that you lived? I was happy before you were born. If I pretend that I never knew you, would that make me happy again?

Where are you among those faces, Billy? There are so many people surrounding me, but I feel so alone. I can sense their awkward hesitation; they don't know what to do to help me.

I want to tell them to hug me—I'm missing that physical touch from my child. I want to tell them that I may cry when they hold me, but that allows me to release my tears.

I'd say to them, "Don't avoid me because you don't know what to say. Say the things you've said to me before; you don't have to be inventive. If your words offend me, I'll forgive you because you were the one who was there when I needed you. But you really don't need to fill the lapsed moments with words. Just guide my way in silence with an attentive ear, a warm embrace, and an open heart. If I say I'm okay, I'm not. Don't judge me, don't rationalize, and don't tell me I can have another child.

"*Confirm my pain by giving credence to my feelings. And the tears, especially the tears from your eyes, comfort me. Then, I'll believe that you truly remember my child. Mention his name. Now that he's gone, I need to hear it more than ever. You're not reminding me of his death. How could I ever forget it? I might cry, but that won't hurt me. The dams need to be opened before the flood of my tears spill into my life at a later date; at a time when I have no shoulder to cry on. You don't have to make it better, nothing will. Just be there.*"

Chapter 15

DICK

*O*thers took care to feed and clothe Danny in the first few weeks, because your mother and I were physically unable to. His appetite resembled ours; he was even disinterested in the sugary fruit snacks you had both enjoyed before, Billy. Everything that reminded him of you, he either avoided or tried to mutilate with his plastic sword.

In public, Danny usually appeared unfeigned by his loss, so some of our friends believed that he was too young to be affected by your death. But your mother and I could see the pain through his animated grin. And we believed that Danny's greatest fear was losing the security of his parents as he knew them.

Through books and pamphlets, valuable bereavement gifts supplied by friends and family, we tried to educate ourselves on childhood grief. The literature directed adults how to explain to their child, respective to their age group, how the human body ceased to function—instead of saying he or she *went to sleep* or that we *lost* a child. One could imagine a parent's attempts at bedtime after the analogy of death to sleep or the child's fear of being misplaced.

I learned not to say *God took your brother* or *God wanted your brother in Heaven,* which would only initiate Danny's fear that God may also want him. Also, the importance of being forthright about the death, funeral, viewing and interment was stressed. Children know when something is wrong and keeping secrets will only make them uneasy. However, the most important suggestion of all was for the parents to be physically and emotionally available to them. And though we were ineffective in many ways for Danny, we were still able to hold him with a loving desperation.

Danny confronted us with questions throughout the day, and we would answer them methodically, without contemplating what was being said, because that was all we could manage. Through our responses, we were forced to speak out loud what we needed to accept ourselves, taking pains at each word.

Like your mother, your big brother held on to the guilt of your death, Billy. He would daily beg her for another brother, but this time, he promised, he would watch him more carefully. He asked her if God was chasing after you, so you wouldn't go in the mud puddles in Heaven. He was the oldest, the strongest—he believed he should have saved you. No matter how she tried to relieve his guilt, he stubbornly maintained that it was his fault that you died.

"Honey, you couldn't have saved Billy. It would be your fault only if you had walked out on that dock and pushed him in." Exasperated with her attempts to appease him, one day, she finally stated the obvious—and so he did back at her.

"I did push him in! I did. I walked out on the dock and pushed him!" he insisted, because his need for her to know his guilt was strong. He believed that he had magically made you die because he had, on occasion, wished you were gone after a normal fit of sibling rivalry. In his mind, he had pushed you in, although he had been nowhere near that dock.

The greatest impulse for Danny to express his sadness came when your mother freely expressed hers. When she spoke of her emotions, he felt the liberty to release his. Besides, it was useless to try to hide her grief from him. When she cried in front of Danny, he would unfailingly wrap his arms around her neck and stroke her hair to console her. And sometimes, there would be a hint of a smile on his face. It seemed as if Danny felt comfortable with her tears; I believe he actually welcomed them. You see, she cried for him when he couldn't. But at the same time, your mother would need to reassure him that she would feel better again. He needed to know that she was able to take care of him no matter how irrational she appeared.

In addition, your brother needed to know that your mother loved him the same as she did you, Billy. I imagine this was because your picture was displayed in every room, and her conversations were always about you. So she tried to be more careful about being consumed with your death, while telling Danny that she loved you both equally because of your differences. These became more evident than ever, because Danny was her reason to live and you had become her reason to die.

"Aren't you glad I didn't die?" Danny would often ask her. The fear of his own death overwhelmed him. So she would hold him in the security of her lap to reassure him.

"Honey, I'm so glad you didn't die… And you won't die for a long, long time," she would tell him while praying that this would be the case. "And when that happens, I'll be in Heaven with you," she promised, knowing it was true because she would voluntarily follow if Danny died before her.

We learned through your brother, Billy, that young children can't maintain continual sadness; they intersperse their anguish with reprieves of levity. When Danny received an answer from us that was unpleasant, he would briefly cry on our shoulders and in the next minute, run away from the source of bad news to escape. Danny would defy the truth by absently playing with his toys or reading a book. It was as if he was enjoying the full run of the house and our undivided attention until your return, Billy.

Then, when he realized you weren't coming back, his play would turn violent with guns and swords aimed at the real monsters of his mind.

He spent endless hours at war with his action figures, role-playing the scenes of your death as he imagined it. Within a few months, your mother bought him multiple new plastic toy actors, understanding his need to safely express his anger through his plastic allies.

At times, your mother found Danny sitting motionless and staring into a world she couldn't enter. Then she would play a game by offering him a "penny for his thoughts." In the guise of fun, he would share his thoughts with her and eventually accumulate a large peanut butter jar full of pennies. I guess you could call her method Freudian bribery.

Then Danny would whisper in your mother's ear "I miss Billy," and then they would hold each other and cry. He told her that the thing he missed the most about you, Billy, was taking baths together. He said that the biggest change in his life since you left was the *quiet* around the house.

Sleep became less fitful for your brother after his vision of you, yet he wouldn't allow your mother to sing lullabies at bedtime anymore. I imagine the songs reminded him of you, Billy. *Somewhere Over the Rainbow* was definitely not allowed. So to calm his nerves and soothe his thoughts before bed, she would massage his back every night until he gave in to sleep.

Even though your mother took off work for the first few weeks, she continued to bring Danny to his daycare for a few hours each day. The separation was hard for her, but her "how-to-grieve" books suggested maintaining a normal routine for a mourning child.

When they entered the daycare on those mornings, the children would overwhelm her and Danny with questions. "What happened to Billy?" and "Is Billy coming back?" One small boy with a bowl cut of dark straight hair posed the same question each day. "Where's Billy?" That's all he would say. No matter how many times she explained Heaven and death to him, he still repeated the same question each day.

Like me, Danny appeared more cheerful when given a reprieve from the depression at home. But he had clearly become a different child; dark circles had appeared beneath his eyes and his lips naturally drooped downward while in thought, indicating a weight on his young mind.

Though your mother read books on how to help him get through his grief work, she found that there were no fast solutions. She searched the bookstores for children's' literature on the subject of a sibling's death. But she only found topics on deceased pets and grandparents, which didn't touch on the emptiness Danny felt without his little brother. Nevertheless, her narration of these books encouraged him to speak about you, Billy, and helped him sort out the inner turmoil in his mind.

I was Danny's reprieve from his grief. With me, and like me, he could pretend things were the same as before. To her credit, your mother knew how to help your brother express his loss, Billy. This is why I saw no need for him to go to a fifty-dollar-an-hour play therapist.

~ ~ ~ ~ ~

"It's not the money. He'll get better with time. He's a smart boy," I whispered before taking another bite of roast beef. As always, we were sitting in front of the television for our family dinner, using the coffee table to hold our place settings. I took the last sip of my milk and glanced at Danny, whose attention was on the movie, oblivious to our conversation.

"What is it, then? Danny could be traumatized forever by Billy's death, and it isn't going to hurt him any to see her." She spoke softly, yet with resolve, while filling Danny's plate with more mashed potatoes, the only part of the meal he consumed.

"I don't believe that Danny's mental health can be remedied by a stranger."

"But it can be monitored by one. She can tell us how he's doing and if his behavior is normal for a child who is grieving. I know that we're the only ones who can help him through each day, but the therapist can show us how. She can help *us* help *him*." When your mother became dramatic, I knew the battle was lost. So I conceded again.

So once a month, Danny started visiting this play therapist, whose one-hour sessions objectively portrayed the progress he had made since the last. This psychiatrist's therapy with Danny consisted of idle chatter and extensive observation of the manner in which he played with the numerous new toys at his disposal. Because of this obvious reason, he enjoyed his monthly appointments with her.

After Danny's sessions, the therapist would explain to your mother that he had an excellent concept of what happened to his brother and with that, harbored some anger inside. But, she explained that Danny's reaction was normal. Since you died, Billy, we learned that anger is normal. Confusion is normal. Guilt is normal. Insanity is normal.

The therapist taught your mother how to safely dissipate Danny's anger by encouraging him to hit pillows against the couch, throw balls of crumpled paper against the wall, and scream at the top of his lungs while confined behind the closed door of our bathroom. That last one also worked well for your mother. In the end, I had to admit that these sessions were well worth the fifty dollars an hour.

Even though I had agreed to the play therapist, your mother knew I was opposed to the children's bereavement support group. Despite my convictions, she continued to bring your brother there every week. She told me he needed to meet children who were the same as he was—three-year-olds with complicated adult emotions. After those sessions, his nightmares started again, and so did his questions on death. I knew in my heart that his fears were initiated by her stubbornness. All the children in his group had lost parents; why wouldn't he be terrified?

Now that your brother knew of the existence of this creature called death, he was horrified that it could possibly take us, too. He said if we died, he didn't want anyone taking care of him but us. He wanted to be "home alone," like the movie. I didn't know what to tell him. How could I promise him that I would be around for a long time when I had learned that life's plan can change so quickly?

At times, when Danny felt your mother and I were emotionally gone, Danny developed a strange routine of trying to keep us from physically leaving him. A day didn't go by in those first few months without him tying your mother or me to the kitchen chairs or any other stationary object that we sat on. To prevent our escape, he would use a scarf, jump rope, or shoestring, looping it around us until there was only enough length left to tie a three-year-old knot.

Because of your mother's open displays of emotion and her insistence on the therapy group, I blamed her for his obsession. We were equally adamant about protecting your brother, Billy; the irony was that our methods were the antithesis of each other.

JoAnn

A MOTHER JOURNALING THROUGH GRIEF

Wherever I go, I feel you by my side; you're always in my peripheral vision. But when I turn around to see you—you disappear. The sensation teases me through-out the day; you're always within my reach, but I'm not able to touch you. Who said that life is short? Mine is seeming to take forever.

Your daycare director educated her staff on children's bereavement to help with the ease of Danny's return to preschool. When he brought home hand-crafted cards that the children had made there, we sat together and I read them to him. They were all filled with innocent concerns and memories of your antics, Billy.

I was proud of myself for keeping my composure through all but one. When opening that folded blue construction paper, I noticed only two words scrawled in big, black crayon across the length of its page. So I read them out loud to Danny.

"WHERE'S BILLY?"

KEVIN
THE FISHERMAN

The fish weren't biting on either side of the dock that day. I often wonder how many lives I would have changed had I cast my lure under the neighbor's dock versus the Emerald Lake channel. I know I would have changed at least one.

But that's hindsight, and I've been able to let it go. But I still can't silence the scream. When I turned around from my line to see her, there was a child in each of her arms and her head was thrown backward in pain. She was like a wolf howling at the moon or a dog struck by a car—a beastly sound, I thought, incapable of coming from a human.

I didn't know why she was screaming, but I knew she needed help. Without thought, Ray, Paul, Todd, and I ran to her.

Chapter 16

DICK

When I finally persuaded your mother to hire a sitter one Saturday night, we didn't stay out long because I tired of her calling home every fifteen minutes. I wasn't concerned about Danny's safety, because I couldn't imagine being struck with the same tragedy again. Besides, we hired a very competent girl who was reliable and loved our children. I have to admit, she was much like Denise.

Although I continued to coax your mother on outings with other couples, her behavior made her a bore to be around. At the time, I resented her for this, but now I see her behavior as a filtering tool. She definitely scared away our platonic acquaintances.

We had tremendous support from all our friends at first, but many became distant with time. I was surprised and hurt by the people who stopped calling. Before your death, our relationships solely comprised of entertainment and alcohol. I still needed that, but your mother was overly sensitive to laughter and showed it. Even though I could pretend to join our friends' frivolity, they must have noticed that I had changed, too. So they eventually avoided us. I was hurt by their distance, but understood their sentiments.

You see, we had been exactly like them only a few months before; young and light-hearted, often avoiding serious matters. But your mother and I had been transformed with your death, Billy. We had matured in one day, and they had not. Even though their support was abundant in the first few months, our presence became an impediment to their gaiety as time moved on. So many of their invitations eventually stopped. I was surprised by the identities of the friends who avoided us, though I should have known all along whom they would be.

Would I have been a devoted friend had this happened to them and not me? I'm not sure of that answer. Would I be a devoted friend if this happened to them after your death? Yes, definitely yes.

One of the most difficult adjustments I needed to adapt to was the alteration of my vocabulary. After eighteen months of saying, "my boys" or "my children," my tongue would often stumble with correction as the words left my lips. But to your mother, Danny would never be an only child, even though she had to stop herself from setting four places at the table.

She learned that this exclusion from her life was called a secondary loss. The primary loss was you, Billy and everything about you. Even though she appreciated Danny more than ever, that space labeled "Bam-Bam Billy" could never be occupied again. You could never be replaced, but her secondary losses could. Someday she wanted to say "children" and speak of her "boys" in plural. Danny could have a playmate again. She could set another place at the table. This is why she longed for another baby.

When your mother was not at work, Danny and she were inseparable. If they needed to part temporarily, her good-bye was said as if it was her last. They connected emotionally through their combined tears, the inevitable product of Danny's questions on your death. They connected physically through tactical closeness, each needing that physical touch of reassurance—if it were only to have his hand entwined in hers throughout the day or their feet sandwiched together under the covers at night.

Danny often crawled into bed with us to nestle in the concave of your mother's curled body. Finding it difficult to sleep with his constant movement in our bed, I suggested he sleep in his own, but your mother disagreed. So your brother would often take my place in bed in the middle of the night, while I would migrate to the couch downstairs.

I knew she was merely existing for your older brother, because she didn't seem to notice me at all. So to avoid Danny being smothered by an overprotective mother the rest of his life, I agreed to have another child.

But when we made love for the first time since your death, it was as if she finally invited her mind a release of emotions. I should have been offended, but wasn't. Her wall of denial was torn down for a moment, and she couldn't stop crying afterwards.

JoAnn

A MOTHER JOURNALING THROUGH GRIEF

How can the hours seem endless but weeks pass without notice? Why does my heart carry the fresh wounds of your death, but it seems like an eternity since I last held you in my arms? I feel powerless over the hands of time; I want to flip the pages back like a calendar on a wall. You're the same age, size and shape that you'll always be. No growth into childhood—a frozen picture in a frame.

How can I fully comprehend that you're gone, Billy, when my mind protects me from that very concept? I have to keep reminding myself that even if my questions are answered, you still won't return to me.

PATTI
BRIAN'S MOTHER

What an amazing week! When you opened your eyes, you could talk, Brian, but most of all, you recognized me. It had been so hard for me to watch you suffer through the awful nightmares…or were they visions? My heart hurt for you when you would scream in your drug-induced coma about demons and monsters. But that too has passed…thank you, God!

Even though the doctors say that your emotions and reasoning skills may be affected, I can't help but imagine that my intelligent seven-year old, who could always outsmart me, will return. But if that doesn't happen, Brian, I don't care. I'm just so happy you're alive—that's all that matters.

I hear the laughter of a child and turn around to see
You reaching out your little hand while running next to me.
The patter of your footsteps is like the beating of my heart.
We're never far apart.
—Billy's Song

Chapter 17

DICK

*E*ven though her manager had granted her an extended bereavement leave from work, only six weeks after your death, your mother returned to flying. Her decision was influenced by a few acquaintances, who foolishly thought that her job would keep her mind off you, Billy. They didn't know that method only worked for me.

It was definitely premature for her to return to flying. But her absence was considered unpaid leave, so she couldn't use her sick time—even though that's what she was, emotionally sick, and she would agree with me. Luckily, the generous memorial cash contributions from friends and family covered the expenses for your funeral and burial. To be truthful, I was relieved when she returned to work, as well as embarrassed that both our paychecks were needed for the upcoming monthly bills.

So each morning, your mother followed the sunrise into work, searching for you in the orange clouds of the dawn. Where was Heaven if not there? She would identify the shapes of the clouds as an outline of your face or a scrawled message as if they were divinely placed there just for her. By that time, she believed that every atypical circumstance was a sign from you. She had found you in an isolated raincloud while gazing out the bedroom window one night and believed that goose feathers that washed onto our beach had been placed there by you. The cottonwood tree's seeds that covered our yard were definitely a message. During that time, she could have found the Virgin of Guadalupe in the outline of a tablecloth coffee stain.

Her first day back to work was an annual training day when flight attendants review their procedures for emergency situations, which had never occurred in her twelve years of flying. While driving through the rain on her way to training, she prayed that she would not to be seated next to some frivolous coworkers. Straining to see past the water on the windshield, she worried about losing her composure during the CPR drill in a classroom full of strangers.

Glancing at the rearview mirror, she noticed a tailgating car and realized she was driving too slowly for the left lane, which would have never occurred before your death, Billy. In fact, she was more prone to drive well over the speed limit. But her life had slowed down and so had her driving habits. She decided to move over and let the world go by.

While changing lanes, she glanced at the miniature mirror on her visor. Your image momentarily appeared. You were smiling at her, and your feet were dangling from the car seat, kicking back and forth. Even though the vision was there for only a moment, your voice stayed.

"Oh, Ma...maa...." Your voice seemed to come from nowhere discernible, yet it was all around her, inside her head, very close, and clearly yours. She naturally answered back.

"Oh, Bill...lee..." Every time she answered you, your voice cadenced back.

"Oh, Ma...maa...." Your voice called to her until she turned around to find the back seat empty.

Your mother walked into the overly bright training room with red, swollen eyes. She anxiously scanned the room for a quiet, discreet table at which to hide. Then she saw her angel-with-metal-wings sitting next to an empty chair.

Out of hundreds of possible training dates and nine-thousand flight attendants, Jeannette happened to be among her thirty classmates. Was she only wishfully imagining the Virgin of Guadalupe in a coffee stain this time? Maybe not.

~ ~ ~ ~ ~

When your mother returned to flying, she was still unable to show any resemblance of a grin.

"Hi, I'm JoAnn." She spoke slowly in monotone as she poked her head into the cockpit on her first trip back. The young copilot turned around to face her.

"I'm Scott....Hey, smile! It can't be that bad!" he teased with a hint of a Southern drawl. He beamed at her with an idiotic grin waiting for her reply.

"No, I don't believe I'm going to smile today." Her eyes reverted from him to the floor. His smile turned to feigned worry, and he reached out to pat her on the back.

"Oh yeah, that's right, the Minneapolis flight attendants don't smile, my condolences," he said with a smirk. Within the airline, there was sometimes an unexplainable rivalry between crew bases, especially against the largest mother hub.

His condolences, she thought, *how many times have I heard those words in the last few weeks?* Your mother felt a surge of anger surface in a flash of red.

"No, maybe we don't smile all the time, and I'm definitely not going to waste my energy smiling for you when my son drowned two months ago."

After dropping her bomb, she marched out of the cockpit, leaving the mutilated copilot staring gaped mouth at the empty doorway. I would bet that he never asked a flight attendant to smile again.

Poor guy, he wasn't the only one who insisted on telling her to smile. There were numerous occasions this was requested by unsuspecting passengers on their way to a sunny destination. Her response was always brief, but more cordial than her first to the copilot. She often wondered why they would ask that of her and not of the male flight attendants.

She noticed that the passengers had a negative reaction toward her unless she forced her lips into a strained grimace. Even some of her co-workers seemed uneasy in her presence, so avoided her. Never before experiencing this reaction, it left her feeling alone and isolated.

At times, she would fail to find you in the dawn's sunrise on her way to work. Then her anger would surface, and she would struggle to keep her grip on the wheel while mentally shaking her fist at God. By the time she arrived at work, her emotions were drained. This left her facing the passengers with a dry, tear-stained face, passing out peanuts in a zombie-like trance. It was helpful that her job was usually routine. Yet, if there had been an emergency evacuation, instead of leading the passengers safely out of a flaming fuselage, crying "Come this way!" she would have stood immobile in the midst of the burning wreckage, thrown her arms out to the heavens and screamed, "Please, take me!"

The first time her plane soared above the orange clouds of the sunrise, she was disappointed that she didn't find you there. She must have anticipated you romping above the puffs of mist in a place where Heaven should have been. It was at that moment she had searched everywhere to no avail.

Your memory consumed her throughout the twelve-hour workdays. The pain would flow in continual, intense waves, impelling her exhausted mind to eventually shut down into a total stupor. This would leave her unable to focus on even the smallest task. She made her routine simple; navigate the endless aisle, fill beverage orders, escape into the bathroom just in time to release her tears. Serve, cry, serve, cry. After every trip down that aisle, she would stare at her distorted, tear-streaked face in the unisex bathroom mirror and try to muffle her cries so the passengers in the last row wouldn't hear her. At those times, she would see your face in hers, Billy, silently crying through the glass window of your daycare, crying for her to come back. Every morning, she use to cry, too, but continued to drive away, leaving her child behind. The guilt gnawed at her and justified every tear she shed.

She found herself envying the elderly passengers because they would most likely see you sooner than she would. She was envious of families with more than one child and knew they would most likely never experience the death of their offspring. You see, she had been like them only a few weeks ago—smug, feeling deserving of her two little boys.

She saw toddlers with blank stares and joyless faces and couldn't help question why God had let you die and not them. What more could they offer the world than you, Billy? And when their eyelids were closed as they slept in their mother's arms, she saw your body in your coffin. You had been a light sleeper, so she had rarely seen your face during sleep except there in your death.

She had struggled through the long hard months of infancy and the many sleepless nights of your ear infections. These eventually lessened, and you became easier to handle as you went from an infant to a little boy.

You had been sleeping through the nights and becoming more enjoyable each day. She never reaped her rewards; all her efforts were wasted.

Sometimes she could identify the vitality and delight that had been yours in a toddler's face. At those times, she would ache to hold the child in her arms, needing to feel that weight on her right hip again. But she was afraid if she did, her tears would scare the child and she would feel a rejection of you through them. So from her cart in the aisle, she would gaze into each small child's eyes, searching for some sign from you. And when the children smiled back at her, it was as if they were telling her that all was well with you. You see, those children were the closest things she could find to Heaven on earth. But even though their innocent spirits were similar to yours, they were never the equivalent—they were never you.

Complaints from passengers were simply disregarded. She had no empathy for those who didn't receive their choice of chicken or beef or for those who were denied the opportunity to hang their oversized bags in a garment closet. Even the trivial lamentations from flight attendants made her feel as if no one had been affected by your death if one weekend of work was a major burden for them.

There were a few coworkers she had once considered friends and now avoided her for lack of appropriate words. Some would whisper about her, believing she was out of hearing range. This confirmed to her that she was at fault for your death.

When she would tell new acquaintances that her son had just died, some ignored her words and changed the subject. One flight attendant merely walked away without comment, as if your mother had the nerve to darken her life with such a tragedy. Some would reason, out loud, why her loss could never happen to them.

"That's why we don't live on a lake."

"I'm glad we don't have anyone watch our children but my mother."

"You know, they have swim classes for toddlers now. My daughter's enrolled."

And then your mother would recognize the arrogance that had once been hers.

While she could feel the shallowness of those who hadn't experienced a loss in their lives, she could also feel the depths of emotions in those who had. There were a few coworkers who would listen, sympathize, and cry with her while they were seated together on a three-by-two-foot board in their seat belt restraints. Flight attendants often call this "jump-seat therapy."

Some spoke of the glories of Heaven, giving her comfort with the description of your new home, Billy. Repeatedly, she would retell her story to every coworker—some whom she never saw again nor remembered when she did. Even though she may not recall those flight attendants or the details of their conversation, she always felt a deep gratitude to the remembered hearts who were willing to share her fresh pain on every take -off and landing.

When she met new crew members, she found that questions, once socially routine, became difficult for her to answer.

How many children did she have? Did she *have* you anymore, Billy? Were they asking as if you were a possession, as if she could still hold you in her arms? If that were the case, then she would be forced to tell them she only had one child. Or were they asking her if she gave birth to you, took care of you, loved you, and still did? Were they asking her if you still existed as her child? Then she had to claim that she had two, even though the void of your absence was palpable. If their queries stopped there, the answers were recited as before your death, but usually the most difficult question followed.

"How old are they?" Then she would stumble over the weeks she had stopped counting.

Yet she didn't mind them asking about you, Billy, because you were always on her mind. She needed to tell the world about you and, like a couch psychiatrist, led her coworkers to that most relevant topic. Somehow she could turn any discussion into a synopsis on your death.

Even a "How are you?" would be answered truthfully. "Lousy," she would say. And if they choose to venture farther, they were in for a lengthy, emotional monologue. She had a consuming urge to relive your death story through the constant retelling of it. I don't know whether she was trying to narrate her way out of denial or attempting to rearrange the ending.

For the first month back at work, she managed to fly one-day trips, which brought her home every night. She felt that an overnight absence from Danny would be unbearable and what little sanity she had left would completely take leave when confronted with your death in a hotel room. Then the four walls would close in on her again.

When she couldn't avoid overnight trips any longer, she found that it was in her hotel room where she would feel the darkest corners of her grief. While yielding to the invasive memories that came flooding out in waves, she quickly logged them in your baby book before they were lost. She would place your picture on the nightstand next to her bed, because she was afraid that if she didn't dwell on the features of your face, she would forget that, too. Your favorite stuffed monkey was always placed next to your picture. "ChiChi," as you called him, was a brown fuzzy marsupial holding a pacifier in his little paw, which had come in handy during the late hours of the night when you lost yours in the crevasses of your crib.

At the end of her trips, when the airplane and your mother were on their last leg, a sudden tingle of anticipation would consume her. While walking through the terminal to the bus stop, she unconsciously felt a lightness in her step. Weaving her way through cars in the employee parking lot, her heart quickened, and she felt an alien levity. Only after climbing into the driver's seat of her car did she become aware of the reason for her unusual eagerness—the anticipation of a reunion at home. Then her elation would take leave, and reality would overwhelm her. You were not in the clouds; you were not at home.

JoAnn

A MOTHER JOURNALING THROUGH GRIEF

How does summer end without the beginnings of autumn? One minute Danny, you, and I were playing in the water under the hot sun, then I turned my head for a moment, and you were gone—leaving Danny and me alone, watching the leaves turn colors. Summer vanished and took you with it. The cool days of fall are leaving you behind while I move unwillingly into the month of September. I want to stay in that illusive place, suspended in the warmth of summer with you. What happened to August?

Remember when I bruised my nail the day you died, Billy? I lifted you from your car seat as I closed the door with my hip. My finger was smashed between the door and metal frame, leaving a black contusion at the bottom of my nail bed. But I never let go of you. Now I look at that scab, which has inched its way to the top with growth, day by day, marking the passage of time, moving upward until it will eventually be gone. But I want it to remain under my nail bed forever— maybe then you'll stay too. I'd like that moment to return; I want to slam my finger in the car door again because I was holding you in my other arm.

Now it only leaves me to wonder how my nail can continue to grow when you aren't—making me feel detached from my own hand. How could that bruise still be evident on this finger in front of me, when I'm not the same person I was then?

Chapter 18

*I*t had happened to me before, viewing the last scene of a movie while never watching the first, knowing the conclusion without ever knowing the plot. But I had never felt the need to view the entire script after learning its ending. That's why your mother's obsession puzzled me. After walking into the theater at the finale of our personal horror movie, a compelling force drove her to understand what had led its outcome. Maybe that was because *The End* was printed on the screen, without the inclusion of *and they lived happily ever after*.

The storyline of your death occupied most of your mother's thoughts. In her attempts to rewrite the inadmissible conclusion, she tried to find the perfect screenplay—one that assured her that you hadn't suffered.

Even though each new piece of information disrupted her imagery of your last moments, the true story line of your death was more important. However it transpired, she was determined to know every dreaded detail of the script. So she sought the program for the final curtain call of your life through hospital, emergency helicopter, paramedic, and personal eyewitness reports.

There were many actors performing in the last scene, and she attempted to interview them all. With the discovery of each new character, her list of names grew—a cast who had never known you, but expended every effort to save your life. The knowledge that you were not alone comforted her. Above all, she needed to see the faces surrounding you at a time when she imagined you were looking for hers.

But through her search, she had yet to learn what Danny had seen of your death. Your brother could only speak about the events preceding the discovery of your body in the lake. His narration always stopped short of the water's edge.

As the story unfolded, the *what-ifs* grew in number. She didn't know what to do with her regrets, because they came to mind without warrant. This wasn't a circumstance that could be remedied by another action or rectified by a spoken word—it was too late, it was forever conclusive. But try she did.

In her efforts to seek out an explanation for your death, she started attending mass on Sundays. This only led to her pitiful presence in the back pew, crying with an indecipherable Bible clutched in her hand—ignored by the uncomfortable parishioners around her. To her disappointment, I wouldn't attend mass with her. I couldn't reach for God at the same time I was pushing him away.

The church's Woman's Guild attempted to befriend your mother by inviting her to a tea. She looked forward to that day, hoping she would be enlightened by divine answers, but she found none there. She merely found herself surrounded by mothers with perfectly intact families of two, four, or five children—after all, it was a Catholic gathering. And there she sat with tea in hand, feeling insufficient with her remaining child and wishing for a stronger beverage. She was looking for an answer to your death everywhere she went, Billy, which was beyond the powers of those well-meaning parishioners.

Her desperate search led her back to confrontations with God. When reading the Bible, she found confusing phrases and contradictions. There were many ambiguities in the words: "for those who sleep with Jesus" and "the dead are conscious of nothing." And the tenets of Mormonism and

Jehovah's Witnesses claimed that you were only "sleeping" until the end of the world.

Weren't you playing on that big play-gym in Heaven, like we told Danny? How could every deceased person be sleeping until the end of the world? She couldn't fathom how you could be oblivious of her, when sometimes she felt you so near. On the other hand, if you were cognizant, how could you not want your Momma? You would have to feel as if she deserted you.

Did you leave your physical body behind and only carry your intelligence to Heaven, or was everything we taught you destroyed with your body and only your spirit salvaged from your incapacitated brain? And if your spirit was not saved, then every vague soul was the same there and your unique personality was gone forever.

On the other hand, if everyone was uniquely different in the heavens with their own spirits intact, owning their personal emotions and memories—how could they all be happy and content? How could you not miss her now, Billy, if you were the same eighteen-month-old child going through a separation-anxiety phase? So she found that her mortal reasoning was deficient for understanding your presence in the next world. There were too many contradictions.

Even though it was a fashionable belief, your mother was uncomfortable with the possibility of reincarnation. She believed that the concept was disrespectful of the person you were and allowed no value to your distinctive personality. She believed that you were physically *and* mentally attached to your heritage by the sum of the genes and your upbringing by your mother and me. No one else could be you, and you could not be anyone else. Besides, when finally reaching the afterlife, she couldn't fathom God trying to explain to her that you weren't there because you were, say, a philanthropist on a mission trip in the Amazon.

When she listened to Christian radio, it gave her the anticipation of a reunion with you. Because these sermons gave her a glimpse of hope, she wanted to believe the entirety of their beliefs, but couldn't. A few of the preachers declared that your communications to her, the only hopeful thing in her life, were a trick of Satan. And she needed to hear from you even if it was through a psychic, which the self-proclaimed prophets on the radio denounced. They preached that it was a sin to attempt to speak with you, Billy. So she merely concluded that *their* misguided ideology was a trick of Satan.

A coworker told her that when you died, Billy, God gave you a perfect body. In turn she would ask, what could be more perfect than the dimpled hands and sparkling eyes of an eighteen-month-old child? She was informed that your soul would meet your old body from the grave and she would recognize you in that heavenly place of the afterlife. So how was God to put it back together from its ghastly decomposition?

Some people told her that your death taught us that life was precious, and she would insist that it only preached that life was insignificant and our bodies easily dispensable.

She was told that good things would come of it, as though anything could make up for your death. And there were many who said that you were in a "better place." Then she would ask them how any place could be more comforting to a toddler than the bowl of his mother's lap.

Some assured her that you lived on in her heart, when she had only known you through your body. She didn't want you in her heart, but in her arms. A mother's relationship with her toddler is not comprised of spoken words, but instead, of caring touches and loving embraces.

Your mother felt a driving desire to know everything about your new daycare and a deep frustration at the lack of information. Even Jesus' apostle, Thomas, needed to physically place his fingers in the wounds of

Jesus' flesh to believe. She wanted to see your bed, playroom, and your caretakers. But the tangibles weren't there for her.

When people told her to be content with the time she had with you, she responded that she wished that you were never born only to be taken away so early. Your memories, Billy, weren't cherished, but only painfully led her thoughts back to your death.

She was told by a devout Christian that peace could be found by "praising God," but that was a remote possibility in light of her unanswered questions. Many told her that "God doesn't give us what we can't handle," as though the bereaved parents who had gone over the edge of sanity or committed suicide had "handled" it. When she was told that it was "meant to be" or that it was the "circle of life," she would recall how one small variation in the sequence of events could have prevented your death.

On the other hand, if your death had not been divinely planned, then chance was the culprit, which made her responsible, because then it was an accident and it could have been prevented. Her guilt could have been eliminated if she believed that your death was in some big master plan. But she embraced her own guilt because she didn't want to hate God as much as I did. She wondered if she was vulnerable to tragedy because she hadn't been strong in her faith lately and was susceptible to Satan.

Had Satan caused your death because of God's absence? It was implied by some that you were taken from her as punishment for her past sins. She almost accepted that rationale, knowing that she was far from sinless. But then she wondered why God chose her, she wasn't the only sinner. And even if she were, why punish Danny for her sins? Why punish every person the lost opportunity of knowing you? Reflecting on the numerous benevolent, God-praising parents who had also lost children, the punishment theory didn't wash either.

Some told her that prayer heals all, but then she would remember her prayers in the sheriff's van on the way to the hospital. Hadn't she prayed the right way; hadn't she prayed hard enough? She couldn't believe, anymore, that God would change events by merely asking. And if things were "God's plan," how could praying help?

Nevertheless, your mother still believed in miracles, but there was some reason God didn't grant her one on that day. She believed that your accident was not "meant to be," but God choose not to save you for some omniscient reason. And at times, she could not help but resent Him for that.

But even through her curses to the heavens, she told people that God was holding her hand on the rocky path of bereavement. There was no conceivable way she could have survived without divine help. But instead of feeling blessed, she felt that He owed her that. So ungratefully, she was guided by God's gift of strength through the only Hell she believed in — life on this earth.

~ ~ ~ ~ ~

He was standing by your crib on your bedroom. Even though I hadn't seen it for a while, I remembered the doll Danny was holding. Your mother had bought it before you were born, Billy, to help in his transition to a new sibling. He had often rocked the doll and changed its diapers when your mother was busy with you.

Danny was moving the doll over the bars of your crib. Even though he was mumbling to himself, his voice had been audible from our bedroom across the hall. I peeked into your room as Danny animated the doll's movements, one leg at a time, down the side of the crib.

"I want to go swimming, Dawnee." I heard Danny project a falsetto voice to the doll. I squatted down to his level and gently placed my hand on his shoulder.

"Hey, Bud, what's the baby doing?" He turned toward me with wide eyes, noticing me for the first time.

"I'll show you." He dropped the doll to the floor and grabbed my hand. Leading me to the closet, he frantically looked inside.

"He's not there, he's not there..." Panic grew in his voice. His small hand gripped mine so tightly that I'm not sure I could have freed it without force. So I followed him throughout, the house in search of you, Billy.

We looked in every closet, under every bed, behind every door. Then he'd whisper, "He's not here...he's not here..."

"Billy....Billy! Where are you?" Danny's voice yelled throughout the house as I followed him. He pulled me down the stairs and then led me to the dining room by the screen door. He searched out the window, scanning his eyes across the water beyond.

"Did you and Denise look for Billy, Bud?" I interjected.

"Yes! We looked in the closets, in EVERY closet, we looked FOR-EVER... and Billy wasn't there, we couldn't find him, Daddy. We looked around the house, in the high street, then in the brown street, then the garage." Then his voice broke, and he looked up at me with moist eyes and started crying. I knelt on the carpet by the door and pulled him into my arms. We rocked together, and I felt his warmth on my chest and his wet cheeks on my shoulder.

"I'll bet you were really scared when you were looking, huh, Bud," I whispered in his ear. He raised his head so he could look into my eyes. What I saw was complete terror.

"Yes, I was so scared, Daddy! And then 'Neese screamed, and screamed and screamed and *SCREAMED*, and it hurt my EARS." His volume escalated with each word. Not knowing what else to do as his cries grew louder, I smothered him in embrace. Holding him tightly, my tears mingled with his as he replayed the events of that day. I held him that way until his sobs turned to hiccups.

~ ~ ~ ~ ~

Like your mother, Billy, I tried to sort through the trite justifications for your death. Contrarily, I could only conclude that the nasty consequences of life were either the destiny of circumstantial fate or the result of our own conduct. God had nothing to do with it. I was stuck with the phrase, "shit happens" after seeing it in bold letters on a car bumper in front of me one day on the way to work. This was the only explanation I had, because your death was the shittiest event in my life, and I was beginning to realize that it had truly happened.

JoAnn

A MOTHER JOURNALING THROUGH GRIEF

"God grant me the serenity to accept the things I cannot change." Those words were printed on a cookie tin a friend brought over today. The serenity to accept... It will take more than serenity for me to accept your death, Billy. I swear I never will.

Someone stole "ChiChi" from my mailbox at work. I wish I could tell that person that they didn't just steal a replaceable stuffed toy; they stole my child's memories.

There seems to be a persistent lump in my throat at all times. It increasingly grows larger until it chokes the air from my lungs. When I cry, the blockage dissolves momentarily as if it were made of tears. But it inevitably comes back — gradually growing again like a malignant tumor.

I've heard it takes more energy to frown than to smile — I've disproved that theory. I find it very difficult to smile, but my grimace comes naturally. My emotions run up and down like a schizophrenic's. People stare at me wherever I go. Do they know it was my fault? I guess I could be labeled a paranoid schizophrenic.

Since your death, the baby monitor has futilely scanned your room in search of your voice. At first, I could actually hear you call through the static and would have to stop my habitual urge to respond. After eighteen months and numerous battery changes, I finally packed it away. Even though the baby monitor is silenced, like a cruel joke, I'm still awakened by your cries every morning at 5:30 a.m. And throughout the day, I find it hard to ignore the fire truck sirens that scream past our home, resonating the horrors of that day.

In the evening while in my bed, I still stare at the image of that drifting boat on the shores of that peaceful lake and try to bring myself back to a place of tranquility. But with the passage of time, I'm unable to escape into the picture on my wall.

RAY
CAYMAN'S MASTER

Like most black labs, Cayman loved the water. So I would often take her to Troy and Paul's house, which was on the point of Cook's Bay and Emerald Lake Channel.

That day, I was on the dock throwing the ball into the water for Cayman while my nephews, Kevin and Paul, and their friend Todd were fishing beside me.

Then I heard the scream.

At once, I turned toward the direction from which it was coming and saw a girl with a child in one arm and a limp baby in diapers in the other. She was walking out of the water on the neighbor's shore, painstakingly, trying to hold both.

I yelled at Paul to call 911 and then ran over and took the limp boy from the girl. He was so blue. I laid him on the ground, opened his airway, gave him one breath, and started chest compressions. Kevin was at my side.

"Man, I don't know if I can do this, Kev," I doubted myself out loud while I made small compressions on the child's chest. Kevin immediately stepped in and took over the mouth to mouth.

Cayman sensed the anxiety in the air and began to frantically run around us.

"Todd, please get her out of here!" I remember yelling. *This is working*, I thought. *The baby's color is coming back.*

It had been at least five minutes of compressions before a man, who introduced himself as a doctor, appeared at our side. He put the baby on the deck of the house and took over the breathing for Kevin while I continued the chest compressions. Then I looked up and saw the familiar face of Tim, a Mound firefighter whom I knew personally. His eyes were wide in disbelief.

"Tim, help!" I screamed as he took over for me. When I walked away, my body started to tremble and I allowed my tears to flow.

What could have been one of the best days of my life, saving a child, became my worst. If only I had seen him come out of the house. Then I would have taken him by the hand and brought him back home— changing everything.

Instead, I've replayed that day a hundred times through the years. A news article on a drowning, a child in the water playing…something will trigger the memory and then it will consume me. The scream—the limp, blue baby. I wish I could forget. I've tried. I can't.

Chapter 19

As there was no stopping of time, Danny turned four years old on the 17th of September.

"Why am I still little?" he asked me on the morning of his birthday. Pondering the question, I acknowledged that my son had been forced to psychologically mature beyond his chronological years, which had left him wondering why his body hadn't caught up. Our dilemma was always to distinguish whether Danny's idiosyncrasies were a product of his age or the trauma of your death.

Games were played, faces were painted, and a few of our leftover friends, the Worley's, hired a clown for Danny's birthday party. He seemed to enjoy the activities and the gifts. At our request, Uncle Dave and Aunt Jeanne gave him a globe of the earth. Having a difficult time understanding that you were gone from "this world" forever, Billy, your big brother needed a visual aid to help sort out his imagery. You see, his world extended approximately to the end of our block, so in his mind, you were hiding just around the corner.

At the end of the day when all his buddies were gone, your mother found Danny absently staring at the globe, slowly turning it around with his little fingers.

"Did you have a nice birthday, Honey?"

He continued to stare and turn the globe around and around as though looking for something.

"You made Billy die," he stated quietly, but firmly.

"Sometimes, I feel that way, too," she whispered. It was easy to hide her pain from him at that moment, because she almost felt relief from his statement. Her secret was finally revealed; Danny had stated what she had known all along.

"You weren't there. You could have saved him." Danny grabbed a new plastic sword he had received as a present and started slaying the couch as his mother had taught him—hitting it over and over, stopping only after becoming exhausted from the effort.

"I hate God! He should give me my brother back! I hate Him!" He breathlessly laid his head on the couch. Your mother kneeled down to Danny and held her arms out to him.

"Sometimes, I feel that way, too. Come here, Sweetie," she whispered and he leaned into her body.

"Let's cry, Mommy. Cry. Okay?"

"Okay, Honey." So she did with permission from her eldest son. They cried together with uninhibited tears. It was Danny who said it first.

"I f...feel like I'm going to cry forever!"

And your mother knew exactly what he meant. So she prayed, this time, to relieve her son's sadness. She wanted more than anything, even more than your return, Billy, to take the hurt away from him. But then where would she have put it?

When their cries eventually turned to sniffles, Danny raised his face to his mother's and wiped the tears from her cheeks with his little finger as she had done so many times for him. She smiled at him.

"When you're done crying, Mommy, you get strong. Crying makes you strong." She gave him a little hug and nodded at her wise four-year-old.

~ ~ ~ ~ ~

It wasn't until fall had blown its cool breeze that your mother visited your grave for the first time. Until then, she had ignored the fact that your body rested there, so it was Danny's insistence that led her through those formidable gates again. He wanted to see where his brother's "old body" was. I felt no desire to go with them.

She parked the car on the dirt road that encircled the cemetery, and searched in the direction of where your grave should be. She thought that the site would draw her without direction, but found it hard to distinguish your grave from the others at a distance. Remembering that St. Joseph's Home for Children was directly across the street, she aimed for that focal point.

To reach your gravesite, Danny and your mother navigated down a narrow path with gravestones perfectly aligned on each side. As they neared the end, your gravestone stood out among the others because it was the newest and was contrarily misaligned. Yours deviated out of the row by two feet to allow a nearby tree its space. It was just like you, Billy — to be "out of line." The diseased elm at the head of your stone was marked for destruction with a big red X painted on its side. Not wanting to lose that staunch guardian at your grave, your mother tried to rub the bold impression off, only managing to break two fingernails in the process.

Before they left the house, she had tried to explain to Danny that he wouldn't be seeing you at the grave, but her attempts had proven futile. When they arrived at your gravesite, his demeanor changed from anticipation to disappointment. They sat and embraced on the grass in front of your grave. Then he brightened and pulled away from her.

"Read all these names for me, Mommy. Read this name! " He pointed at the gravestone next to yours. Danny frolicked among the gravestones surrounding yours, as your mother read off the names for him. Periodically he would return to yours, Billy.

"And this one is my brother's!" he proudly exclaimed, as though you were a member of an elite society. *This is as it should be*, your mother thought. She wanted the place of your gravesite to be a peaceful, bonding experience for him.

While watching her eldest play among the headstones, she remembered the purpose for the vault in which your casket had been placed, and she could pretend for a moment that you were the same as before — unblemished, waiting to be reunited with her. But, when she placed the daisies on your grave, she took care not to step on the spot where you lay and fought the image of six feet of dirt separating her from her son.

JoAnn
A MOTHER JOURNALING THROUGH GRIEF

Every night I pray that you'll come back in my dreams, Billy. But when dreams of a reunion occur, they're nightmares. Your body is always eerily disfigured — rotting, back from the dead. And your brain is always damaged by your drowning.

But I'm not afraid of your deformities, because when I hold you there in my sleep, all the pain that has become a prime player in my life disappears as if it had never been there in the first place. Then in the morning, I wake up at 5:30 with the weight of your body gone and your voice calling from your crib across the hall.

Even though your voice comes more softly and with gradual abatement, it continues to wake me without the aid of the baby monitor. I've discovered that it originates from my heart and not your bedroom.

So in the morning, I stay in bed unresponsive to your calls while imagining my movements to your room. I see myself leaning over your crib so your little fingers can wrap themselves around my neck in efforts to climb out. When I concentrate hard enough, I can almost feel your body in my arms.

And then some mornings, when I lay in bed, I can actually feel you kicking against the walls of my uterus as you did as a fetus — the tactile, warm sensation of pregnancy. With my hands resting upon my stomach, I can feel the pulsating movement of your body inside my womb. The impression is so strong that I imagine a new beginning to redefine the ending. The only rational explanation I have for this experience is to liken it to the phantom pain experienced by amputees when a limb is abruptly severed from their body. A part of me has been lopped off, but the sensation of its presence and the pain of its detachment are still there.

Your body inside me surprises and comforts me, so I desperately hold onto that warmth until it subsides. Eventually, the feeling dissolves into a weightless void. As if falling from a cliff, that deep, sinking feeling engulfs me again. Then I want to crawl back into the lesser of my nightmares.

Chapter 20

DICK

I t was early October when your mother laughed again for the first time. By that time, her cigarette habit had become a renewed addiction and she was puffing at least ten a day. To buy a carton would force her to admit her addiction, so instead, she would make several trips to the local gas station to replenish her supply.

~ ~ ~ ~ ~

The bell jingled overhead as she opened the door and left the cool outside air. While approaching the elderly man behind the register, she noticed a woman at the counter wearing a cashmere sweater, angora hat, and reeking of money. A toddler stood by the woman's side, holding her hand. Your mother thought, *this woman has more riches than she's aware of,* while she sensed that familiar empty space beside her.

The woman was peering over the cashier's shoulder through the window, waiting for the gas nozzle to click off at the gas pump as it filled her BMW. Your mother shifted her weight from side to side impatiently.

"Probably not a good idea to do that, Miss," the elderly cashier joked with the woman. "Last week a young man drove off without disconnecting the hose. The hose broke off, spilling gasoline all over the ground. Now, I'm well into my sixties, but you've never seen an old man move so fast!"

He laughed heartily, and the woman laughed with him. "There's your total now, $21.39, Miss."

The woman chuckled, "Oh, my goodness, I'll bet you see some strange things in here. What was he thinking of?" She opened her wallet and handed the man the cash to cover her gas.

"He didn't even notice it, just went and drove off. He's probably still looking for his gas cap!" They both laughed too loudly. Your mother interrupted.

"Could I just get a pack of cigarettes? I'm in a bit of a hurry," She tried to contain herself. The woman looked down her nose at your mother, noticing her for the first time.

"It was quite difficult, but I'm so glad I quit that nasty habit years ago," the woman said while nodding to the cashier. He nodded back in agreement.

"Well...," your mother vowed self-righteously, "I just started a few months ago, and I'm up to almost a pack a day."

"Why, for God's sake, would you ever do that?" the woman asked, not really looking for an answer and clueless to the trap your mother had set.

And so your mother dropped the brick, "Because my son drowned."

At that, the woman took one step back, her jaw dropped, and the condescending smile vanished from her face. As she murmured her condolences, she abruptly grabbed her child's hand and practically dragged him out the door, trying to get as far away from your mother and her tragedy as possible—as if she would "catch" something from just being near her.

While your mother paid for her vice, she glanced out the window as the woman hurriedly climbed into her car. The engine revved loudly, and the woman rapidly drove away from the pump to which her BMW was still connected by the gas hose. The hose tore away from the gas pump, spilling gasoline across the pavement. The elderly cashier frantically dashed outside to save his gas pump once again.

He does move fast for a guy his age, your mother thought as she chuckled and an unusual smirk appeared on her face.

Through her naughtiness, your mother had discovered humor in her life that day. Yet, when that laugh finally surfaced, her guilt did, too. Not the guilt of tricking that poor, unsuspecting woman, but the guilt of enjoying life when her son could not.

JoAnn
A MOTHER JOURNALING THROUGH GRIEF

Some people have asked me how I could possibly get through the death of a child. For this, I have no answer, but know that there are few alternatives. My heart keeps pulsating, the world keeps rotating, and the bills kept rolling in. My only choice is to cash in or to keep living. Without consciously being aware of it, I must have opted to live. But without Danny, I fear the former choice could have been taken.

Danny is my reason to get out of bed each morning. I feel as if I'm striving to keep up with him as he moves forward; he's living my life for me. He is my life. Sometimes I stare at him as if in a timeless void, just to watch him walk, talk, and breath. I'm amazed by his energy; he is so vital and alive. And when I hold him close, I can feel that pulse of life I'm lacking. At those times, I can't help but regret the precious moments I missed with him when I was preoccupied with you, Billy. And vice versa.

When I feel as though I can't make it through another day, I pray for help. At those times, I always find the will to survive momentarily. But in the next breath, I'll curse God for not saving you. My goal is to be as sinless as possible in order to assure myself a place where you are, Billy. So I play the loving Christian through a heart that overflows with uncertainty. I guess you could say I'm using Him.

Chapter 21

*T*hat fall, our family's grief-infected minds also diminished our bodies' immune systems and every virus that passed through the air jumped at the chance to invade us. A bug would usually start with your mother and then take its turn on Danny and then come to me, only to make a full circle and infect her again. It was an endless cycle; grief was eating at our insides like dry rot.

Danny was still seeing his play therapist once a month. But to my relief, his children's bereavement support group was over, which eliminated one point of contention between your mother and me. Danny's games became less animated, and his anger seemed to subside. Although he spoke of you often, Billy, Danny avoided mention of that horrible day. And he still insisted he had killed his little brother by neglect when, in turn, your mother believed this was her crime.

To your mother's amazement and dismay, the world hadn't ended yet. But the fog was lifting, and by October, she could feel the entire pain of your absence. She would sleep in later each day, because your voice was gone from your room across the hall, and your vanished spirit made the house feel empty.

The impulse to push back chairs and shut doors behind her diminished, and she finally disposed of your medicine from the refrigerator door. Although seeming infeasible, she cried more frequently. It's been said that "tears are the telescope through which man sees into Heaven." But if this were true, your mother's view of your new home would have been a wide-screened panorama. Though I tried to empathize with her at these times, I was tiring of her behavior. I wanted her to push the tears inward as I did.

Never having experienced grief before, I found it wasn't the sole emotion I had imagined it would be. I thought a bereaved person would immediately plummet into a deep depression, but gradually and steadily emerge over time. The gradual uphill climb I anticipated developed into hiked miles up the steep cliffs of reality when waking up every morning. Then I would scale down the valleys of lost memories, crawl through the deserts of shock in a trance, and then skip through the delusional flowered fields of a hopeful reunion. I would often find myself sliding off the edge of denial into a dark cavern of depression. This only led me to travel the same path over and over again. There was no goal, no sequence, and no glimpse of an end to the journey.

Although the most prevalent emotion I felt at that time was anger—at whoever I could assign it to; God, Denise, my friends, or your mother. And I could only freely express my anger while drinking. My anger was evident because I directed my feelings outward, far away from my heart. But your mother, Billy, didn't express her anger at all, but nourished it inside her. Psychology theories have stated that *anger* turned inward is *depression*. But I believe the anger she directed inward merely manifested itself as *guilt*—an anger toward herself.

At times, I was much like your brother, Billy, ignoring my grief when I could. I had to be strong for my family, and your memory didn't allow me that. When sober, I didn't speak of you in public, avoiding the un-manly tears that would inevitably come. But when I denied my emotions, they eventually exploded at a later time, while drinking, through the fragile wall I had built.

When I came directly home from work, I sometimes found your mother crying in a chair. When she wasn't crying, her heavy sighs continued to irritate me, mainly because I couldn't fix her pain. I thought it would be easier to forget you, Billy, if I artificially numbed myself. So I sidestepped your memory by spending less time at home and more time at the bars where there was no mention of your name.

I avoided the empty stillness of our home to venture to loud, gay places where I thought I could ignore you. But ironically, the very place I sought refuge would become my emotional outlet. After a few scotch and waters, I could never contain what I had gone there to hide. For the price of a few drinks, I would talk about you and cry—never remembering the embarrassment of my tears the next day. It was cheaper than a therapist.

On one of those evenings as I was driving home from my favorite local pub, the Wayzata Bar & Grill, I noticed two geese on the road. The male was on the right side of the street and the female on the left, separated by a precarious stream of traffic. Unable to navigate the span, they honked deliriously at each other through a barrier of speeding cars. So I thought of my marriage.

Before your death, your mother and I believed we were alike in our values and viewpoints. Our few differences had always been regarded as delightfully trivial. After all, isn't it the similarities that usually motivate a couple to marry? Oddly, the mutual loss we shared accentuated our differences.

Your mother and I couldn't seem to span the differences, so we found ourselves like those geese, honking at each other through the obstructive barrier of our own personal bereavement. When I was at the top of the roller coaster, she was at the bottom; we were unable to time our ride to meet in the middle. She was on the North Pole while I was on the South, continents away from each other. When she was the high tide, I was the low tide—being carried away by two different pulls of gravity. We were both drowning side by side in the currents, with only enough strength to keep our own heads above the suffocating water. And we were afraid to reach for each other for fear that we would pull the other under.

Our grief seemed personal—not in a secretive way, but uniquely experienced by the individual. Although we had each loved you with the same intensity and suffered through similar memories, we ultimately had to fight the wages of grief-war with our own arsenal.

She needed to talk about you to everyone, anywhere, anytime. I hesitated to mention your name for fear of losing control in public. Guests would still come to the house to console her because she was the one who welcomed the mention of your name and the tears that followed. When I was at work, my co-workers would ask me how your mother was coping, while ignoring the hidden anguish a bereaved father experiences; which was fine by me because this enabled my denial.

I resented her insistence to commemorate you in every thought, object, and occasion, Billy. And your mother resented me for the omission of your name. She desperately wanted another child, and I vacillated on that decision weekly. And that further embittered her.

She wanted our lives to change, and I wanted our lives to continue where we left off before you wandered into that lake. She believed we needed to change and improve ourselves in order to assign your death some purpose. I wanted our life to pick up where it left off, confirming that your death was a senseless act of circumstance.

There are some dismal statistics on the fate of bereaved parents. It has been reported that 75 percent of all bereaved couples divorce within two years and 90 percent have serious marital problems within a few months of their child's death. So we became a statistic and emotionally divorced ourselves from one another while still occupying the same living space.

JoAnn
A MOTHER JOURNALING THROUGH GRIEF

You were asleep in my arms; I could feel your weight as if you had never left me. Then I noticed the tube running into your stomach, suctioning the feces you had swallowed in my womb before birth. The tube was sucking the fluids in and out, in and out. When you opened your eyes, they were round, white, opaque balls. Then the tubes started growing like vines, wrapping themselves around me as the fluid within them turned to red. They menacingly circled us while I tried to protect you by holding you closer. Sucking, sucking blood around, in, and through you and me, tightening, squeezing my breath from me. Fluid ran in and out of your body into mine, out of my body into yours. I felt your rotting skin give way in my arms. I couldn't hold on to you. You were slipping away. I could hear the tubes still sucking, in and out.

Then I woke up in my hotel room. My arms were empty, but, still, I could hear it. The sucking… in and out. I ran to the bathroom, where the sound seemed to come from. I looked for you there, but only saw the hot water spigot gurgling over the sink. Sucking…big time.

When you were born, they tore you from my body to suction your stomach as you cried for me. You cried until you heard my voice. I'll stop crying when I hear yours. When they suctioned the dirty water from your stomach when you were dying, Billy, were you crying for me then? The alpha and omega of your life.

RANDY
THE DOCTOR

It happened on the day of the triathlon during the summer of my third year of residency. The race went well that day, and I looked forward to a well-earned break. A beautiful sunny day, a lake, a boat—my favorite things and everything I needed to relax and recover.

The engine dutifully guided my 16-foot Sea Ray into a quiet cove. I surveyed the surroundings and dropped anchor near an outer bank. As I settled onto the cushions of the forward berth, the boat bobbed gently in the water and a warm, soft breeze moved the waters waves against the hull. The rhythmic movement and soft, lapping sounds soothed my weary body. Slowly, exhaustion gave way to a restful nap.

The light breeze continued to gently rock the boat, tugging at the anchor line until it slowly gave way. While I rested unaware, the Sea Ray had drifted over a mile. Not far in nautical terms, but far enough for me to hear a very different sound.

I was startled when her scream woke me. Not screams in plural, but **a** scream—one continuous, excruciating wail. Dazed and confused, I pawed my way to the nearby boat rail and scanned the horizon, trying to find it s source. I studied the surrounding buoys, channel markers, and landmarks. Where was I? Who was screaming and why?

Then I saw her standing in the water with her body bent over. At first I imagined that she had, perhaps, a water toy in her arms. As my vision cleared from sleep, I saw that it was limp and dangling…a doll or stuffed animal? Then in horror, I saw him. I still see him.

Your costume was a pumpkin in the picture on our wall
Now it's in a box of memories lying crumpled in a ball.
Why do monsters come from graveyards
With death's goblins everywhere
When my baby is sleeping there?
—Billy's Song

Chapter 22

DICK

*I*t was the holidays that reminded us most of the passing time. Before the shock had worn off, Halloween was upon us. It had been over three months since we had lost you. What a funny phrase—as if we misplaced you. We always knew where you were. Yet, I found it hard to say that you were "deceased," because your energy could never stop or cease. The phrase "crossed over" seemed more appropriate, yet that sounded a bit over the edge for me.

Some people proclaim that their loved ones "pass away," which sounds more like an intestinal disorder and doesn't make any sense. And you didn't pass away quietly, Billy, you went away with a bang. So if asked, I just told people you had died. Even though the word was unpleasant to them, it was my reality.

Your mother was unable to look forward to anything, except a drag off her cigarette or a desired pregnancy. Her periods were often late, but always arrived, as if to tease her with their bloody appearance. Though their occurrence dampened her one remaining expectation, it relieved me.

I didn't deny her my affection or myself sex, but I mentally crossed my fingers after each time we made love. That was my secret from her; I did not want another child. Though I was only thirty-eight, I felt too old to have another baby. I had aged a lifetime since your death. Above all, the responsibility frightened me. I couldn't keep you alive, Billy; how could I be trusted with another child?

Even though your mother resisted moving on with time, she knew that small advancements were needed to physically continue her life. Everyday feats, taken for granted before your death, were slowly attempted on good days when she could muster the courage. She forced herself to venture to places where your memory pained her most. The zoo, the beach, the mall, and numerous other backdrops to the scenes of your short life were not avoided.

But every action she took and every purchase she made was in memory of you, Billy. In the absence of diaper changes, bottle preparation, and all the vigilance required for a toddler, she found herself with idle time. The urge to tend to your everyday needs became a compulsive force that wouldn't diminish. So symbolism became very important as a substitute for her physical labor.

She bought everything in baby-boy blue. She changed all her passwords for her accounts to BILLY. I often found her in your bedroom, leafing through pictures and negatives, reproducing them over and over again. We still said "Billy's room" when speaking of that bedroom with the babyless crib. Everything in it was frozen in time; to a happier day, just the way you had left it. When she purchased something for Danny, she did the same for you, Billy. We still had two of everything. For her, not doing so would mean that you no longer existed.

The urge to preserve your memory continued to be her obsession. So when a baby product manufacturer advertised a contest for *Baby of the Year*, she couldn't resist entering your pictures. Her desire to have the world come to know you drove her forward. Besides, she couldn't imagine losing the contest; in your death, your beauty reached beyond all others.

So she purchased eighteen bottles of baby oil to provide six proof-of-purchase seals to accompany each of the three photos she sent in. While stuffing the proof of purchase seals along with your photos in an envelope, she imagined your picture displayed on every baby product in that formidable aisle five of our grocery store. Even though she cherished the consolation prize of a T-shirt with your life-sized picture on the front, she felt disappointed. And whenever she would chance upon those unused baby oil bottles in your dresser drawer, she felt their rejection of you. Instead of the company's logo on the back of the T-shirt, it should have read, "My child died and all I got was this lousy T-shirt."

JoAnn
A mother journaling through grief

The dark vampires, ghosts, and goblins have garnished the world. Halloween is quickly approaching, bringing with it mutilated corpses and evil phantoms residing in burial plots much like yours, Billy.

How could the dead be evil, when you are one of them? At every simulated coffin and graveyard scene, I've attempted to cover Danny's eyes. He's come to believe that cemeteries are holy, tranquil places—which is the notion I'd like him to keep. But I've found it a futile battle. Even his daycare staged a "haunted house" last night with young innocents dressed as the dead. I must have been crazy to agree to Danny's role as a vampire in a casket. Maybe I just didn't have the heart to object to his much anticipated role.

Even though it snowed a record 28 inches on Halloween night, I was able to drive my SUV to the daycare center for Danny's haunted house debut. In the corner of the darkened classroom, I watched in horror as he climbed into the casket and patiently lay motionless for the next group of children to walk in. For a moment, it was your body there in the casket, Billy. So I waited in the corner with my hand over my mouth, struggling to keep my silence—privately relieved each time Danny would pop up to scream "Boo!" to each group of children that entered.

He needs to be light-hearted and play as he did before your death, Billy. So I allowed my emotions to turn numb and tried to block out your image every time he crawled back into the coffin. Over and over again, clothed in a black cape with face painted green, Danny would reveal his plastic fangs in a grimace to the unsuspecting children. With each repetition, it became easier for me. It's like this with your memories too, Billy. Each time I cry over them, they become a tad easier to deal with the next time they surface.

After all, it was great to see him having so much fun. But with each costumed child who entered the room, I still felt the urge to wipe off their paint or peek under their mask in search of your face.

Chapter 23

DICK

Y our mother succeeded in persuading me to attend a meeting of The Compassionate Friends, a national support group for bereaved parents. It was your mother's third meeting; it was to be my first and last. My grief was my own; it was futile for anyone else to understand it. Besides, I didn't feel comfortable in a room that seemed to pulsate with grief. The pressure of over sixty bereaved parents in one place suffocated me, making me feel that at any minute the walls of the church hall might explode.

Your mother found something different there. Unlike others outside this club, who would safely change the subject to Danny once they learned of your death, the members of Compassionate Friends wanted to solely hear about you, Billy. She was pleasantly surprised at their interest when, usually, the mention of her youngest child was met with unease and discomfort. Yet, when finally given the chance to speak your name, she found herself at a loss of words.

We all wore nametags on our chests with our child's name and eternal age on it. One by one in succession, each parent attempted to stand up from their chair and proclaim his or her child's name, age at death, and manner of death. Some could talk at length uninhibited, some could only accomplish their child's name with tears choking their words, and others merely stayed silently seated. I was one of the latter, Billy, as I sat in my chair trying to stifle my emotions. But your mother stood up in to proclaim your name.

"Our son Billy drowned three months and twenty days ago at the age of eighteen months." Her voice shook while she confirmed your death to all. Then she asked them how long this unbearable pain would last, and they told her at least a year. She asked how long she would ache for your touch, and they told her forever.

At the conclusion of the meeting, your mother engaged in conversation with her new-found friends, as I avoided them. I discretely slipped away to the exit, impatiently waiting for her to join me. With my hands across my chest, I fidgeted uncomfortably from one foot to the other, trying not to make eye contact with anyone. When I spied a photo album lying on a foldout table before me, I quickly used it as a shield to avoid being approached. It appeared to be the group's memory book, and so I became immersed in it.

Innocent faces confronted me, portraying the life of a child on each page. Some wore diapers, some wore graduation gowns, and others wore wedding gowns. Some pages were yellowed from years of exposure and some were a bright white with the freshness of pain. I felt your mother's arm around my waist.

"I find it very hard to feel sorry for myself in this room," she whispered. I nodded in agreement.

We stood with our arms around each other, silently leafing through the pages of the photo album. She removed a blank white sheet from the book to bring home to attempt to create a page for you.

For days, she tried to design that page of your life, Billy, but found it very difficult to fit it all on one 8X10-inch area. You see, you didn't belong in that book, anymore than she belonged in that room with those unfortunate people. You were coming back, you were special, and nobody could love a child as she loved you. She was not like them.

Though refusing to be a member of the club, a compelling urge drove her to condense your life on that page. So without me, she returned to that church hall the next month to place your story in that book of death.

JOANN

A MOTHER JOURNALING THROUGH GRIEF

For months I've managed to avoid aisle five in the grocery store; the baby aisle. But today, I absently entered it while on my way from the dairy section to the register. Even though the rest of the store was busy with shoppers, there was no one else in that aisle but me. Just myself, the baby food, the diapers...and that run-a-way balloon. It was hanging, half-deflated, at eye level in the middle of the narrow pathway. The attached string caressed the ground, balancing the balloon in the center of my view. Then I noticed the words on it "Thinking of You." Still alone in the aisle, I approached the balloon and touched its round, smooth sides, almost feeling a vibrant connection to you. You know I'm thinking of you, too, Baby.

Your father and I were as close as we'd ever been immediately after your death, Billy. We became one within our grief. I remembered what had made me fall in love with him — that kind, compassionate, ethical, respectful, responsible, patient, laid-back boyfriend of yesteryear.

Things are changing. He's talking less about you and staying away from home more often. Somehow I don't blame him; I'm not the same woman he married. But how can he disregard his pain, how can he tell people he has only one son?

Sometimes I wonder if he even wants another child. I feel him pulling away from me while he comes home later every night.   He's not making the same money from DevCom as he use to. Is it the economy, is there a recession... or is it his depression? Maybe if our finances were better, he would be more eager to have another child. Please, God, let me win the lottery so I can have a baby.

I got my period yesterday. No baby this month, I guess. So I cried most of the day, couldn't even hide it from Danny this time. He took a picture off the shelf and handed it to me. It was of the three of us, Billy. You, Danny, and I on the

4ᵗʰ of July, only nine days before you died. In the picture, the camera captured the oblivious innocence in our smiling faces—so unaware. As Danny placed the picture in my hand, he said, "This is when you were happy all the time, Mommy."

To my credit, I can sometimes stop the tears and smile. But I still wonder, when I have a good day, am I truly getting better or am I just denying that you're gone?

A turkey's in the oven, the table's spread for all to see
The yams are ripe for eating, I feel love surrounding me.
Lord, why can't I be thankful — my faith, please be restored
When my family's no longer four?
—Billy's Song

Chapter 24

DICK

*E*ven though the sun shone bright, there was a chill in the air as I stood over your grave with the bouquet of daisies in hand. The world was moving forward into late November. At that time, your Great-grandma Cencic's home country of Croatia was being invaded by the Serbs, the NBA's Magic Johnson had tested positive for AIDS, bringing greater awareness to the disease, a fired postal worker went on a shooting rampage at a time when this was a novel idea, and to top it off, Sonny Bono was elected to US Congress.

A time to be thankful…Would that time ever come for me?

I barely noticed the many good circumstances in our lives that November, even though my father had undergone successful treatment for his prostate cancer and my sister's melanoma was arrested by the removal of the menacing mole on her back and the radiation that followed. But selfishly, I would have returned every blessing just to have my child back. God could have saved you and he chose not to.

The daisies had been hard to find during that time of year, but your mother insisted that I buy them for my first visit to your grave. The wire stand on the bottom of the vase buckled as I forced it into the frozen ground next to the condemned elm tree. The boughs of its branches displayed a few remaining leaves salvaged from the cool autumn. Each one was painted with a colorful rainbow of orange, yellow, and brown, brazenly announcing the passage of time since your death.

Be thankful. For what? Despite our family gathering the day before with the lavish meal and loving support, Thanksgiving had been a non-event for me.

Merry Christmas! Happy Holidays! Joy to the World! *Bah, humbug!* No sooner had Thanksgiving Day passed, when the Christmas season arrived. The superficial gaiety of every greeting, caroled Noel, and jolly Santa Claus contrasted with my morbid apathy. The forced, heightened animation drove me into a cynical disposition.

Toys, presents, clothes, sales, money, things and more things. All the materialistic pleasures people charged on their plastic would eventually be boxed up or discarded, except for the clothes on their bodies in the darkness of their graves—just like my son.

He is the Christ Child, the Savior, the Reason for the Season, Jesus, the only hope for me to see you again, Billy. Your mother often prayed and thanked Him for being born—someday making a reunion possible. For me, accepting the birth of Jesus was as difficult as believing in Santa Claus that Christmas. It took a reaching for the intangible to believe, a desperate clinging to an unproven theory that I couldn't quite grasp. So I let my beliefs slip away from me, having no room in my life for both my faith and my resentment. I was adverse to that year's Christmas celebration, knowing you would never sing a carol, ice skate outdoors, decorate a tree, or sit on Santa's lap again.

My anger followed me as I turned toward the car and left the spot of your frozen bed.

JOANN

A MOTHER JOURNALING THROUGH GRIEF

The cold days of this winter continue to be the most difficult season of my life. Nothing excites me but having another baby. I feel unloved. Have I always felt this way or did it happen when you died, Billy—when I lost someone who loved me unconditionally?

Last week, you would have sung "Jingle Bells" at the Christmas program with the other toddlers. While I sat in the metal chair in the musty basement of the daycare center, I imagined you losing patience in the middle of the song and running down from the stage with the other kids following right behind. And I still would have been so proud. While the little girls on stage looked and sang like little angels, I remembered that three-year-old girl in the park just two weeks before you died, Billy.

She was alone at the playground, so I looked around for a parent. After searching the park to no avail, I noticed a woman watching out the window of her house across the street while talking on the phone. How many times had the mother let the little girl go to the park alone? I remember self-righteously thinking; I would never let you or Danny wander that far from a watchful eye. But in retrospect, Billy, I've done far worse—I let you die.

That day in the park, you and that little girl smiled at each other, and then, to my surprise, you started showing off. It reminds me that I'll never see you get married. You'll never have any children of your own; never kiss your first girl. You'll never get your driver's license, ride your first bike, fly in an airplane, own your first baseball mitt, or see your first movie. I was planning on buying you a tricycle this year for Christmas. I was planning on you living.

TIM
A FIREFIGHTER

It's amazing that I heard the call at all, being that I wasn't consciously listening to the radio at the time. It must have been the address that drew my attention…Wilshire Boulevard…just a few blocks from my house. I knew I could make it there before my buddies would even get to the fire station. I flew through the door and never ran so fast in my life.

The sitter was sitting in the grass at the side of the house, holding a young boy in her arms. After all my years as a fireman, I had never heard such gut-wrenching cry. Three men surrounded the toddler, who lay on the deck of the house. One person breathing for him, and I recognized an exhausted Kevin Berg doing compressions. So I took over for him.

"It's okay. You'll be fine, little guy" I reassured the baby as I pushed on his chest, though his eyes were unresponsive.

I tried to memorize that boy's pictures at the funeral. He had lively blue eyes and a mischievous smile in the photos, but that's not the face that continues to enter my dreams.

It's okay. You'll be fine, little guy. I still hear the cries of the sitter while I keep pushing on his chest. But there's still no movement, just the face of death.

Chapter 25

DICK

*I*n comparison to the last Christmas, our decorated house appeared much the same—hiding our transformation with its adornments. Only the decorated tree was slightly different. It stood in the same corner, but was trimmed contrary to the year before. The ornaments, which were once hung higher than four feet to escape your wandering hands, Billy, were all hung below those four feet, since Danny insisted on independently decorating the tree himself.

With the uncasing of each ornament, we silently reflected on the memories of the Christmas before: your keepsake rocking horse from Godfather Dave, the wooden teddy bear from Grandma Deveny, and the red metal jingle-bell you tore from the Scotch pine limbs last December claiming it as your own. They all blended together with the newly purchased angels. Being that angels were trendy at Christmastime, your mother bought several of male gender to garnish our home and represent you in your absence.

Lacking a fireplace, the four Deveny stockings were hung from the top of the hutch as usual. Yours was a temporary felt sock with the word BILLY hand-stitched by your mother on the top cuff. We were still waiting for an intricate cross-stitched replacement that your godmother, Aunt Sue, was in the process of designing. Between chemo treatments and work, she had found little time that year for needle-pointing, so your stocking was delayed. It appeared that the completion of your life superseded the creation of your Christmas stocking.

On the table adjacent to the tree, your mother placed your picture and a glass candle holder in the shape of a bluebird. The candle burned every day of December, and your mother would sit and stare into its glowing flames, searching for her personal light as the world outside continued its joyous intentions.

That Christmas, your Aunt Kathleen gave your mother and her sisters a set of small, handcrafted wooden elves. Each elf had a different letter printed on its square block-body, so in sequence displayed a word. Your Aunt Jeanne's elves spelled JOY, Aunt Kathy's elves spelled FAITH, Aunt Theresa's PEACE, and Aunt Jennifer's spelled NOEL. When opening her package, your mother anticipated five elves portraying the word BILLY. So she was disappointed when she turned the four wooden faces around to read the word HOPE. She contemplated the meaning of the word.

Through the early months of your mother's grief, her emotions would beat on her as if she were the sole target in a dodge ball game. Depression and guilt hit the hardest at the forefront—intermingled with an assault of other various feelings. Jealousy, sudden levity, denial, and vacant stupor would visit her briefly without command. But neither she nor I ever felt fear. Fear was lacking, not because we felt invincible, but because nothing could hurt us more than your death. Nothing could touch that place deep in our hearts when there was nothing left there. Even our own deaths were not feared. There's nothing like the tides of your own child's death to squelch the flames of your own.

While studying the word HOPE in front of her, she tried to comprehend its definition. As she couldn't feel fear, she couldn't feel hope. The word was meaningless, just black print on the white pages of a dictionary; green marker on wooden elf bodies. Fear and hope were indefinable to her.

~ ~ ~ ~ ~

When your mother visited the shopping mall with Danny that Christmas season, the trip reminded her of presents not purchased. In the past, she had often frequented malls with the sole purpose of entertaining her boys. The active hallways would fascinate Danny and allow you an endless raceway, Billy. Your brother would walk at her side, trained to grasp one hand on the buggy at all times, while you were temporarily strapped inside. When the buggy stopped for even a moment, you would wiggle out of your confines and try to escape to great adventures.

Your threesome would always visit one particular toy store that had a hands-on policy for children. Even you, Billy, couldn't destroy the child-sized gadgets lining its shelves. Your favorite toy was a wooden workbench painted in the primary colors. You would sit in front of it for an unusual length of time, pounding the hammer on its colorful pegs. Though it was a basic workbench I could have made myself, it was priced at thirty dollars. Because of the cost and on principle, your mother had always refused to buy it for you.

So when coming across that workbench's idle mallet that Christmas of '91, she used her plastic and brought it home to place under our tree. When Christmas Eve Day arrived, she realized that your gift would remain unopened.

~ ~ ~ ~ ~

"I'll be right back, this won't take long," She reached for her ski jacket and grabbed her keys. As she opened the door, a subzero blast entered through in a miniature blizzard of icy snowflakes.

"My mother's expecting us at five for dinner..." My voice hung in the air as the door slammed shut behind her. While Danny and I waiting impatiently at home, she searched for a recipient for your gift, Billy.

With resolve, she systematically drove her Honda through the winding streets of our little town. Clutching the rim of the steering wheel, she squinted through the frozen windshield in search of the perfect house.

Finding a small, dilapidated home with toddler-sized toys strewn throughout the fenced-in yard, she parked on the narrow street and approached the door with the present in hand. The green paint on the door frame was peeling and the storm window had a crack inching its way through the center. Through the doorway, she could hear children screaming, a female voice commanding attention, and a male voice attempting to converse above the others: the sounds of a family. After trying the inoperative doorbell, your mother softly rapped on the door to no avail. Then she forcefully knocked against the hard door frame until her frozen knuckles felt the impact.

A large woman suddenly appeared at the doorway. Surrounding her were three young children spewing a clamorous array of high-timbered shrieks.

"Shush...be quiet. Tommy, settle down!" The woman wiped her hands on the towel that hung from her apron. "Can I help you?" She looked at your mother with leery, questioning eyes. Your mother placed the package adorned in Santa Claus wrapping in the women's hands.

"Please take this gift," your mother mumbled, her eyes lowering to the toddler attached to the women's beefy leg. As she turned around with envy and left the poor but complete home, she felt some closure with her Christmas Eve donation.

The woman looked out her doorway at the stranger who climbed into her car and drove away. She opened the gift tag on the present and read, *"To one of God's children, from an angel named Billy."*

~ ~ ~ ~ ~

On Christmas Day, your mother replaced the brown, withering Thanksgiving daisies at your gravesite with a wreath bearing miniature toy soldiers and a blue gingham bow. While all the other wreaths at the cemetery had red bows, yours needed to be different, because you weren't the same as the others. The elm tree stood bare and tall surrounded by a white carpet of snow, making more evident the red X printed on its bark.

"Can we ever dig up Billy's old body, Mommy? Can we ever see him again?" Danny asked while attempting to scale the tall, staunch Deveny gravestone.

"No, Sweetie, I'm sorry. We can't. Remember, this is Billy's 'old' body? It doesn't work anymore. He has a new one now in Heaven."

"I wish I was Superman so I could see right through the ground!" He yelled while jumping as high as he could with his arms extended toward the stone's top. Failing to fly, he eventually gave up and returned to your mother's side at the grave. With Danny's proclamation, her guilt surfaced; she had always regretted excluding Danny from viewing your body at the funeral home.

"Remember Adam and Eve, Honey. Adam was made from dirt and Eve from Adam's rib..." Then she stopped herself. Her son needed tangibles; he was a four-year-old who had had to learn too many abstract concepts in the last few months. The story sounded ridiculous even to her.

"It would only be my fault if I pushed him in, right, Mommy?" Danny now stood by her side, asking for atonement.

"That's exactly right, Danny," she answered him with resolve, and as always, there was a release of tension in his shoulders. She stooped down to his level and wrapped her arms around him. She reminded him that wishing a brother away doesn't make him die and wishing a brother's return doesn't make him come back.

That's why she refused to pull the other half of the turkey wishbone on Thanksgiving Day. And that was why she couldn't bring herself to throw a penny in the wishing well at the mall like the other shoppers a few days before. Their wishes could be granted. If she couldn't wish for the only thing her heart desired, there were no wishes left. But she was careful around Danny not to show her cynicism. She didn't want him to lose his dreams just because she had lost hers.

JoAnn

A MOTHER JOURNALING THROUGH GRIEF

Your Aunt Jeanne helped me pack up your things today, Billy. As I placed each item into the boxes, memories came to mind without warrant.

When I opened that colorful pop-up book and saw your fingerprints, I remembered how you had ripped out the moveable pieces to get a closer look. As I held the torn corners of each page, they warmed my hands in the chilly air of the garage and an image appeared to me: Danny on my right side and you on my left, sitting in our allotted spots on the couch in the living room. I leafed through the soiled pages, and for a moment, I was reading to you under the warmth of the brass lamp. Then suddenly the blanket of reality loomed over us, shattering the scene into tiny fragments and leaving me kneeling on the cold cement floor of the garage, leaning over a cardboard box.

Memories are like this for me. Not bitter-sweet, but sweet-bitter. They arrive sweetly and then the bitterness bites through, leaving a lingering, acrid taste in my mouth.

It seems odd that your possessions filled only five boxes, because my memories of you are so much more. My mind can't convince my heart that you'll never need those objects again, so I'm saving them for you on a shelf in the garage. I can't bring myself to give them away, to be used by another toddler fortunate enough to live when you should have.

So by placing them on that shelf, I hid your memories in my box of denial. I'll keep them in their concealed container with the knowledge that they'll be waiting for you in the dark recesses of a garage—waiting for me to find an appropriate place for them in my life. The sweater that Grandma Deveny gave you, the squeak toy that Grandma Kuzma bought, your dinosaur socks, your little baseball jacket and the "Where's That Puppy?" book, marked by your curious fingers and chewed on by your teething gums. Your tooth marks were still there.

Is this all that's left of you? Where's Billy? Yes, little boy, I wonder, too.

Chapter 26

DICK

"I want to see Inspector Dog, Mommy! Nathan, do you want to see Inspector Dog? Come on, Mommy!" Danny grabbed her hand, trying to pull her through the corridors of City Hall. It was Safety Day in our little town of Mound, so there were numerous parents and children moving along side them as they weaved their way through the hallways. The atmosphere was filled with energy; every child was excited to see a police car, fire truck, and, most importantly, a large costumed dog dressed like a spy.

Your mother let Danny invite his best friend, Nathan, because she still felt more comfortable having two at her side. And sometimes she would pretend the playmate was you, Billy, when strangers commented on her two little boys. Through fantasy, she could relieve one of her secondary losses.

It was disconcerting to me when she would continue to imagine you were still there. And the recipients must have thought your mother's actions were delusional when she would sign your name with ours at the bottom of thank-you cards. We kept receiving notices for doctors' appointments and mailers for children's shoe sales addressed to Billy Deveny, because your mother wouldn't notify them of your death. And she saved these letters in your ever-growing death binder. Because you were acknowledged by the United States Postal Service, she felt that they were evidence that you still existed.

With the exception of one bank teller at the drive-up window, who continued to hand her two suckers even though only one child sat in the back seat, most people excluded you. There weren't many who understood that she still had two children.

"If your mother dies, do you say you have no mother? No, you just say she died. People know you must *have* a mother; someone gave birth to you. I gave birth to two sons. I *have* two sons," she would tell me. "I'm not denying Billy's death by the inclusion of his name. I'm fully aware that he's gone," she insisted.

As Danny led her by hand through the hallway of the police station, she glanced at his blackened fingertips. She had subjected him to the free fingerprinting the police department was offering, believing she could save him from abduction that way. It was always the worst-case scenario for her. She had become quite overprotective of Danny, finally understanding that a tragedy could happen again.

Even though I believed that Danny was progressing wonderfully, your mother was still worried about the nervous habits he had picked up since your death, Billy. He had started to suck on his thumb, hands, or clothes, leaving the area around his mouth continually chapped. When he became anxious, sometimes a back rub would help. So every night your mother would continue to massage the knots out of his tense little muscles.

Throughout the day, he asked endless questions about which animal was more powerful than the next. *Is a cougar more powerful than a tiger? Is an eagle more powerful than a vulture?* And so it went until he got them in their sequential order of physical aptitude.

He had also found a new aspiration in becoming a garbage man when he grew up. Because he watched in wonder every Monday morning as our trash collector lifted heavy cans above his head, Danny surmised that he must be the most powerful person on earth. Danny's obsession with tiers of power led your mother to believe that your death, Billy, left him feeling helpless and ineffectual.

So your mother practiced some amateur psychology techniques by letting Danny make more decisions. He could choose between at least two sets of clothes and two brands of cereal in the mornings. But mostly, he enjoyed it when she let him direct her car into the garage.

Acting like a flagman for a Boeing 747, he would stand safely on the sidewalk next to the driveway with a miniature American flag in each hand. Using different signals for stop and go, your mother followed his commands—even if it seemed to take eternity to move five feet. She detected a sense of control in his eyes as he guided the massive car into its allotted spot.

At City Hall, while the threesome followed the masses of parents and their children, she felt the completeness of two small hands in her own. When the trio neared the large double doors leading to the outside, she heard a familiar escalating humming sound. Her body tingled with vibration as the sound got louder and nearer. She let go of the boys' hands to muffle the rotor's pulsating beat from her ears. While staring with apprehension out the door toward the parking lot, she saw a familiar metal beast leave the ground.

"Look Mommy, a helicopter!" Danny pointed and screamed with glee, but she couldn't hear him over her own thoughts.

"Wait for me! Please, I'm his mommy...please come back!"

~ ~ ~ ~ ~

By the onset of the New Year, your mother learned the meaning of post-traumatic stress syndrome. Even through her efforts to confront the memories of your life, she found some experiences were deeply buried in her subconscious, only to be unexpectedly retrieved by a sudden smell, noise, or vision.

The pulsing sound of a helicopter left her scanning the skies for you. The sirens from the rescue vehicles left her holding your imaginary body, rocking, and reciting the *Hail Mary*. The sucking of liquid through tubes brought images of your body on that hospital bed.

A shopping trip turned to mayhem one day when Danny played hide-and-seek in a clothing store without your mother's knowledge. A stifling pressure of anxiety mounted into an uncontrollable panic as she circled the forest of clothing racks in search of him. She transformed into a lunatic in front of store clerks and shoppers because she was able to vividly imagine the sudden loss of her remaining child. These experiences awakened sleeping emotions and moved her back to a place and time she thought she had left behind.

In January, your mother tried professional help, which only resulted in the young counselor crying along with her. The counselor listened and empathized, but she couldn't remedy it. And your mother could talk forever, to whomever, about you. There was nothing that a counselor could teach her that she hadn't experienced herself or had read in her how-to-grieve books multiplying on the dresser next to your crib.

In the end, your mother still maintained that counseling often benefits the bereaved. But she was blessed with supportive friends, family, and jump-seat therapy, which served to be more effective and financially reasonable. But patient and attentive as they all were, she eventually came to bore herself with the same repetitive concerns and questions.

Being a very private man, I didn't believe in counselors or psychiatrists. I was the only one who could remedy my own pain, and I didn't need to talk about it. Besides, it was as difficult for me to mention your name, Billy, as much as it was to constantly hear your mother speak of you.

Every month, your mother's mood would brighten after intercourse and plummet at the onset of her period. In riding her conception roller-coaster, she was experiencing the reverse of PMS. And I couldn't help but feel that my sole purpose was to provide sperm. Then a week before your second birthday, Billy, your mother told me she might be pregnant.

JOANN

A MOTHER JOURNALING THROUGH GRIEF

Creak...creak...creak...creak. The noise was coming from outside. I looked out the living room window and saw you on the play set in the backyard, swinging back and forth, back and forth.

Creak...creak...creak. As I ran out the door, only the top of your curly blonde head could be seen; your face was limply buried in your chest. Your chubby little legs and arms were hanging loosely from the swing seat. As I got closer, I noticed that your flesh was blue. Your eyes stared vacantly at the ground while your body swung back, creak... and forth, creak. Back....creak, and forth, creak. I reached out to you to stop the noise, but felt your flesh give way under my finger tips. Then I woke up.

Creak...creak...creak, I could still hear it. I sat up in bed, placed my feet into my slippers, hesitantly making my way downstairs. Frightened and anxious, I moved to open the shades of the living room window. The swing was idle and empty while the hanging flower pot on the eave swayed—creaking in the wind.

The sunrises, which at first reminded me of time passing without you, don't bother me as they used to. They're preferred over the darkness. But I still long for you throughout the eternal hours of the each day. Longing—what an appropriate word. I hope time isn't going as slowly for you, Honey.

Everyone thinks that you're gone for good, Billy, but I know that somehow I'll see you soon. Sometimes I find myself privately dwelling on my little secret, that I'm merely playing a game. Until I see you again, I'll pretend to go through the motions of a bereaved mother who has lost her baby. And when you come back, people will tell me that I misled them with my little joke, that you had never died at all. I imagine that they'll be indignant because they wasted their empathy on me for all those months. What a wonderful joke that would be. This is how I feel on my good days.

Then on my bad days, when the ache escalates, I reach for my last life-line. I call to Jesus or God; it doesn't seem to matter which one. Then I find myself in a place not of this earth—serene with a contentment that I've only felt in a dream. At these times, I can almost hear, "There is a better place." Then I find myself in that light again and I'm momentarily rescued.

I'm five days late on my period, which is very unusual. That makes me feel wonderful...and guilty. I'm not replacing you, Billy; I'm replacing my secondary losses. You were ripped out of my arms, and there my love dangles in midair. I have so much more to give.

It makes me smile to see you dancing, joy glowing from your face
When I gaze into the flicker of the candles on your cake.
You came to me a miracle; you left me so much more.
Happy Birthday, my little boy.
—Billy's Song

Chapter 27

DICK

"*Everything grows and grows. Babies do, animals too...*" From the overhead speakers, Raffi's recorded voice crooned to a crowded room filled with mothers and their children. All joined in with the popular melodies, which brought enjoyment to the kids and parents alike. Danny snuggled into the bowl of your mother's crossed legs as she sat on the cool cement floor of the large auditorium. Her arms enveloped his body while the January winds howled outside.

After your death, Billy, Danny and your mother were left with ample opportunities to spend quality time on field trips and community activities. That winter, one could often find them at their designated spot in that room or sliding down the snow-covered first green at the local Burl Oaks Golf Course. Sleigh rides, museum tours, and community activities filled their days when I was at work and she was not.

Despite their busy schedule, she was determined to perfect Danny's swimming skills for obvious reasons. Once a week, in the humid clamor of the Mound Westonka High School swim pool, she would watch her four-year-old cling to the side tiles of the shallow end—while the other children in his group concluded their lesson on the diving board at the deep end. Danny had become an adept swimmer, but would not risk a journey to that dreaded end of the pool. Our little guy knew what had happened to his younger brother when he ventured *too deep in the water*. In hindsight, that may have been a bad choice of words your mother and I attributed to your death. So session after paid session, Danny would be held back from the next level due to his resistance to the deep end of the pool.

"*Everything grows...Sisters do, brothers too...*" Danny was smiling with sheer delight while clapping his hands to the beat of the music, as your mother shuffled her bottom over to allow another mother and her two small sons a space next to them. She couldn't help but notice the totality of their family. Yet it warmed her heart to see Danny happy again, so she disregarded the silhouette of her past and donned her mask of denial. Warmth penetrated her heart as her oldest son looked up into her eyes with laughter. She felt blessed as she touched her stomach and almost felt the new baby growing inside her. *Two weeks late, it had to be a baby,* she thought.

"*Everything grows...Anyone knows that's how it goes...*" The chorus sang on as she remembered your second birthday arriving in a few days.

I'd like to proclaim that your mother was *okay,* which she told others only to relieve their discomfort. But if I did, I would be narrating a fictional account of her grief. Yet a possible pregnancy had definitely buoyed her spirit, even though it froze mine. Now, I guiltily recall ignoring her or changing the subject when she spoke of it to me. So she spared me and kept it in her thoughts while walking through life with her head held higher and a new lightness to her step.

"*A blade of grass, fingers and toes, hair on my head...Everything grows...*"

Were you growing in your heavenly home, Billy? Were you keeping up with all the other two-year olds seated around her in that room, leaving her to miss every new word spoken and physical feat accomplished in your afterlife? But with the absence of your earthly body, you could only be growing in intellect. Would she meet you on the day of her death as a wrinkled old lady with a fading mind and you an 18-month-old child who could outsmart her? Heaven forbid. On the other hand, she didn't want to miss your growth into adulthood. There was no best-case scenario to her fantasies.

Your rapidly approaching birthday turned out to be a more difficult occasion than Halloween, Thanksgiving, or Christmas. What does one do for a child's birthday in his absence? A child's second birthday—a day to celebrate the physical and emotional growth of the past and the novel learning experiences of the future. A time to reflect toward another year filled with wondrous changes and milestones. Conversely, for her and me, it was just another reminder of the early conclusion to your life.

"Two little ducks went out to play, over the hill and far away..." she breathed a sigh of relief as Raffi began a new song. His melodic voice mingled with a chorus of little voices to fill the room.

"Mother duck said, 'Quack, quack, quack, quack'..." she watched Danny, smiling, as his body swayed with the music. The high-pitched volume of the juvenile vocalists escalated. *"...but only one little duck came back!"*

The walls of the room moved in closer as a tear welled up in the corner of her eye. She grabbed the hand of her most prized earthly possession and shimmied through the knee-high toddlers and their parents.

"Excuse me, please...oh my, I'm so sorry. Excuse me, excuse me, please..."

"Why are we going, Mommy? I want to stay 'til he sings *Baby Beluga!*" Danny yelled over the music.

"Not today, Honey," she told him, sounding calmer than she felt. Just as she exited out the doors of the auditorium with Danny in tow, her fragile mask of denial shattered and a tear escaped down her cheek.

Please don't grow up, Billy....I don't want to miss you growing up.

JoAnn
A mother journaling through grief

When people ask me how I'm doing, my response has graduated from "lousy" to "okay." I guess you could call that progress. I'm physically surviving and merely coping emotionally. Even though I sense a dark blanket floating over my head—dangling, ready to smother me—I don't feel that anvil on my shoulder anymore.

I can bring myself to wear earrings and a little make-up now. I found the perfect tear-proof mascara; maybe Maybelline needs a spokesperson? I'm smoking more, but have gained two pounds back. Sleeping long and hard—it's the only time I don't think of you. Even though I still see your face when my eyelids first close at night, I can hold back the tears at work. I can smile, a little; laugh, a little. I can read books that don't pertain to death now. I can watch television and tune your little face out. I can shave my legs now. Little by little, step by step. I feel as if I'm going through physical therapy.

RANDY
THE DOCTOR

She was still screaming when I noticed the four young men run to her from the next yard. Something seemed very wrong. Instinctively, I climbed over the railing of my boat and dove in.

The warm water consumed me and cleared my head. I began to swim. Stroke, breathe, screaming…stroke, breathe, screaming. What a paradox— a few hours before, I had been racing for the finish line after months of preparation. Soon after the triathlon, I was racing to a different goal, in a different way. I was moving impulsively with a very different intensity; anxious, confused, and straining. I knew that this was serious—very serious.

I welcomed the silence of the water each time my head went under. *Focus, just get there. You'll know what to do,* I thought to myself. Stroke, breathe, screaming…stroke, breathe, screaming. Each time I came up for air, my panic intensified, which motivated me to swim faster. *What will I find when I get there?*

I arrived at the water's edge and climbed up the steps into the yard. There lay a small child, dripping wet and motionless. My training kicked in; access, decide, *act.*

The neighbors seemed relieved by my arrival, because one of them immediately moved aside as I took over mouth to mouth. *Look, listen, feel. No breath, no pulse. No signs of life—yet.* Breathe, one and two and three… His stomach was distended. *Where's an NG tube?* Vomiting. *Stay on it,* I thought to myself. Spit, rinse, back on it.

"Does anyone know his name?" I asked the bystanders between breaths. I heard the answer as I worked. So I whispered in his ear, "This will be okay, Billy. You'll be okay."

Chapter 28

DICK

I could see our house on a high, rocky cliff as I looked up from my small fishing boat, floating on a vast sea. The thunder was deafening and the torrential downpour of rain made the vision of our house seem far away and blurred. I put my hand above my brows to prevent the drops from blocking my view. Its harvest-gold sidings started to peel off one by one from the force of the wind, precariously falling down the cliff into the water near me. The boat tipped from the onslaught of waves, demanding that I hold on to the sides in fear of falling overboard. The rock foundation upon which the house was anchored gave away, bringing the house toppling down—falling on top of me.

"Guess what day this is?" With a start, I opened my eyes to see Danny shimmy onto the bed. "Billy's birthday!" Danny looked upward as if gazing through our bedroom ceiling. "If I were Peter Pan, I'd fly up to Heaven and bring Billy back!"

"Let's get some breakfast, Bud," I rolled over slowly to sit up and felt that familiar stab of pain through my lower back. *Man, I feel old.* As I shuffled down the steps with Danny at my heels, I could hear the sounds of your mother in the kitchen, clanging dishes and running water. Because our dishwasher had broken again the month before, I was in the process of finding a used engine for it. I thought of the impending pregnancy and saw a flashback of our home toppling down the towering cliff. We couldn't afford another child.

The climate of the car leasing business had changed that year, and dealerships were squeezing out the little guy, which was me. As an independent leasing company, I provided more personal services for my customers, such as delivering every new car to their driveways. Yet the consumer was wooed by the big guy's lower prices, which I couldn't match. My mind was, more often, preoccupied with finances than your death, Billy.

One would think with the absence of your diapers, pediatrician bills, and food, that the total expenses of the household would have been lowered. But with photo reproduction costs, the symbolic angels and bluebirds bought, group therapy bills, a library of grief books purchased, funeral expenses, days of work your mother missed, bouquets of pricey flower arrangements ordered for your grave and eighteen bottles of baby oil, grief was extensively more costly and much less rewarding than the presence of our child.

I should have been able to file a lawsuit against God for mental anguish and financial loss in the nearest heavenly court of law. Or, at least, the monies for flowers, statues of bluebirds, and all the grief books your mother purchased should have been deductible according to tax laws. And it would have only made sense to write off eighteen bottles of baby oil as bereavement expenses on Line 36b of our returns for that tax year of 1991.

I scooped Danny into my arms as we navigated the last stair.

"Oh, no, here comes *The Claw!*" This was always our little game, years before Jim Carey showed up on the screen. So in turn, Danny's face lit up with feigned fear. I froze my hand into a distorted talon. Hovering it over him, I tickled his tummy until he gasped for air through his laughter.

Man, how I love this boy, I thought.

~ ~ ~ ~ ~

It was below zero that mid-January day as the car engine rumbled on idle. Even though I had avoided visiting your grave, your mother had insisted on stopping on our way to your Grandma Helen's house. My breath's moisture glazed the car window with frost, so with my glove, I cleared an area to look out.

Through the porthole of ice, I could see your mother plod through the snow drifts toward the Deveny grave plot. She methodically lifted one boot in front of the other to clear the snow banks, nearing the spot where she imagined your grave should be. As soon as one boot cleared the top crust of the white covering, it would then sink deeper into another mountainous pile. *Symbolic of our grief*, I thought. She was wearing layers of mismatched accessories with the oversized ski jacket that I had given her during a happier, wanted pregnancy. *Please, God, she can't be pregnant – not now*, I prayed silently.

"Happy Birthday to you, Happy birthday to you…," Danny sang behind me in the back seat, gazing vacantly at his new plastic Ninja Turtle figurine that he idly fingered in his hand.

She stood in front of the marked elm tree. Unlike me, she felt comfort at your graveside. I watched out the window as she moved into action, fervently digging her mittens into the tiers of heavy snow.

"Come on, Bud. Let's go help your mom," I opened the car door and a blast of frigid air rushed in. With Danny at my heels, I grabbed the shovel from the trunk of the car and navigated along the imprint of your mother's footsteps.

When reaching the gravesite, I gently moved her aside and pushed the shovel's blade into the crusted snow cover. I dug at the base of the elm tree until the warmth of my body underneath my down-filled parka dripped with sweat and the stone was finally revealed beneath our feet. My breath was labored when I stopped to watch your mother discard her mittens to free her hands.

Her fingers opened to reveal a miniature toy truck. And there it idly sat in her opened palm, waiting for a taker. She wanted to place it in your pudgy little hand and watch it come to life; instead, it sat there as an inanimate object. It had no home; the physical object couldn't go to that obscure place where she imagined you would receive it. Indolently, it sat in her red palm where small flakes of frozen snow fell around it and then vanished through the heat of her flesh. Before her numb fingers were unable to, she tied the attached wires of your birthday present next to a red and white tin soldier on the wreath and stood back to view your birthday present dangling on the garland. She made a mental note to save these toys for Danny and the new baby before the groundskeeper removed the wreath in the early spring.

"*Happy birthday to you. Happy birthday, dear Billy. Happy birthday to you.*" Danny stood between us with one arm around my knee and the other around your mother's thigh, while his song hovered with condensation in the frigid air.

Your mother arranged a party for you on the day you would have turned two. Being that the *Happy Birthday* song was inappropriate for everyone but Danny, your Aunt Jennifer played guitar and sang *Billy's Song*. Your Aunt Jennifer had composed this song soon after your death, Billy. Then she had recorded and given your mother a cassette tape copy. Every day on her way to work, your mother would listen to the song and mentally create a new verse for every holiday that arrived without you. In doing so, she would release her demons before arriving at the airport. A comatose state was preferable to a time bomb of bottled tears. So as Jennifer sang at the guitar on your second birthday, the Kuzma family joined in. But then, the Kuzma family always joins in.

I often felt that being with your mother's family was like going to a musical production. When one would expect a prayer, conversation, or farewell, an illusory orchestra would start in and Grandpa Joe would burst into song. The Kuzmas weren't professional singers, but they sure loved to belt out a tune, in or out of harmony. So we all sang for you, Billy and, on that special day, the Devenys even joined in.

I watched my family: your Aunt Susie, who was in remission from her melanoma; my sister Diane, with a good heart but usually trying to run the show; my fragile mother, still losing weight after the news of Susie's cancer; and my father, age 83, shuffling through the room telling another lame, but charming, joke.

My father was 48 when I was born, and I remember, with regret, the embarrassment I felt in grade school when my teachers would refer to him as my grandfather. I watched your mother while she laughed with him. *We couldn't have a child; I couldn't have a child at my age. I don't have the energy.*

As soon as we arrived at your grandparents' house and the families gathered, your mother placed a video in the VCR to show scenes from your life. I tried to look away or at least move into another room to no avail; it had a magnetic pull on me when I heard your voice for the first time since your death

Your animated image filled the TV screen, and I had to hold myself back from reaching into that box of wires for the softness of your flesh. After studying your two-dimensional pictures through the past six months, I had forgotten your three-dimensional characteristics. Your movements on the screen were a reminder of all that was not grieved for yet. You were so amazingly alive; I felt alone in the room with you.

Yet at the same time, I was horribly surprised at the limits of your physical form before me and wondered how that eighteen-month-old boy on the screen of the television could be the whole of my grief. Where was the rest of you? The image before me was inadequate; it couldn't portray what we had truly lost.

Even though our families were viewing the same video, they seemed to fidget with boredom—or was it unease? Despite their feigned interest for your mother's benefit, no one seemed to grasp the unique character of your spirit. Even our immediate families hadn't come to know you during your eighteen months of life. At the same time, I was as guilty as they were in my failure to bond with my nieces and nephews. We had all contemplated the death of our parents, but took for granted the existence of the children. I turned off the VCR.

"It's not over, Dick," your mother snapped. She was dressed in baby-blue tones and wore a button with your picture on her lapel. She reached for the control.

"Settle down....I'll turn it on later. We're going to light the cake now," The edge in my voice revealed a patience tried.

"Don't tell me to settle down," she whispered harshly and glared at me. Just in time, your Grandma Jen appeared at my side.

"Time for cake! Everyone come into the dining room!" She took Danny by the hand and he followed alongside her.

For the occasion, your Aunt Jeanne had created a cake in the shape of a lamb. Surrounding the bottom of the coconut frosting serving as its fleece, fresh daisies lay on the platter on which the white lamb sat. As we sliced the first piece, I remembered your birthday the year before.

The sequence of snapshots your mother took on that day showed your attempts to devour your first birthday cake. The photos, which now hung next to your crib, depicted chunks of chocolate swirl in your hair, ears, and eyes. White icing was spread over nearly every body part, except your two-toothed grin.

Danny had excitedly anticipated your second birthday party, so when the event concluded without a *Happy Birthday* song, games, presents, or candles, his disappointment was evident. By the end of the day, he was disheartened by the lack of gaiety at the unusual birthday party for his little brother.

"Why did Billy go in the water, Daddy?" Danny asked me that evening as we sat together on the couch watching the television. His questions about your death had abated by that time, so I was caught off guard.

"I don't know, Bud. Maybe he just wanted to go swimming," I reasoned. *Brilliant*, I thought to myself. Despite my lame answer, he was content with it and redirected his attention back to the television.

What did happen, Billy? I doubt that you fell off the dock, because you were incredibly coordinated for your age. I often imagined that you would have been an excellent athlete. When you climbed down our deck steps, you would always shimmy down the side, instead of going down the longer correct way. In whatever you did, you took the most dangerous, fastest route. There was only one occasion when I spanked you on your diapered bottom; it was the day you tried to navigate our steps down to the lake. To this day, I don't know why I did that, never having believed in the effectiveness of corporal punishment. Did that slap on your diapered bottom teach you a lesson or did it only teach you defiance and resolve? So I imagine that you took the neighbors' steps instead of ours. Is that what you did, Bud?

You may have climbed onto their dock, bent over to reach for something, and then fallen in. Or were you shimmying down the side into the water, not knowing or caring how deep it was? Or you could have merely waded into the water from the neighbor's beach. Were you splashing in the water when a large boat came tearing through our channel, unmindful of the slow-wake laws? Did you get knocked over by the waves it left in its passing?

Through all the scenarios that could have transpired, there's one that plays foremost in my mind. I see you opening that screen door and then turning around to quietly close it behind you, giggling at the trick you were playing on Denise. Then you run down the neighbors' dock and jump into the lake, barring all consequences.

Why did you go into the water, Billy?

JoAnn

A mother journaling through grief

*You were two years old, and your curly blonde hair had turned to a dark brown —
as I always thought it would, because you looked so much like your dad. You
needed help using the toilet because of mental and physical handicaps from the
drowning. So Danny was on one side and I was on the other, supporting your
little arms. Then I saw the bugs.*

*They were centipedes with thousands of spindly legs, first crawling on your
back and then on your legs. As they multiplied, they started to swarm your face. I
frantically brushed them off and slapped at the ones on your back, taking care not
to hurt you. Your skin started coming off with the bugs and I tried to scream for
help, but nothing came out. Then I awoke.*

*Even before my eyes opened, I could feel the blood between my legs. No baby.
Why, God? I feel overly sensitive; everything's too bright. I'm numb, in shock; the
familiar feelings after your death, Billy. I'm grieving the child I could have had.*

*No one will ever inhabit the world as you did, Billy, but I need a baby to love
again...and Danny wants a brother. Though I try to push that sensation of
emptiness away, it's most piercing when I watch Danny playing catch with a
baseball off the garage roof or throwing his football the short distance it would take
to receive it himself in our front yard. That hole in the middle of our family is most
profound at these times.*

*God, why do you punish Danny? He's a good little boy; he deserves a little
brother. There's so much on his mind, but I can't get him to talk. Even though
your dad and I try to hide our disagreements, I'm afraid Danny may be sensing
the friction between us.*

*I dream of bugs often. Is this recurring nightmare a result of suppressing the
images of your rotting body? I fed you, cut your nails, wiped your bottom,
brushed your teeth, washed your hair—and it's all being eaten by bugs. I can tell*

myself that your spirit isn't there, but isn't your body a sacred thing? Should God let it be eaten by bugs?

Why didn't Dick want to bring the kids on the boat that day? Damn him! Why didn't you perform a miracle, God? Damn You! Why didn't Denise lock the door? Damn her!

Remember when your leg got stuck in the blind cord? I had always draped the rope up on the valance so that wouldn't happen, but that day, you managed to climb onto the chair and reach it. When you calmly called for me, I looked around the corner from the kitchen to find your body dangling by one foot. Your torso was hanging upside down and only your shoulders were resting on the chair. But you didn't cry; you knew I'd be nearby. You always trusted me to be there...and I wasn't.

Why didn't I tell Denise to lock the door? Damn me!

Now you'll never come back. Where are you? Can you hear me? I don't feel you anywhere anymore.

Oh, little Valentine, sweet Valentine. Please mend my broken heart,
Wrap your arms around me dear, as though we weren't apart.
Cupid, pull your arrow back and let my message fly
To my angel in the sky.
—Billy's Song

Chapter 29

DICK

*Y*ou opened the screen door and ran toward the lake. Holding my arm as a barrier in front of Denise, I motioned for her to stay back. This was my job. Waiting until your head submerged beneath the water, I then sprang into action. I felt the coldness on my legs when I reached the water's edge and entered the wet surf. I could feel my body bending over and felt my hands grasp underneath your armpits through the wetness of the water. My fingertips touched your soft skin, and I could feel the surf's resistance as I lifted your body out of it. Your head emerged from the water while I reached in and pulled you out. It was just as I had always imagined; what I longed to do on that dark, sunny day. Reach in and pull you out.

That was the first and last dream I had of you, Billy. I remained on the couch, which for many nights had served as my bed, and stared at the spider web in the corner of the ceiling while taking in a feeling of accomplishment. I was there; I had saved you, remedying our family's grief. A sense of closure followed me throughout that snowy February day. But at the same time, I wished that I could save my marriage with just one dream.

To your mother's credit, she finally learned how to stuff her emotions in public. This was due to the reception she received when displaying her true feelings; which was either one of pity or aversion. So she learned how to protect others by her silence and pretended to enjoy our Saturday night dates.

Your mother and I had grown even farther apart in our grief. For my own sanity, I wanted to grasp on to any last remnants of familiarity. So I spent more time with my bar buddies, while pretending to be the same person I was before. Now, I can clearly see why the distance between your mother and I grew. I'm sure that my emotional escape was the major contributing factor. But in my defense, her transformation had sent me running.

An accurate description of your mother before your death would have been an eternal optimist. Any negative turn in her life was justified as fated for some beneficial reason. If her car went into a ditch on a deserted road in the middle of a sub-zero January night, she would contend that a worse accident must have been waiting up ahead. While standing in four feet of snow, your mother would have patiently rehearsed the story to entertain a future audience until help arrived. Possibly, she would have humored herself by returning to a pleasant notion, like being blessed with two little boys. Your mother had what I called a "happy gene," a natural tendency to gravitate to levity.

I know that she tried to fight the negative thoughts after your death, Billy, but she was unable to find anything advantageous about it. There was no worse accident up ahead. She couldn't believe anymore, that fate was just—that fate was kind.

Because my attempts at emotional support were ineffective for your mother, she continued to seek comfort at The Compassionate Friends meetings. Though seldom participating in their discussions, she benefited by hearing other parents' horror stories. At each monthly meeting, she marveled at the varying levels of grief in every familiar face that faithfully returned. The vintage members arrived with offensive gaiety and the new members hesitantly shuffled through the door, bearing the ashen tone of shock on their faces.

Even though death made them all equal there and they accepted your mother as a member of their club, she told me she didn't feel like one of them. She still couldn't admit that she was a bereaved parent.

~ ~ ~ ~ ~

This time, she stood alone at your gravesite. Her hands met the bitter February air as she peeled them from their gloves and groped into the confines of her jacket pocket for a small, plastic teddy bear. It held a tiny red heart in its paws with the words "BE MINE." When she saw it in the drug store, it reminded her of the red and pink papers hearts you and Danny had made at the kitchen table only one year before. The hardened glue and red glitter were still embedded in the cracks of the table's oak finish at home.

She looped the wire hook attached to the teddy bear around a bough on the wreath above your grave, and it dangled next to the Christmas tin soldier and the miniature birthday truck. Her thoughts drifted to the day we brought you home from the hospital and she placed you in Danny's arms for the first time.

"He's not Jessica's, he's not Beth's, he's not Deanna's....." Danny was positioned on the couch with his arm propped upon a pillow, gently holding your body in crook of his elbow. He delicately ran one small finger from the top of your head to your toes, while listing every person he had ever met in his two-year-old world. "He's not Nathan's, he's not Victoria's...HE's MINE!" Danny proclaimed happily.

Your mother knew it was wrong to think of you as a possession, Billy. But, like Danny, she felt that you were hers in every sense of the word, and she had been robbed—robbed of hearing your first sentence and seeing your ninth tooth surface.

Like a portfolio of term-life insurance, you were her asset that God was banking in his trust until her own death. Where was her certificate of ownership? Was it possible that God would forget your spirit among the millions of others vaulted in his care? Panic consumed her and shortened her breath in the cold February air.

JOANN
A MOTHER JOURNALING THROUGH GRIEF

I was pushing you in the stroller through the streets of my hometown. I looked down at the sidewalk below me and remembered every crack on those rural streets.

I slowly plodded along, as one often does in a dream, struggling to put one leg in front of the other as if they were wrapped within sheets of bedding. I finally reached the front door of my past—my childhood home. When arriving there, I made my way around the stroller to lift you out, but found it empty. You must be in the house, I reasoned. So I left the empty buggy behind.

Walking through the door of my mother's bedroom, I noticed her old mahogany dresser. Somehow I knew that your new address was inside those drawers. One by one, I heaved handfuls of baby clothes out of the drawer onto the floor. Even though the floor was covered in little shirts and trousers, I couldn't get to the bottom. Where was your address? I had to find it. But I couldn't reach the bottom; beneath one layer of toddler clothes was always another.

A stern woman wearing a uniform walked in through the door and told me she was now your foster parent because I had been neglectful. She told me about your favorite foods and that you had grown two inches in the last seven months—smirking while taunting me with the milestones I had missed. I grabbed her by the shoulders and screamed,

"Where's Billy! Where's Billy!" I woke up before I could find your address in those drawers.

I turned 37 today, but feel as if I'm pushing 60. While I unwrapped the paper on the gift boxes from your dad and brother, I imagined you popping out of each one. You're the only present I really wanted. Some days are like this, Baby; the grief feels fresh, as if you died yesterday.

Did I slap your hand too much, Honey? Did I make you cry? Did I hold you enough? Why can't I remember comforting you? I know I did. Did I give you the toys you wanted, or did I give you something else to pacify you? Was I home enough? Did I give you a good life?

Someday I'll hold you again. Someday I have to, or death wouldn't be any fairer than life.

RANDY

THE DOCTOR

Breathe, one and two and three…breathe, one and two and three. In between breaths, I started to bark out directions.

"Let me know when the ambulance arrives… and send someone to the road to help them find the house! We can't waste any time!" I then noticed a young man who was on the phone with a 911 dispatcher. I realized I might know the physicians working in the Emergency Department that day. I took the phone from him and dialed the numbers I had memorized.

"Randy, what are you doing there?" I heard my colleague say.

"Long story—I'll tell you later. We need help. This is a field resuscitation of a child—two years old or so. He's unresponsive, but has a slight heart beat. He needs a hospital quickly. Is there any way to get a helicopter here?"

"I'll check." He put me on hold for seconds, but it seemed like an eternity.

"Yes, we can get one for you, Randy. Arrange for a landing zone nearby."

Thank God, I know these people—a helicopter isn't always sent out.

Then I thought of the parents. The parents, oh, my. Another realization.

I continued the mouth to mouth. *Breathe, one and two and three.*

When the Waconia medics arrived, I readily handed the child over to them and followed the stretcher to the ambulance out front. I watched while the sirens blared and the vehicle sped away. *Blessings, little guy. You're in good hands.*

All of a sudden, I had nothing to do. My part was over. *It's up to them now.*

I brushed the grass off my knees and walked slowly back to the house. *My God,* I thought, *what just happened?*

Many were still milling around the lakeside of the house, but I noticed the sitter first. She was entirely speechless, inconsolable, horrified—in shock.

The neighbors, sheriffs, and firefighters were still all there, and so we thanked each other. But in between our words was an awkward silence. Silence, words—they meant the same. Nothing, really. We felt unspeakably incomplete. There was no closure.

And there was still the sound of screaming. But this time, it was ours. Silent, yet louder than ever.

Chapter 30

DICK

When you're Irish, St. Paddy's Day is the major holiday. Many Irish and "non-Irish" use it as an excuse to drink to excess, myself included.

But in your mother's case, St. Patrick's Day of 1992 only marked the passage of time and dredged up a feeling of regret, even though I had been the one who talked her into going out the last year. Billy will be fine, I told her, even though you had gotten second-degree burns on your hand moments before we left you with Denise. In my defense, you weren't crying when we left the house, but your wails could be heard through the phone receiver when we checked in an hour later.

Your mother had a tendency, at that time, to remember her failings above her sacrifices. She was sure that Parents' Anonymous, an organization to stop child abuse, had sent her a pamphlet in the mail because they heard of her neglect. She questioned if Denise knew you could open that screen door, and if not, then it had been her job to inform her. Accusations seemed to surround her even when there were none. It was apparent that the guilt was diminishing her self-esteem.

So it was your mother who felt a stab of remorse on that St. Paddy's Day. There was no returning to make it right. So her self-imposed atonement was to stay home with Danny, and let me go bar-hopping with my Irish friends.

~ ~ ~ ~ ~

"How can you be so sure that we can't communicate with Billy, Dick?" Your mother was brushing her hair at the double sink in our bathroom, while I prepared for an evening of beer, corned beef, and cabbage. Even though it was mid-March, the weather outside our home was gentler than the inside climate. I glanced at her in the reflection of the mirror as I navigated the razor along my chin.

At my objections, your mother was considering the use of a medium to provide the contact from you that she needed so badly. She insisted that there was no alternative but to accept the bridge between the living and dead.

"Those psychics and mediums are all phony. They generalize and probe until they get some clue from the bereaved to make an educated guess, until eventually they guess or luckily hit on the truth," I stubbornly insisted.

"I've felt Billy, Dick and I've heard him as if he's right next to me."

"That's your need, Dear." I said gently. "You need it so badly that your mind is tricking you." I rinsed the whiskers from my razor and turned off the running water.

"We don't know everything yet, Dick; we still have a lot to learn about the spiritual world. Facts can't explain it," she gathered her long hair away from her face, tied it with a band, and turned to me in earnest. "Look at the past. No one knew about the properties of fire, the solar system, or light and sound. There's so much we don't know about the afterlife today." Now her voice was louder and higher.

"I still don't believe in giving those scam artists our money," I made an effort to lower my voice in correlation to the decibels that hers was raised. This seemed to be my role, to diminish the intensity of an argument, although my composure (she would say apathy) would upset her more. I wiped the remaining shaving cream from my face and left the room to dress as she followed after me. While I searched through my drawers for a clean pair of boot-cut jeans and the green sweater reserved solely for St. Paddy's Day, she made her way around the bed to other side of the room like a boxer positioning in the ring.

I shook my head sadly. Why did I always have to play the devil's advocate? I knew you existed, Billy, you had to. But you were gone from my life—you had to be, because I missed you so much. Besides, I couldn't admit that you might be able to contact me from the grave, because the wall that protected me from intense emotions couldn't be torn down. It was safer that way.

"Well, it's important to me." She was standing at the dresser with her back to me. She picked up the plastic bluebird that rested there and shook it roughly in her hand. "Damn it, it's broken. It's supposed to chirp when you pick it up." Besides smoking, she had also taken up cursing since your death.

"Is the battery dead?" I maneuvered my arms through the sleeves of my shirt and positioned the collar around my neck.

"No, I just replaced it…again." Her face rose from the bird, and she stared at me with her vivid blue eyes. "Why don't you want another child, Dick? We already had two, you agreed on two before, why not now?" She was waiting, demanding an answer. *Damn, let's get back to the bluebird and the psychics,* I thought.

"I'm too old; I don't want my child growing up with an old dad." Thinking of my eighty-three-year-old father, I methodically buttoned my shirt and diverted my eyes from hers.

"You're only a few years older than you were when we had Billy, and I want a brother for Danny so badly…" She was forcefully shaking the bluebird, while I interrupted her.

"And I definitely do not want another, so who wins and who loses here?" My voice rose as my temper flared. In response, she threw the bird on the floor and ran out of the room, slamming the door behind her.

I could hear her sobs through your bedroom door and imagined her rocking in the bentwood chair with your blanket in hand. I bent over to reach for the bluebird, which she had so vehemently thrown, and gently placed it back on the dresser. I sat on the bed, placing my face in my hands.

Why did she always make me feel like the bad guy? I had a right not to want another child. I couldn't keep you alive, Billy, how could I be trusted with another child?

"I miss you, Bud," I whispered.

From the dresser behind me, the bluebird chirped.

JoAnn

A mother journaling through grief

Even though Dick says he doesn't want another child, he seems to be meeting me halfway by not preventing it—but I'm still not pregnant. Danny was a pleasant surprise and you, Billy, happened on the first try. Your Aunt Theresa's pregnant. You owe me a child, God, not her.

I feel powerless, I'm doing nothing as my biological clock ticks and my eggs shrivel up and die. Every day, I dream of another child to make us four again. I feel a burning envy whenever I see a pregnant woman's bulging stomach. Not one of them could appreciate another child as much as I could. And nothing irritates me more than the complaints from these mothers. They dare stand in front of me, whining about their burden of pregnancy or child rearing. Don't they know that it's more difficult <u>not</u> to raise your own child?

I want to be one of those undiminished families; I envy their lack of financial problems. Why are neither the riches of family nor money my blessings, as both are theirs? Is God playing favorites? I use to write off my trials as being "for the better." Now I see them as an injustice—the luck of the draw.

Sometimes I can't help but be angry with you, God, for dealing me those cards. If I praise You with hopefulness when my period is late, why can't I curse You when the blood starts flowing again? If I credit You with my blessings, why shouldn't I accuse You for my afflictions? In the same vein, if I reverently thank You for the gift of my oldest son, why can't I, in all rights, damn You for taking my youngest?

The tears still warm my cheeks remembering the happiness I lost,
Just like the Mother Mary as her Son died on the cross.
Easter brought you gifts of bunnies
And gave you life that never ends,
And I'll rise to hold you again.
—Billy's Song

Chapter 31

DICK

*Y*our burial plot seemed to have a magnetic pull on your mother. Giving in to the urge, she continued to visit the cemetery on every Hallmark holiday, leaving a trinket on your wreath in the winter and a bouquet of daisies at the base of the condemned elm tree on the warmer days. During her pilgrimages, she often discovered freshly picked daisies left by her sister, Jeanne, or a small jar of pansies from your Grandma Helen.

Your headstone was exposed through the vanished snow and, as she neared it, she saw that the wreath was gone. She had waited too long—the soldier, truck, and teddy bear had all disappeared with the wreath while the condemned tree faithfully remained at its station. With a small Easter bunny charm in hand, she honored the faithful guard's loyalty by force-fully piercing its bark lapel with the wire attachment as if it were a medal of honor.

Sunday is Easter. God gave His only son so we would not perish. He forgave our sins, so we could continue to live. She paraphrased the Bible and ques-tioned God. *I should thank You for that gift; but, how did You suffer through Your son's ordeal? You're omniscient; You can see everything. You were with*

Your son on earth and again after he died. You were never without him. Mary stood by the cross in anguish, knowing it would be eternity before Jesus and she would be reunited. When did You suffer, God? Some say that You suffer when we do. Then let me take my grief in second person as You did.

She finished securing the wire into her staunch, devoted friend, leaving the smiling Easter bunny to dangle precariously above your grave. Easter should have been the most meaningful holiday ever, but your mother's cynicism had emerged—leaving a skeptic shaking her fist at God, daring Him to punish her again. *Maybe I'll burn in Hell for my anger at you, Lord,* she thought. *That is, if I believed in a Hell outside this earth.*

Her boot had stubbornly sunk into the muddied dirt, so she forcefully freed it, leaving its impression before your headstone. Then she turned away from your grave and back to her mandatory life.

JoAnn

A MOTHER JOURNALING THROUGH GRIEF

Two children walked in circles around me; I needed to keep turning to follow their movements. The one child who was moving clockwise looked like you, but had a vacant look in his eyes. With little energy, he continued to move slowly around me while dragging his feet. I could tell there was something wrong with him.

The other was moving counterclockwise, stepping lightly with high energy. He was your age, but didn't resemble you at all. Still, I accepted him as you, because he had your spirit. I kept turning to try to see the both of you, getting dizzy with my own movement. My vision became blurred, until the two images merged into one. And for a brief moment, I saw all of you. Then I woke up. Were these your body and soul?

I can't seem to stop the memories of your death from entering my thoughts, Billy. Talking about it helps, so I continue to reach out to anyone who merely pretends to listen. When I sense their boredom, I search for another attentive ear. In the constant retelling of my story, each memory is mourned as if it has its own life. By my sadistic repetition of it, the memory becomes a bit less brutal.

But with every detail successfully grieved, there are always more waiting around the corner. There seems to be no end to the novel recollections that surface to my awareness. One at a time, they either creep into my conscious thoughts or suddenly lunge out at me when least expected. But fortunately, they rarely manifest themselves into a combined assault.

Like an old trustworthy employee, a physically instinctive or spiritually divine receptionist seems to be individually admitting them from my waiting room of memories into my office of grief work. So I'm able to "treat" one before the next appears through the door. There's never more than one scheduled at a time. It's as if I'm becoming a doctor of "griefopathy" with an overflow of waiting patients.

JEFF

A FIREFIGHTER

Sometimes days are just not meant to be normal and such is the case for most volunteer firemen. On that day, a call came in as a possible drowning. I arrived with my crew to a scene that proved to cause years of heartaches.

When we arrived from our station just a few blocks away, it was already a very troubling, chaotic scene. Present was a firefighter who lived up the street, a doctor, and numerous others who were frantically attending to a small child. Of all scenarios…a small child…the worst for a firefighter.

The majority of us have children of our own and situations like this prove to be the most devastating—especially when the outcome isn't good.

Since many people were there trying to save the child, I turned my attention to assist and organize in any way I could. Then I heard the sirens from the approaching paramedics. Upon arrival they, too, learned of the incredible efforts already in progress.

I remember keeping an ear open for calls about Aircare, the helicopter unit that would be coming from an area emergency trauma hospital. When I was informed that it had indeed been called, I instructed my crew to establish a landing zone for the helicopter. We then gathered ourselves and relocated to a soccer field two blocks up the street, awaiting the ambulance carrying our young patient. Both ambulance and helicopter arrived simultaneously. We carried the young boy to the Aircare crew, loaded him up, and watched as they lifted off. I silently cried as I watched the helicopter disappear over the trees.

Little did I know how much the last few minutes would impact the rest of my day, the rest of my life. Since then, little things that happen can bring me back to that moment—the images seem to be seared into my brain. How, in God's name, could something like this happen? I believe God truly has a plan for everyone…but I want to ask Him, what does a situation like this teach us?

Chapter 32

DICK

hat day, the USA Space Shuttle Endeavor was making its maiden voyage from Cape Canaveral and the Mall of America was nearing completion. There was still monumental rioting in the streets of Los Angeles after the police officers in Rodney King's beating were acquitted. And just the month before, Ross Perot had announced his run for presidency against Bill Clinton and George H. Bush.

The sun was bright and the air was warm as your mother and Danny returned from a shopping trip that May morning. The water from the melting snow was dripping from the eaves onto the sidewalk in front of the house. There was a change in the air; the coming of summer. Danny spoke first.

"This is the best day I've ever had, Mommy!" He looked up at her with his face beaming. He grabbed her hand and skipped up the cement sidewalk toward the house. She smiled back at him, thinking about how wonderful it was to see him happy again. Nevertheless, there were still times when he'd fly off the handle over trivial setbacks. But then she was like that, too. *Maybe someday our emotions will level out*, she thought.

She had always loved the warmer weather and the end of winter, but her feelings were conflictive that spring. With the smell of the new grass and the warmth of the bright sun also came the memories of the previous summer. With the days becoming temperate, the lake had dissolved the melted ice and opened its taunting mandibles in clear view. When your mother stepped out from the security of our house that spring, the memories seemed to close in on her.

Recollections concealed behind the stagnant days of winter were pried open by the vigorous energy of spring. She thought of your little Mickey Mouse sandals—one packed away in a box and left behind, the other one, you must have taken with you. The aroma of the suntan lotion spread on Danny's back, the vision of her summer clothes revealed from storage boxes, and the sound of waves slapping the rocks—all brought forth scenes from a past life.

Last summer, the shock of your death had shielded her, leaving her unable to mourn all these sights, sounds, and smells of better times. Now that the spring sun thawed the winter air, it revealed the summer that never ended—the summer that faded away with you in the middle of July.

She had always loved the spring and the summer that followed, but that year, she wanted to stay in the bleakness of the winter. She didn't want to confront the vitality of the spring days arriving without you. Besides, the winter's sunless aspects mirrored her new persona; sunny days were a contrast to her mood. And she couldn't imagine Heaven as being the "better place" when the sky was bright and the world was beautiful. How could eternity be complete without Danny, you, and her splashing in the water under the warm sun?

Even through her despondency that spring, it was a time of angelic portents, omens, and divine communication. Whenever she felt she couldn't go on, a sign was sent to prove that you still existed. The bridge between Heaven and earth wasn't a surprise to her, because she was already somewhere in the middle. She also felt that she was due the positive circumstances, so she thoroughly expected them.

Daisies would appear in the most unexpected places and bluebirds would suddenly fly onto a nearby perch. Even though she was elated by every encounter, her cynicism would eventually override the magical communications. She must have learned this stubbornness from me, as she clung to her pain and minimized the heavenly indications. I imagine you, Billy, looking down at us with that old wooden spoon in hand and asking God, "They don't get it. Can I please whack them over the head just once?"

When climbing the front steps with Danny still skipping at her side, she noticed a piece of paper hanging from the doorknob. Upon closer examination, she discovered that it was from the Mound Police Department.

"What's that, Mommy?" Danny questioned as she removed the official notice.

"There's a lost item at the police station that belongs to you." She read the note out loud. "Please claim it at your earliest convenience."

When she finished, Danny and she simultaneously looked at each other with anticipation. For a brief moment, they had thought of the same notion—both imagined the recovery of their most-desired lost possession.

In reality, the item turned out to be her misplaced cell phone. When she presented the claim check to the officer at the Lost and Found window, he searched behind the counter through his cabinets of lost goods and pulled out the cell phone with the claim check attached.

But what she and Danny had imagined for a split second was somewhat different. They imagined that the officer would pull you out of one of those drawers, Billy, and set you on the counter. And there you'd be sitting with your eight-tooth smile and a little tag tied around your ankle reading, FOUND.

~ ~ ~ ~ ~

She sat on her beach blanket on the sandy public beach two doors down from our house. That June day, the beach was filled to capacity with parents and their children.

She diligently watched Danny while he built his sand castle at a safe distance from the water. Even though her focus was on him, she couldn't help but notice the young boy a few feet in front of her. He was dark skinned, with straight brunette hair, looking nothing like you. Yet she recognized the familiar motions of the eighteen-month-old child.

She studied the movements of his hands, that thick, clumsy manner in which a toddler shovels sand into a pail. An audible gasp escaped her lips as she remembered your similar movements in that spot only a year ago. She put a hand to her mouth to stifle it and looked around to make sure nobody heard her. But the toddler was the only one near enough to notice the sound. He looked up in surprise, and then with concerned innocence, when he saw your mother's pained face. Dropping his shovel into the sand, he straightened his short, chubby legs into a stand and waddled over to her beach towel. He placed his face a few inches from hers and looked into her eyes with empathy.

"Owie?" he asked, without blinking. And when she looked into his eyes, she saw you, Billy.

"Yes, Sweetie, owie in my heart," she told the beautiful creature sent by God. Confirming what she already believed, he gave her a face hug.

JOANN

A MOTHER JOURNALING THROUGH GRIEF

I was confined to a jail cell. It was only one among many in a long endless row, all filled with women who were also sentenced for being unfit mothers. But I was the only one who wasn't allowed to see my child on visiting day, so I must have been exceptionally negligent.

As I watched the other inmates leave their cells, I screamed through the bars, pleading with the guards to release me until only a whisper came out. I could hear your cries in the distance, but I couldn't get to you. Even my fellow inmates gave me accusing sneers. They laughed and told me I'd never see you again, and you'd eventually forget about me. They told me that I was just like them, condemned to my cell for life; confined by my guilt forever.

With the passing of Mother's Day and no pregnancy in sight, I finally took apart your crib in your bedroom, Billy. Your dad wanted it gone long before, but patiently waited until I was ready. But I didn't want his help; it was something I needed to do myself.

With each twist of every bolt that held your bed's support, I painstakingly admitted that I was a member of The Compassionate Friends. I couldn't deny it anymore; I was a bereaved parent.

When I removed the mattress from its frame, I found three pacifiers underneath. It was as hard to box them up as it had been to throw away your medicine from the refrigerator, Honey.

It seems that when material items have memories attached to them, they stop being physical objects. They become more than just plastic, metal, or wood. They have a life of their own, because your hands once touched them. It's as though your energy was transferred to them, so they come alive like a spirit of yesterday's memories. They emit a comforting aroma, a familiar ambience, and sometimes a painful reminder.

KEN
THE SHERIFF

When I arrived at the house from the station, the first responders were working on the child and plans were being made for a helicopter to transport him. I felt bad for the sitter, but I was shift commander that day, and it was imperative to get information that only she knew. *Where were the parents? Could they be reached?* And sadly my other thought was, I had to get the parents back home to see their child. It was a bad situation.

When the mother arrived in the water patrol boat, I ran up the dock to meet her and then brought her around the house to the water patrol van I had parked in front. After just missing the helicopter at the soccer field, I then transported the mother and Sheriff Rankl to the hospital. Due to the risks involved, it wasn't protocol to have a witness or victim in the back seat of a patrol car while "on the red." But I needed to get the mother to the hospital to say goodbye to her child before he was gone.

I glanced back on occasion to assure everything was all right, but it was the nature of the job that allowed me to concentrate on the radio and the road ahead while the mother rocked her imaginary baby in the back seat. I couldn't help but momentarily think of my own boys back home; they were about the same age as the Deveny boys. I had to shake off that thought. You see, first responders learn to fend off their emotions in order to do their jobs—we have to set our feelings aside so they don't burn our insides out. But I only had seven years of practice at that time.

A few weeks after that day, I visited the older Deveny boy and brought him a "comfort teddy bear"—a program that the Water Patrol Station had just initiated. It must have been the thought of my oldest without his younger brother that motivated me.

After thirty years of calls like that one, I became very efficient at not letting the job get to me—or so I thought. So it came as a surprise to me when, two days after my retirement from the Water Patrol, my wife said I finally got my smile back.

Chapter 33

DICK

"**N**athan and I built a HUGE sand castle today, Mommy…it was bigger than Stephanie's. So she was mad and knocked ours down, and Laurie gave her a time-out!" Your mother was sitting in her hotel bed propped up by two oversized pillows. She held the TV remote in hand and turned the audio to mute as Danny's voice prattled through the receiver. She was comforted by the delight in his voice, a new-found energy of yesterday.

He's going to be all right, she thought. Danny continued.

"…and I was the only one who hit a HOME RUN in T-ball today… Can I bring my bike to daycare tomorrow?" She clicked through channels with one hand and reached for her steaming Earl Gray tea on the night stand with the other. As Danny jumped randomly through various subjects, she noticed my voice in the background.

"What's Daddy saying, Honey?" She put the remote down at her side.

"Okay, I'm coming, Daddy! Mommy's on the phone… GUESS WHAT, Mommy?! There's water dripping from the ceiling in here, and upstairs is all wet and…."

She threw off the covers and jumped to the side of the bed.

"Get your dad on the phone, Danny… Now!" She turned the television off and began pacing the confines of her hotel room with the phone pressed to her ear.

Life showed us there would be no sabbaticals that summer of '92. Even though he had turned on the faucet upstairs before we left for daycare that morning, it really wasn't Danny's fault. The city had turned off the water main for repairs without notifying us. Why would a four-year old need to turn a faucet to off when there was no water coming out? When the water main was turned back on later that morning, the water had flowed all day until I arrived home at 6:00 pm. By then, the damage had been done.

When your mother came home from her trip the next day, she discovered that the diamond was missing from her wedding ring. Even though the ring wasn't adequately insured and we had to live in a house with bare, wet floorboards for weeks afterward, your mother and I didn't feel overwhelmed by these events. These inconveniences weren't significant because they couldn't top our threshold of loss, which was set quite high at this point. We couldn't help but wonder if God was shedding us of all our possessions to reveal what was truly precious in life.

Okay, I wanted to say, *we get it already.*

After your death, we had learned to prioritize our lives into tiers of importance; the damage to our home and the loss of the diamond were at the bottom and the health of our family was unchallenged at the top. We had learned that material items were perishable and had no status on our pyramid of priorities. Small setbacks didn't bother us anymore, because we hadn't recuperated from the big one yet.

JoAnn

A MOTHER JOURNALING THROUGH GRIEF

We received the helicopter bill in the mail today. A teasing reminder that arrived almost exactly one year after your death. Although our medical insurance will inevitably pay the bill, I was taken by surprise when I opened the envelope. What do you remember about that awful ride, Honey?

At times, I can't envision the distinct features of your face, Billy, and that scares me, although the pain is far greater when your memory is vivid. Still, I force myself to remember each notion in detail by writing it in my journal. Now that I've filled your baby book with my ramblings, I'm well into a second notebook.

I've followed all the directions in my library of books on how-to-get-through-grief-in-ten-easy-steps. I've challenged my grief in a direct approach and have chosen not to go around it. But sometimes it makes me feel as if I'm stuck in the middle of an eternal maze.

Wasn't one year supposed to be that magical milestone of recovery? I've found that there's no expedient way through this. I also know that time alone won't heal my grief, but time is needed to accomplish the required grief work. I have to be patient with myself.

CHAPLAIN GREG
THE MAN WITH JESUS EYES

My digital pager went off while I was visiting an elderly hospice patient who was sharing his life review with me. The words said, ED ASAP. I knew that page well. I also knew that when the Emergency Department staff wanted support quickly, something significant was going on. After saying my goodbyes to the patient, I hurried down the stairs to the ED. Before entering the room, I first paused, as always, at the door for prayer. I asked God to go with me through those doors to whatever need awaited.

Being deeply aware of my own need for help from God in these situations, I always ask to bring His presence while I am present with those in great need. After finishing my prayer, I took a deep breath and entered the stabilization room.

I saw a young mother holding a her small child. She was crying, at times wailing, so I knew the child was gone. As I approached them, I thought of Isaiah 41:10.

Fear not, for I am with you; do not be dismayed, for I am your God.

I put my arms around her, and even in his death, we shared the beauty of her son. She told me that she was feeling faint, so I held her closer. Then we rocked together and cried. I remember my tears, the mother's tears, and the tears of the nurses and hospital staff surrounding us as I prayed.

Hear my cry, O God; listen to my prayer. From the ends of the earth I call to you, I call as my heart grows faint: lead me to the rock that is higher than I.

Chapter 34

DICK

*Y*our mother continued to memorialize your life that summer. She had a maple tree planted at your daycare center, a nearer location to our home than your distant gravesite. The daisies surrounding its base could be seen from the busy street we both traveled daily. Perennial daisies were strategically planted on the lakeside of our home where the sun cast its light on their flower bed for approximately one hour and twenty minutes during the month of July. From 3:40 p.m. to 4:50 p.m., the sun's rays represented the exact time of the onset of the rescue attempt to your recorded death.

As the anniversary of your death approached, your mother couldn't stop her mind from reliving that day. Like a reel of film, the events surfaced, replaying the story from the morning when you awoke to the fatal finale. As the passing days brought her closer to July 13th, an urge to alter the events escalated in her. This left her with a desire to mark the day with some event, so she arranged for a mass to be said in your memory.

"Somewhere a child has risen, someday I will rise….." Your Aunt Jennifer started singing at the altar with guitar in hand at exactly 4:50 p.m., the exact time of your death. The church was filled with people and, with the aid of the song sheets in front of them, their voices joined in on the refrain of *Billy's Song*.

Jennifer's fingers moved nimbly over the acoustic guitar strings and her voice was rich with feeling while singing all eight verses for the filled pews. Afterwards, she acknowledged that it was her finest performance ever, but thoroughly accredited her talent to divine intervention on that date of your death.

"*...to meet you gladly, my precious Billy, my precious Billy.*" Reading from the duplicated sheets before them, our guests crooned from the filled pews. Your mother's escalating anxiety, which had led up to that moment, abated with the conclusion of each verse. And her apprehension ended when the song did. It was too late to edit your script; you were still gone. So in that moment, she stopped searching for the circumstances of your death and allowed the plot to stay as written.

~ ~ ~ ~ ~

"*Our Father, who art in Heaven, hallowed by Thy name...*" That night your mother recited her usual prayer at Danny's bedside.

"God isn't listening, Mommy," Danny said firmly. "You're just pretending. If he was listening, he would let Billy come back." Danny's defiance surprised her as she tucked the blanket around him in bed.

"But remember when God let you say good-bye to Billy?" she reminded him. Danny's eyes widened and a grin appeared on his face.

"It really happened, Mommy. I wasn't dreaming. I walked down the stairs and Billy came in the front door. He was bigger than Dad! He said, 'Good-bye...good-bye,'" Danny whispered hauntingly. Then Danny's smile faded, "Why didn't Billy stay, Mommy?"

That night I contemplated the distance we had come in the past year. Our family's immune system began to function again, warding off the viruses that had consumed us before. However, the last year had definitely taken its toll on Danny's physical development—he had not grown in height in his fifth year of life. The nutrition he took in must have been solely applied toward his mental stability, because he had made great emotional progress by his brother's first death date.

Danny spoke of you more casually, Billy, and without tears. He had fewer episodes of hyperactivity and crying outbursts. His movements were not as restless or animated. However, he still believed your accident was his doing. Therefore, I knew he'd be forever transformed by your death.

What frame of personality would Danny have if you had not slid that door open, Billy? Danny's path of development had been detoured, creating a different person than was previously fated. He was more mature and contemplative than his four-year old counterparts. I often wondered if his character would be deeply enriched or traumatized into deviant behaviors as a result. If you hadn't run into the water, Billy, would he have been more carefree? Would he have had such an attraction to toddlers?

I often caught him staring at a small child with amusement. His eyes would always be transfixed and his expression affectionate while studying the familiar actions of the toddler. But I could always see around the smile on his lips into his pained eyes, which portrayed a void he longed to fill.

Your Aunt Kathy once told us that there was a piece to our family puzzle missing, and someday we'd find it in Heaven with God as its keeper. Then we'd place it back in its rightful spot and feel like a family again. Then, I guess you could say that, we would see the "big picture." But in the meantime, that one piece of our puzzle was still missing, creating a black hole in the middle of the total panorama.

An improvement in your mother's physical health was also evident. She was maintaining her weight and the dark circles under her eyes had diminished, allowing her to physically blend with the living world. But, I knew that her body was healing more rapidly than her heart. I often wondered if your mother's transformation would create my preferred outcome. I wanted her happy again, but didn't want her changed in the process.

On the anniversary of your death, your mother also tried to sum up the lessons of her grief. For one, she had discovered the significance of her children and the insignificance of other earthly events beyond them. Above all, the most profound lesson she had learned was that you were not coming back.

JoAnn

A MOTHER JOURNALING THROUGH GRIEF

I watched the doctor near me while slowly climbing up the stairs from the basement. He was carrying something in his arms and, even before he reached me, I knew it was you. Your face was bloated and blue, and your skin seemed to be rotting from your body. But still, I didn't hesitate to take you when he held you out to me. I felt the familiar weight in my arms, but you didn't look the same because your face was disfigured. As I rocked you back and forth, I felt the warmth of your body next to mine.

Too soon, the doctor held out his arms to take you back and, somehow, I knew I had to give you up; you didn't belong to me anymore. So he took you away from me and walked back down the stairs to your coffin in the basement. And you didn't cry when he took you from me. It was as if you knew, as I did, that was where you belonged.

That was one of my good dreams, Billy, because the emptiness I felt when you were taken from me was effaced by the impression you left in my arms. Even though the image of your distorted face stayed with me throughout the morning, I was able to hold you last night.

When I dream of you, Billy, you become the whole of my thoughts. So after I made Danny his breakfast this morning, I sat in the living room, thinking of you and my dream as I stared vacantly out the door that you escaped from. Then they came one at a time; four in all—like a complete family. One by one, they landed on the railing of our deck. Seeing one bluebird is a rare event in our area, but today, four bluebirds came to visit me.

Sometimes, when I see a rainbow or an unusual cloud, I question whether it's a sign from you, Billy. Then I wonder if your dad is right; do I just want it to be so? And then there are times like today, when I see or hear something phenomenal and instantaneously feel you right next to me. And there's no question in my mind. Usually tears well up instantly in my eyes, and then I'll speak to you as if you were next to me, "Hello, Honey, there you are."

PATTI
BRIAN'S MOTHER

As I fed and clothed you in those first few trying months, Brian, sometimes I felt that you were a new birth, a new arrival—someone I needed to reacquaint myself with again.

Now I can't believe that a year has already passed since you were transformed into this new person. Your brain doesn't process information like most children your age, even though we've hired tutors for you. And I'm tired of the many discussions I've had with your teachers, reminding them that you had a traumatic brain injury and you need more help than the others. Above all, your emotions have been affected, and the depression you experience hurts me the most.

My child, who had to relearn the basics of walking, talking, and eating. My wonderful child, from whom I've learned so much: courage, perseverance and, most of all, acceptance.

Chapter 35

DICK

*A*fter that first year, I thought I had navigated my way through bereavement quite well—I thought I was *healed* because I had proficiently hid my pain. In truth, what I had merely accomplished was to create an emotional pressure cooker.

During that first year after your death, Billy, your mother had succeeded in persuading me to attend mass with her on only four occasions: your birthday, your death date, her birthday, and Mother's Day—the day I agreed to abide in her every wish even though she wasn't *my* mother. But your mother was persuasive, so that fall, I started attending mass more frequently with her. I don't believe that my motivation was sincere, because I didn't feel any closer to God at this point. But I seemed to find some comfort in the symbolic Catholic rituals and memories of my altar boy services. I believe it momentarily moved me back to a happier time.

The first time it happened it took me unaware—I didn't see it coming. I should have been forewarned when my complacency tore down the wall of denial I had built. This enabled a sinister entity to slither through the camouflage of life's routine, bearing its fangs while my back was turned. When it attacked me, I became consumed with its presence.

Fear had arrived.

The organ music seemed to escalate as I stood in the pew. My body started shaking and a bead of sweat rolled down my brow. My vision blurred as I tried to stop the hymnal from shaking in my hands. I was consumed with pure fear—naked, unmasked, and unbridled. A sudden urge to flee came over me, but your mother, Danny, and three other people were blocking my escape to the aisle. What was happening to me? All I knew was that I had to get out or I'd scream.

"I need to leave," I frantically whispered to your mother and hurriedly edged my way in front of her and Danny. Her puzzled expression followed me while I stumbled over legs and purses to the end of the pew and headed down the eternal aisle. Bile built up in my throat as I raced outside the church doors. Just before I reached the tarred parking lot, vomit escaped my lips onto one of the bushes lining the walkway. My body purged the acrid fear from deep within my gut and out my mouth, not once but three times, until there was nothing left.

That was not the last time fear overtook me. The next week, it returned even more strongly than the week before, and then again—and always in church. I was confused and embarrassed that my raw emotions could control me so completely. So I told your mother I was just feeling nauseous and must be coming down with some bug. After a few weeks of these episodes, I discovered they only occurred when I was trapped in a pew with no access to the aisle. And the fear always subsided when I was able to leave the church on my own terms.

So these episodes became my selfish motivation to volunteer as an usher. I could walk the aisles or stand in the back near the door, knowing I could escape without notice at any time. Even though I had no name for these events, the fear eventually left me, and I, too, willingly left it behind as my guarded secret.

~ ~ ~ ~ ~

"Can dead people ever talk again?" Danny dug into the dirt near the foundation of our house with his plastic shovel. He and I were having a burial for a dead vole we had found in the yard, an exercise your mother thought would further clarify the concept of death for him.

"Well, Bud, their old bodies can't talk." I picked up the mangled carcass and placed it in the hole we had dug.

"I was really good to Billy, Daddy, wasn't I?" Danny looked up at me with inquiring eyes.

"Yes, Bud, you were very good to your brother," I reassured him and heard the water's refrain as the waves pounded the rocks on the shore.

JoAnn
A mother journaling through grief

The Child Protection Agency took you away from me and placed you in an orphanage because I was deemed a neglectful mother. I pounded on the tall steel gates that stood between me and the ancient two-story building. Ivy covered its sides, seeming to be the only thing holding the cracked bricks in their place. It scared me to think of you in that cold, dark building. I screamed and rattled the gate, but nobody came to let me in. Because nothing was going to stop me from reaching you, I started to climb until the gate became the building. Then I reached an open window to steal through.

The room in which I found myself was filled with children of all ages. Nevertheless, I immediately spotted you standing in your crib in the corner of the room. From a distance, you were two-dimensional like a picture. But when I neared you and tried to pick you up, you came to life. When I looked into your eyes, they gradually began to turn glassy and lifeless. You struggled to escape from my grasp; you didn't know me.

That was a bad dream, Billy.

I feel the wonder of the season and the gift God gave to me
The Babe within the manger, who died to set you free,
The angels sing their carols to you in your home above,
All I can give you is a gift of love ...
                    —Billy's Song

Chapter 36

DICK

Life moved on and the season of *Jingle Bells* and merry Noels began once more.

Beating George Bush and Ross Perot, Bill Clinton had just been elected president, the Church of England announced that it would allow women to become priests, and Dennis Byrd of the NBA's New York Jets was paralyzed by a neck injury.

The second Christmas after your death had arrived, though it seemed like the first because we had missed the celebration of the year before. The Christmas of 1992 brought on a diversity of emotions for your mother. But her outlook was different that year—she briefly set aside her unanswered questions to embrace her faith. Instinctively, she was compelled to grasp her last lifeline, having tried all else to no avail. She read the Psalms from her Bible at night and then set the book upon her chest. It was then she could feel a blanket of tranquility wrapped around her, allowing her to fall asleep without sleep aids.

Your mother tried to imagine a new perspective on life. She kept reminding herself that earth was a temporary station, occupying a miniscule time span compared to eternity. Then she could pretend that her bereavement would be brief; she could analyze it as a challenge, even an adventure.

Much like the pioneers journeying to the West, she imagined the heavenly historians would judge her at the completion of her travels. This was the only way she could envision a different terrain and an eventual end. It wasn't a smooth trail, but the treacherous dips had become shallower.

She continued to attend The Compassionate Friends gatherings, but her reasons for being there had changed. At first, she had strived to set herself apart from the parents surrounding her. Now, she attended the third Monday of every month because it was the only sanctuary where she didn't feel different. The little church hall had become a refuge where she could blend in with the humanity of the bereaved. In becoming a part of that circle, she stepped out of her own little sphere of grief and became aware of losses worse than her own.

Many parents there had lost their only child. Their identity as parents had been diminished, not to mention the alienation they felt at the exclusion of childhood activities, which your mother could still enjoy with Danny. One woman there had two children die within a year of each other from separate accidents. Some children had been abducted or murdered. Within these parents' minds, the fantasies of the unknown must have torturously consumed them.

By that time, your mother had also learned that not one person in that room could fully enter into another's grief. So there was a tendency for some to compare situations and subconsciously believe their loss was the worst. Being so engulfed in their own pain, it was hard for them to imagine anyone else's being more extreme. And your mother admitted that she had been one of those contestants in that unspoken competition.

Was it better to lose a younger child or an older child? She would sometimes notice a disinterested reaction from a bereaved parent when she mentioned your age, Billy, as if she didn't deserve to miss you because you had barely lived. And guiltily, your mother's reaction to a miscarriage was the same, even though she feigned empathy with that parent's loss.

She came to believe that the intensity of pain in grief directly correlated to the strength of the bond in that relationship. Even though she knew that the bond between a child and a parent shouldn't be measured by the passing of time, there are more memories to grieve with an older child—which takes more time.

On the other hand, as a child gets older, a parent gradually lets go a little each year. On a child's first day of kindergarten, a parent releases it to the education system; on a child's first bike ride alone, the parent releases it to the perilous world outside unchaperoned. When a child goes on his or her first date or leaves the house for college, a parent lets go a little more.

She hadn't let go of you, Billy. You were dependent on her for every physical function. Because she had lived with your dependency every minute of the day for eighteen months, your absence was palpable each moment, not just occasionally. Additionally, she often regretted that no one else in the world besides Danny, your caretakers, and I knew you. You weren't loved and missed by teammates, teachers, or classmates.

Why couldn't God have waited twenty more years to take you? You could have had children, and then Danny could have been an uncle. Twenty years couldn't be significant in God-years—but, I suppose, then there would be more memories to mourn. He could have given us only ten more years so I could have coached you in baseball, and we could have witnessed your growth into puberty. A mere four years would have allowed us to witness your first day of kindergarten. I would have cherished one more year just to hear you say, "I love you, Daddy." And if your mother and I had had just one more day, we could have at least said good-bye.

In turn, God could have given that miscarried child the opportunity of his birth and the right for his mother to merely hold him in her arms. Extinguished dreams need to be mourned as well. No, losing an older child is not harder nor easier—only different.

Is it easier to lose a child through sudden death or a long illness? The medical decisions confronting parents during their child's illness could be followed by unwarranted guilt after the child's death. Yet, the death certificate claimed that our child's death was an accident and accidents can be avoided.

If you were one of those children who had a terminal disease for months before you died, Billy, we would have monitored our actions so they would have left us no remorse. Naturally, we would have started to subconsciously grieve at the moment of the diagnoses. By the time of your death, the grief would have been about your absence without the shock of its suddenness. But with no warning, your healthy body was altered into a brain-dead corpse, and our denial took over. By the time we came out of our stupor, most of our comforters were gone.

Yet to watch one's own child suffer would be a parent's ultimate agony. Those parents must die in their hearts a little each day while witnessing their child's slow demise. No, losing a child to a sudden death is not harder or easier—only different.

JoAnn

A MOTHER JOURNALING THROUGH GRIEF

I asked God to give me a dream on your third birthday, and he did. Now I can't help but think of the adage "Be careful what you wish for."

Danny, you, and I were at a large social gathering, a fair of some sort, with games and food concessions. Even though you seemed older than eighteen months, I held you in my arms. We were surrounded by many people who were enjoying the festivities. Your father suddenly appeared at my side, and the completeness of our family stayed with me even after waking.

You were talking in sentences, but in the voice of an eighteen-month-old. I believe I was hearing what you would have said had you lived. I only wish that I could remember your exact words.

I looked away from you for only a moment and then looked back to find you gone from my arms. I screamed your name over and over again, even though I knew I would never find you. The people around me stared, pointing and whispering among themselves—accusing me of losing you again. Then Danny joined in with my cadence as he followed me in search.

"Billy!...Billy!...Billy!" We yelled in perfect syncopated rhythm as though we were merely replaying the motions of that July day. Your father seemed uncon-cerned about what was transpiring; he didn't appear to notice us at all.

"Where did Billy go, Dick? Where did he go?" I frantically questioned him. He merely looked at me as though I were crazy—as though he had never seen you in my arms at all. Then I told him, "I know he's dead, but he's always been around until now!"

When I woke up that morning I thought of what I had said. I've always felt your spirit near me after you died—Dick has not. Now, that feeling has left me as well. What was my dream telling me? Do I need to let you go, Honey, to move on with my life?

Chapter 37

DICK

*Y*our mother and I had both came quite a distance in our grief journey during the second year after your death, Billy. She seemed to conquer the continual melancholy and anticipated life more. We had both learned to move on, despite the longing in our hearts for the contents of the void you left.

Nevertheless, the difference between us lay in the blame. I couldn't readily excuse the cause of your death to the will of God. This is why I believed the fault lay only with the sitter. Your mother felt that she had promised to protect and guide you into the future. She had let you die by not warning Denise about the sliding door—therefore, her unresolved blame led only to herself. Her guilt still consumed her.

~ ~ ~ ~ ~

"Let's talk before we read, Mommy," Danny said to her as she lay down next to him in bed with book in hand.

"Okay, what's on your mind, Honey?" Her upper body leaned back against the headboard while she cocooned his body into hers. He was silent for moment before the words seem to explode from his lips.

"It was my fault, Mommy. If I would have told Denise Billy was gone..." He was kneeling in bed now, directly facing her, as she watched his animation.

"She told me, 'Look out for your brother' and I didn't! I was watching Baloo Bear sing...then when Baloo was done, Denise wasn't there, and Billy wasn't there. I was supposed to be watching him. If Denise would have found Billy sooner, he'd be alive!"

Your mother held him by the shoulders and moved his face in front of hers, gazing intently into his eyes. "*Never* believe that it was your fault, Honey...It was *not* your fault. Denise was telling you to help her look for Billy *after* he disappeared. You were only three years old; it wasn't your job to watch Billy."

"Why did Billy have to die. It's not fair!" He raised his voice with vehemence.

"You're right, Hon, it's not fair, and I'm angry, too."

"At who?"

"Oh, at first God and now myself," she said without hesitation.

"Because you weren't there?" Her six-year-old had guessed correctly. She nodded, afraid her voice would break.

"It's not your fault. We looked all over for Billy. First we went out the front door to the driveway, and then we came back inside. And then we went to the sliding door."

"And that's when you saw Billy in the water?" She prodded and got a nod.

"And Denise grabbed you and you both went to get him?" A nod.

Danny was there. He had seen you in the water.

"But we were too late, Mom. ...Let's not talk about this. It's making me sad." Danny started fidgeting in bed, so she drew him nearer. They cried together until she felt a release of tension in his shoulders, his buried secrets revealed. While he fell into a peaceful sleep in the concave of her arm with a tear still on his cheek, she remembered what he had told her not long ago—"*Crying makes you strong, Mommy.*"

JoAnn

A MOTHER JOURNALING THROUGH GRIEF

Danny still occasionally talks about you, Billy. But at the same time, he's forgotten specific details of your life that I may recall. A fraction of you seems to disappear with each event erased from your brother's mind. But then when he remembers a novel recollection, an incident that only he experienced with you, a part of you comes back to me. These revelations are like precious, limited-edition collectibles, numbered by the days you lived and discontinued by your death.

It's getting harder to put Danny to bed before Dick comes home. Not because your father comes home earlier—with age, Danny is staying up later. To my relief, he didn't notice your dad at the soccer game last night after he had had a few drinks at The Muni.

Usually, I don't confront Dick about his drinking, because he's so sensitive about it, but last night I did. That made him storm off in a fit. Maybe his drinking isn't as noticeable to other people, but all that matters is that it could be to Danny. I don't want Danny to see him that way. I would leave him before I'd allow Danny to be hurt again.

I see your smile in the sunrise
And the twinkle in your eyes,
When I wake up in the morning
When I count the stars at night.
Your laughter follows me in the whistling of the wind,
And your song stays in my heart.
—Billy's Song

Chapter 38

DICK

*I*t happened to her one torrential night in June. Her dream started as a nonsensical imagery—a repetition of the daily drudgeries and unfinished tasks of life. It was one of those dreams that come from the recesses of one's mind—consisting of contained thoughts trapped during the day, only to be released in the night. They come forward in sleep when the barrier of consciousness is down—thoughts swept up in an erratic, senseless sequence like dust particles in the air.

But that night, a deeper notion broke through the cobwebs of her subconscious, shedding its chains to break free and penetrate her dreams.

Lightning struck outside the walls of our bedroom. The boom of thunder traveled quickly over the lake to the bedroom window, vibrating through the frame of the house and interrupting her dream. Even though the obscure dream was gone, she wasn't quite awake. While her eyelids gradually opened, the muted outlines of the room slowly became visible, along with your face.

It appeared in her right peripheral vision, somewhat blurred because of the aura of light surrounding it. It was a familiar light of extreme warmth, and she wanted to stay in its brightness forever. Even though your lips stayed in a frozen eight-toothed smile, your eyes were clearly alive and sparkled with brilliance. Two distinctive words echoed through her mind.

"Thank you."

Even though the words didn't come from your lips, she heard them clearly. She closed her eyes with a smile of contentment and drifted back into a peaceful slumber, returning to her original dream as if she had experienced a brief commercial break.

When she woke the next morning, comforting arms seemed to wrap around her as if she had, somewhere, long ago, been in their embrace. She could almost feel the warmth drive out the cold shame. Like a balloon releasing its air, the knot in her heart relaxed and the pressure escaped.

Thank you.

She could still clearly hear your words. This was all you had said, yet all you needed to convey. With those two little words, she imagined that you had thanked her for your life, her love, and her care. Your innocent gratefulness told her everything she needed to know. You didn't blame her for your death after all.

Your mother had always believed that if she didn't look back on the past, she couldn't learn from her mistakes. And in the same manner, if she didn't anticipate the future, she couldn't prevent her mistakes. After all, that's what it means to be responsible. But why is it so difficult to look forward to make a decision, but so easy to look back and judge yourself? This must be why her guilt was much easier to maintain than self-forgiveness.

In retrospect, I could only conclude that *guilt* is a sentiment of condemning a previous decision with the knowledge of its consequence, and *living* means to make a choice without knowing its result.

So she awoke that morning knowing that the all-consuming guilt was gone. It had been obliterated, atoned for, and exonerated by you. With the absence of guilt, your mother could allow her own healing and accept her own recovery. On that June morning, she chose to live.

JoAnn
A MOTHER JOURNALING THROUGH GRIEF

I wasn't planning to go The Compassionate Friends National Conference in Chicago last week, because I didn't want to leave Danny for the weekend. So when Grandma Jen agreed to accompany us and watch Danny at the hotel, I jumped at the chance.

I signed up for workshops on guilt, anger, after-death communications, and sibling grief. I never felt so close to you and so comfortable with the other 2,000 bereaved parents at the hotel.

We all had our children's photos across our chests and nametags stating the age and cause of their death. Everyone we passed in the halls, sat next to in the restaurant, or stood next to in front of bathroom mirrors, had experienced the death of their child.

On the last day, the 2,000 held hands and we followed ten bagpipers down the streets of Chicago, leading us to Lake Michigan. We placed a wreath, with our children's names attached, into the lake and watched it float toward a symbolic island called "Healing." The energy of our camaraderie flowed through each bereaved parent, and we left a path of tears in the wake of our footsteps as we marched back to the hotel in perfect cadence with the bagpipes.

Chapter 39

DICK

*D*uring the summer of 1993, your Godmother Susie had surgery on a malignant growth that had gradually manifested in her brain. As soon as the obtrusive tumor was removed, she moved on with her life and returned to work only a few weeks after surgery. As your mother watched Susie's bravery and perseverance while battling her cancer, she was shamed into stepping outside her wall of self-pity. This allowed her to notice the world behind it.

Like a cancerous growth, the reason for your death had become a swelling, malignant obsession in her life. Your mother came to accept that the justification would be revealed no sooner than her own death. So she stopped asking fruitless questions. Her journal writing became less frequent and less consuming; she had become tired of the repetitious questions on the pages before her. When her quest was surrendered, her life's clock started ticking again and she started moving forward in time. Her grief hadn't left her, but seemed to diminish in substance. It melded with the many other facets of her character and became a part of her, but not the whole.

She started to experience an alien feeling of desire, a longing to enjoy life again. She started to find pleasure in small, innocent events of life. In a nutshell, she was learning to stop and smell the roses—or as a mariner would say, shut down the engines and drift.

As her weight gradually returned to normal, the change in her appearance became obvious. She could smile and laugh again and even tell a few jokes of her own. Even though she always had witty sense of humor, after your death, Billy, it became drier. Her words were laced with a tad more sarcasm, which was okay, because she was becoming a delight to be around again.

Her turning point had been her dream—or vision, as your mother would claim. So she looked forward to sharing her experience at the next Compassionate Friends meeting. She knew the parents there would believe her, because she had heard similar stories from them.

At The Compassionate Friends' National Conference that summer, she had learned about the high occurrence of after-death communications from deceased children. In a nationwide survey, bereaved parents had received more direct and spontaneous sensory experiences from their children versus indirect communications through mediums or psychics. The researchers concluded that the children either must understand the tremendous need for their reappearance, or that the young are more capable of transcending the wall between death and life than their older counterparts. These communications came most often when the parent had no barriers up and were more receptive to them; in sleep, meditation, or in the *alpha state,* that time between total consciousness and sleeping. And the children's visits always offered comfort, reassurance, and hope to the ones living without them.

I still maintained that parents imagined these visions because *their* need was so essential, though I would never convince your mother that she had not witnessed a message from you. She argued that personal visions have turned many skeptics into believers and that sometimes experience transcends reason. It's a shame that I couldn't agree with her then; it would have preempted a few arguments between us.

So, again, she walked into The Compassionate Friends meeting alone, but this time with the anticipation of retelling her amazing story. Like every other time, she paused at the table by the doorway to leaf through the memory book, confirming that your page was still present in the thick binder. But for the first time, she found herself studying the other pages around yours.

Images of various-aged children filled the sheets, all of them with loving parents, all of them beautiful and alive with spirit.

They are like you after all, Billy, she thought while studying the faces. Then she understood that they were not only like you, but *with* you. They were your playmates now, and she wanted to get to know them.

She remembered the first time she had scanned through that death book. She had noticed then that the album sheets were of varying hues; some were discolored with a dull ache of yellow and some undisguised with the painful shock of bright white. Now the sequence of those maturing pages had changed. Unlike the day she had placed your stark white page next to the faded ones, yours had become slightly yellowed with age next to the bright ones after it. She wondered why she hadn't noticed the discoloration in your page before. Had the distance from your death date been so gradual or was she more aware of the world around her?

She stood at that table remembering the excruciating days that had passed as your page yellowed, and contemplated the days ahead for the artisans of those contrasting, newly designed white pages. She felt a pang of empathy and a desire to relieve those parents' anguish. At the same time, she was grateful that she had already distanced herself from that hellish interval in her life. Forever etched in her memory was the vivid roadmap of the grief terrain she had traveled, and they had yet to. She knew she could help them navigate.

So her accumulated array of self-help books became her curriculum, and the obituaries from the daily newspaper became her guide. She copied poems that had comforted her and educational pamphlets that had reassured her of her sanity. The filing cabinet in your bedroom, Billy, became a bulging bereavement archive, and the bookshelf replacing your crib held an overflowing library of grief tomes. For each obituary portraying the death of a child, she would methodically select the suitable material from her filing system to accompany the sympathy cards she sent to those newly-bereaved parents.

She held a desire to immediately remove their pain, but knew that was impossible. So she forced herself to wait a few weeks after the death of their child to contact them. You see, a condolence card can never be late. Grief isn't like a birthday or anniversary; the occasion will still be there when the card arrives, no matter when you send it. A person can't be late on condolences because there's no such thing as one grief day. Though during that brief waiting period, she often felt like a mother watching her child receive a painful shot from the doctor—standing at a distance knowing that she shouldn't interfere, impatiently waiting to embrace their tears afterwards.

When she did contact those parents, there were only a few who wanted to be left alone in their grief; most eagerly accepted her assistance with extreme gratitude. But your mother had to keep reminding herself that their pain would persist despite the extent of mutual camaraderie. She couldn't remedy it.

Despite her driving need to comfort these bereaved parents, she knew her intentions were not all unselfish. She imagined, Billy, that with each correspondence to a bereaved parent, you would, in turn, meet their child in Heaven. She was merely inviting playmates over for her son.

JoAnn

A MOTHER JOURNALING THROUGH GRIEF

I bought Danny his first pet on his sixth birthday this week. We named him Sammy; this was my first choice of names for you, Billy. Your dad didn't like Sammy, or the five other names I had suggested before we agreed on Billy.

This guinea pig, with a brain as big as a marble, can't do a heck of a lot. But he's the only one who squeals when I walk in the front door after work and coos at me in your bedroom when I feel the urge to let my tears flow there. I believe that I've become more attached to him than Danny has. That guinea pig needs me like you did, Billy.

Chapter 40

*D*anny was sitting next to her in the car holding a beginner reader book. Not only had he learned to read that year, but he had blossomed in health as well. Gaining twenty pounds and growing two inches, he had finally graduated to the front seat of the car. In addition, it had been almost a year since he had been sick or injured. Unlike you, Billy, Danny had become a cautious child, and she thanked God for the reprieve. Even though it was unmerited, she still couldn't help but worry about his safety.

While the leaves on the trees were starting to color that September of 1993, the Mississippi and Missouri rivers continued to spill over the greater Midwest during the largest flooding in U.S. history. Israel's Supreme Court had acquitted a Nazi death camp guard of all charges, and around the same time, LAPD officers were sentenced to thirty months for violating Rodney King's civil rights. On the home front, the Twin Cities lost the NHL North Stars Hockey Team to Dallas, and Minnesota-born Prince changed his name to "The Artist Formerly Known as Prince," or for his close friends, Mr. TAFKAP.

My debt was building and I was hanging on to my leasing company by a thread. I had run out of affordable marketing ideas. Consumers were leasing from the large dealerships, because they were getting lower interest rates from the car companies. To top it off, your mother was taking a pay cut at her airline job.

In that second year after your death, Billy, I was not like your mother. I could not "shut down the engines to drift." I continually worried about our finances, so my throttle was at full speed, still revving up for escape.

Danny put his book down and looked at his mother. "I'm never going to be an uncle, Mommy, am I?" He turned to her and his blue eyes questioned, waiting an answer.

She thought about the innocence of youth and its few finalities; nearly anything is possible when you have your whole life in front of you. Options only start to dwindle as we get older.

Already an avenue has been narrowed in his young life. She thought about her answer to him. *He could be right; he may never be an uncle.* She placed her hand around his shoulder.

"Honey, you could have many nieces and nephews. You'll marry a girl, someday, who has brothers or sisters. When they have children, you'll be an uncle," she lightheartedly assured him. He thought about this for a moment, and then a smile formed on his lips as he looked up at her with relief in his eyes. She smiled back and thanked God for her healthy, bright son and his revival. She acknowledged her own progress as well, and felt blessed.

"I want another brother, Mommy. Can I have one?" She was taken aback at his request. He hadn't asked this for quite some time. Feeling disillusioned with our failure to conceive, she painfully admitted the reality to herself and him.

"I don't think we'll have another baby, Honey..." Then she saw the pained expression in his face. "....but I'd love to be a grandma someday. You can have kids when you grow up!" She tried to put some optimism in her tone.

"When will that happen?"

She realized she had just voluntarily stepped into a quagmire of verbal mud, unable to escape. She stood there for a moment contemplating her next move. She chose to cautiously side-step out.

"Oh, not for a long, long time," she stammered. "You'll be much older, Honey. And you have to fall in love first, and then get married…" She felt the resistance of the mud, "…to a girl."

He turned away in silence for a moment, and then his face lit up.

"Okay, I'll have lots of kids when I get older so you can be a grandma!" She could almost hear the gears churning in his brain. So she quickly changed the subject.

"Hey, do you want to stop for an ice cream cone?"

"Yeah! I want a plain vanilla…a big one!" As his face lit up, she pulled free and willingly walked away from the mess she had ventured into.

~ ~ ~ ~ ~

I repositioned the backpack over his shoulders and pinned the cardboard flyer displaying a bus number on the front of his madras shirt. Your mother held his hand at the curb, glancing in both directions for traffic. There was still a tendency for Danny and your mother to seek physical contact, whether it was holding hands or overlapping legs on the living room couch.

"You would think that the district could figure out a way to prevent a kindergartener from crossing the street to catch the bus. I don't like this. Could you call them, Dick?" When we found our chance, we ran across the street, holding Danny by each hand.

"This *is* ridiculous; I'll call them this morning. Hey, Bud, are you excited?" I gave my son an animated smile, and he returned it.

"I'm going to school! This is real school, not just daycare. Is Nathan going to be there?" He was now hopping up and down with anticipation.

"No, Hon, he's going to a different school. You're going to Our Lady of the Lake. You'll meet a lot of new friends there, and we'll invite Nathan to our house whenever you want." Your mother answered him as she knelt to zip up his windbreaker.

We had decided to send Danny to the local Catholic school, where his class size was half that of the public school. Though funds were tight, we both agreed that ninety dollars a month was worth it.

"How many more years do I have to go to school?" Danny looked at us both waiting for an answer. Your mother and I both glanced at each other and smiled. We mutually felt a connection to each other when sharing in Danny's happiness, when more often than not, there was a tension between us at this time. I answered him first.

"You have at least seventeen years to go, Bud. Is that all right with you?" College was a given, your mother and I both agreed.

"Yeah, that's great. Here comes my bus. Number 242, that's my bus!"

And that's how he left us. He didn't even turn around after we hugged him good-bye. I looked at your mother and saw her eyes tearing up. While watching the bus pull away, she couldn't help but feel that powerless sensation again, and I was unable to stop our son's newfound independence. So I held my arms around her as the bus disappeared from sight. And that's how your mother and I let him go.

Your mother cried on and off through the solitude hours of the morning. She was happy for Danny at this new milestone, but sad for herself. But most of all, she remembered that you and she, Billy, would have been together that morning; she would not have been alone.

Your mother crossed the street twenty minutes before the bus was scheduled to arrive from school. When Danny walked off the bus, her heart leaped at the sight of his grin. She leaned down to hug him.

"Hey, Honey! Boy, did I miss you! Did you like school?" She felt the familiar warmth of his hand in hers as they crossed the street together.

"Yeah, it was fun! We had recess, and math was boring. I have a new friend. His name is Matt, and my teacher's pretty," Danny prattled on, as they neared the driveway

"Oh, and I made this for you, Mommy." He handed her a colored paper medallion hanging from knotted yarn. She turned it over and read:

I survived the first day of kindergarten.

"Didn't you make this for yourself, Honey?"

"No, the teacher said it's for our mothers."

How appropriate, she thought and gave him a hug. Then he threw her a grenade.

"I have to get married to a girl to have a baby, right?" She stopped walking and looked down at him.

"Yes, Honey, why?" She held her breath.

"I'm sorry, Mommy. I can't have any grandbabies for you. I don't like any of the girls in my class. They're yucky!" he avowed adamantly, while his face showed a grimace of concern.

As she studied his resolve, a foreign emotion came forward. A smile appeared on her face, and then a laugh escaped her mouth—that deep chuckle that comes from pure merriment. She hadn't felt it for quite some time.

"What, Mommy? That's okay, isn't it?" He was puzzled by his mother's unusual mirth.

She tried to answer him, but the chuckles kept coming. She bent down to put her arms around him in a tight hug. While trying to catch her breath, she imagined him sitting on a floor mat in his classroom, reciting the ABCs and scoping out potential five-year-old brides.

JOANN

A MOTHER JOURNALING THROUGH GRIEF

"Come out, please, Baby."

The casket was by the wall of your room where your crib used to be. The pulsing of the bulging lid beat in syncopation to a thumping that sounded like a heartbeat. You were trying to get out.

"Come out, Baby. Mama's here." I pleaded.

Yet when the lid started to open, I ran and hid—desperately wanting to see you, but afraid of what I would see. As you shimmied down the sides of the coffin, I watched from the dark corner of the room. You looked the same from behind. But when you turned around and held your arms out to me, I looked away from your face for fear that it would change. I scooped you into my arms and tightly hugged you, afraid to let go. It felt so real.

We stood in front of the full-length mirror and, when I dared to look at our reflection, you appeared whole and beaming with life. You were wearing the soft flannel sweat suit adorned with multicolored sailboats. I knew this was only your image in the mirror and not what I would see if I looked down in my arms.

You looked into my eyes through our reflection and pointed in the direction of Danny's room. I asked if we should check on Danny and you nodded. After setting you down with apprehension, I could only see the top of your curly blonde head as you led me down the hallway. We found Danny snug in bed asleep, but I had a feeling that we had arrived just in time. He was safe now.

Then my father appeared next to me. You reached your arms upward toward him, but he looked right through you as if you weren't there. You didn't under-stand, so I explained that Grandpa couldn't see you, Billy, but would be able to when he died.

My friend, Jeri, appeared in Grandpa's place. She smiled at you and tickled you under the chin as she always had. I was surprised she could see you. By that time, I thought you were my own private illusion. Then Jeri spoke as if reading my mind.

"With this, I can see him," she said, while pointing to her heart.

Then I awoke.

Okay, Freud, analyze that one.

Yesterday was Christmas. Our family included you in their prayers, and your picture was displayed on your Uncle Tom's mantel. One of the baskets from your funeral was used for the cousins to draw names for their Christmas presents. I know those things were only done for my benefit; they don't think of you daily as I do. But that doesn't bother me anymore. It's okay to admit that the world moves on, because I believe that I'm finally moving with it.

Chapter 41

*D*anny did well in school that kindergarten year; the academics were a breeze for him and he made many friends. When the children were assigned to create a book about what they liked to do best, Danny wrote "playing with my brother" and drew a picture of you both, Billy. For Thanksgiving, he made a pilgrim hat for his entire family without excluding you. At Christmas time, he handcrafted a card for the three of us.

I had to agree with your mother, Billy; it was good that he always included you. By speaking and thinking about you, his anger had dissipated. It has been a long road to get to this point, and he has gone through a multitude of crayons, paper, and pillows to take it out on.

~ ~ ~ ~ ~

The damp wind broke the warmth of the early spring air, so I zipped my jacket around my growing frame. Because I was drinking my dinner most nights at this time, I was developing a slight middle-aged gut, something I had never had to deal with before. My high metabolism had always kept me trim, no matter how many plates of meat, potatoes, and gravy I consumed. The ham had been especially good that day, and, as a habit, I didn't hold back.

It was Easter Sunday of '94, and the Kuzmas were gathered outside Aunt Theresa's house for an egg hunt. Danny and his cousins canvassed the yard in their search while the adults watched on the sidelines. There were nine children, ranging from age sixteen down to two. *There should be an even ten*, I thought. *Shoulda, coulda, woulda.*

I watched Danny lead his cousin Bryan by the hand around the yard, helping the two-year old find his egg. Bryan's sister was by herself, searching the bushes that lined the far corner of their yard.

Michelle, too old to enjoy Bryan, too young to relate to Danny. *The same age you would be, Billy.* I watched as Michelle clumsily attempted to keep her candy and prizes within her tipsy Easter basket to no avail. *My, how little she seems.* I thought. *That's how old Danny was when he had to understand your death, Billy.*

I watched Danny's exaggerated smile as he stooped down to Bryan, showing him a green dyed egg with his name scribbled in wax. That was my boy, always acting the protective big brother with the younger children. A stab of bitterness wrenched its way into my thoughts. *He would have been such a great big brother, Billy.* Bryan smiled and ran with excitement over to his mother, your Aunt Theresa, with that same toddler waddle I remember so well. He was the age you would be forever in time. Being adept at doing so by this time, I shook off the self-pity and summoned my son.

"Hey, Bud, come here a sec!" Danny looked up and smiled. If allowed, Danny's diet of the past few years would have consisted solely of Cheerios and fruit snacks, now that his aversion to them was gone. Despite his diet, he had grown to tower over most of his classmates, barring two girls.

He handed the green egg to his cousin, Michelle, and came running to me. I placed my face to his eye level and put my arm around his shoulders.

"I want you to look at Michelle and Bryan, Bud," I knelt next to him, both of us facing his cousins. "Do you know how old they are?"

"Yeah, they're almost four and two. Didn't you know that, Dad?" he teased, and I smiled.

"Do you think Aunt Theresa and Uncle Bill should let Michelle babysit Bryan? Do you think Michelle could, say, try to stop him from running into the neighbor's pool over there?" I pointed past the yard toward the blue-tarp expanse next door.

"You're silly, Dad. She's way too young." We both watched as Bryan grabbed the green egg from Michelle and took off running with his screaming sister at his heels.

"You know, they're about the same age that Billy and you were when he drowned," I cuddled him close.

"But they're so little, Daddy...." As I watched his profile, I could almost see his brain processing the information through his six-year old mind. His brow furled while he stood, motionless, staring at the siblings' evident rivalry. Gradually, the solemn line on his forehead relaxed, and a new life slowly appeared in his eyes. It was the most wonderful thing I had ever seen; Danny's guilt physically took leave.

He gave me a hug and ran to play with his cousins, never looking back. There was a new lightness in his step and a new sparkle in his smile as he ran toward his extended family. I was always amazed at the progress that Danny was making, when all I seemed to be doing is taking one step forward and two backward.

JoAnn

A mother journaling through grief

What would you look like now, Honey? I often wonder because you became cuter every day. I've been tempted to have time-lapse photos done of you at every age, but they would only be fragmented pictures. They wouldn't be connected by the same person because your spirit had never inhabited them. Besides, if I saw those pictures, I would have to grieve over that child at every age without ever having the advantage of knowing him.

It's odd. Since you left me I've wanted nothing more than to see and touch you again. Now I've chosen not to contact you, Billy; not through a psychic, mirrors, nor the flicker of a candle. The forced communication would feel unnatural. It's best to leave you undisturbed in your heavenly home. It would disrupt the important work God must have intended for you—having called you away so soon. I also believe that you'll come to me again with symbols of bluebirds and daisies if needed.

I can't really blame your dad for his doubts. Had I not experienced the proof myself, I would be a disbeliever as well. But I disagree when he says that the signs come merely because of my cravings to see you, Billy. If that were the case, you'd always be by my side. Maybe your rare visitations are condoned and granted with permission from God. Maybe through this mutual and timely consent a divine message is transported to me—and not by a medium's command in front of a studio audience for financial gain.

Chapter 42

"Go, go, Power Rangers!" Disguised in a red suit and cape, Danny jumped from the floor to the coach while brandishing a three-foot rubber saber. Swinging his weapon at the monsters on the television and singing with their battle cry, he spun in the air, only to succeed in knocking a bowl of crackers off the coffee table.

"*Brringg...brringg.*" The phone joined in the reverie.

"Danny! Settle down in there... and turn down the TV!" My hands were immersed in dishwater while I yelled from the kitchen sink. Our dish washer was still inoperable; there were no funds to buy a new one.

"*Brringg...brringg...*"

"Dick, could you at least get the phone... please! I'm in the shower!" your mother's voice yelled from upstairs. On command, I pulled the drain from the sink and turned off the running water.

"Don't worry, it will wait!" I yelled above the Power Ranger's theme song. While reaching for the towel on the counter to dry my hands, your mother leaped down the last few stairs in a fury, wearing a loosely wrapped bathrobe around her body.

"*Brring....brringg...*"

"Don't bother yourself, I'll get it!" She huffed and reached for the receiver on the end table. "Danny, turn that TV down!" Being a rare occasion when his mother raised her voice at him, Danny immediately jumped from the coach to grab the remote.

"Hello?" She unsuccessfully tried to sound inviting, then glared at me before turning away. It didn't unnerve me because I had often been the recipient of those looks by that time. As silence filled the room, her body became still and her expression became one of concern.

"Oh, my God....I'm so sorry Ed. We're coming over. We'll leave right away." Hearing the panic in her voice, I tossed the kitchen towel on the counter and entered the living room.

"Adam's at North Memorial, Dick. He hit a tree with his car late last night and broke his neck." She was staring wide-eyed now, her voice soft. Adam was Ed and Jeri Worley's twenty-one-year old son.

"Oh, my God, how is he?"

"They don't know if he'll walk again, Dick. We need to get to the hospital...I'll get the neighbors to watch, Danny." She ran back up the stairs with the ties of her robe trailing behind.

Ed was my most disagreeable, provoking, defiant, exasperating--yet my most benevolent, compassionate and dearest friend. Funny thing is he would say the same about me. Also, he was often a comrade of my nightly bar ramblings, where I would open my heart through the numbness of my drunkenness. Night after night, he would listen to my anger and not judge me. He mourned the loss of my son along with me, because he was one of the few who remembered you, Billy. And his wife Jeri was one of your mother's dearest supporters. She had been on the top of your list, along with Denise and Jessica, as a trusted sitter.

Since your death and our transformation, your mother and I had acquired some new companions while retaining the old, whose loyal devotion merited keeping. Ed and Jeri were among those ranks, as were our friends, Rick and Shirley.

These friends had always said that they were deeply affected by your departure, Billy. But as a result, Rick and Shirley had divorced less than a year after your death, and Ed and Jeri had separated two years afterward.

We had spent the most of our social time with these couples—boating, partying, dining, or merely playing Monopoly at one of our homes.

It made me wonder, what happened to those "good things" that were supposed to come from your death? Did the lesson of your leaving motivate our friends to review their life choices and leave their spouses? In a nutshell, I learned that bad things could also come from adverse events. So your mother and my social life eventually took divergent roads, and we spent more time with our individual friends than we did with couples.

The bar was still my second home, and Ed was my most frequent companion because this was his favorite pastime as well. I also kept touch with my closest high school and college buddy, Jim Fox, even though he had grown out of the bar scene. He hung by me despite my loss, drinking habits, and financial woes. Rick Meinecke was rethinking his drinking lifestyle at this time, so we often had a safe lunch meeting to reconnect.

Your mother's social group consisted mainly of my friends' ex-wives, Jeri and Shirley and, a longstanding single girlfriend, Sheryl. Needless to say, their discussion, at times, would be analyzing and disapproving of my buddies. And while I supported Ed and Rick with an open ear, their stories seemed to dramatically differ from those of their exes. Though your mother and I tried to remain neutral on these sensitive issues, we usually failed. As a result, our arguments would often bring forth allegiance to our friends on opposite sides of the fence.

So your mother and I were still devoted to the Worleys, as we knew them, and extremely concerned on the event of their son's accident. We knew that we would have to be there in support of our friends, even if it meant a trip to North Memorial Hospital. And it took a dredging of seasoned courage to buckle up our bootstraps and visit the hospital in which you died.

~ ~ ~ ~ ~

I pulled the car into the familiar black-tarred lot and we walked through the formidable doors of the hospital. Your mother carried a bouquet of wild flowers with symbolic daisies sporadically mixed in while we walked through the sterile, narrow hallways. The smells and sounds of the corridors sent her back in a time machine, replaying the events of your death as if three years had not passed. The progress of her grief journey seemed to be obliterated by merely walking through those doors.

We hesitantly opened the door to the family room and embraced the Worleys. When your mother sat next to Jeri, she looked around the white room as though she had never been there before. It was a different room, a different tragedy.

We were still consoling our friends when a doctor walked through the door, but this time, the face that entered was relaxed and smiling. The operation had gone well and nerve damage was minimal. They had drilled holes in Adam's skull to rig a "halo" to stabilize his neck. Although he would eventually regain his strength, he would need to wear this cumber-some contraption for a few months.

After hugging our friends and saying our goodbyes, we made them promise to keep us informed. Then your mother and I quickly escaped the confines of the building, attempting to leave that chapter behind us. Even though we took an unfamiliar back staircase, the memories of that day resurfaced.

Your mother must have been feeling the same, because her tears started as soon as we walked out door of the hospital. I pulled her into my chest, placed my chin upon her head and held her tightly. My bride. I felt her grief and accepted it as my own. Once again, it flowed through us, back and forth, around us; her feeling my grief and me feeling hers. How long had it been since I had held her this way?

I hung my head to avoid detection from any onlookers. Through the haze of the tears brimming in my eyes, I noticed one lone daisy on the sidewalk in our path. While pulling your mother with me, I abruptly sidestepped to avoid crushing its pert petals. It was fresh, as if its stalk had been plucked from its roots only moments before and placed in our path. Was it from your mother's own bouquet that she carried in? No, we had come in a different way.

I loosened my grip on your mother and reached down in front of us. As soon as I clutched its delicate stem in my hand, I imagined your small fingers holding it up to your nose, Billy, as you had done so many times before; breathing in and out, trying to smell its aroma while not knowing which way was correct.

The flower I held was clearly from you, as if you had extended your dimpled fist and placed it into the palm of my hand. You were near; I could feel your presence as if I were holding you and not the daisy. This was what your mother had tried to tell me. I handed the daisy to your mother. Her pained expression turned to one of elation.

"Oh, my God, Dick," she smiled, and tears of happiness replaced tears of sorrow. As we walked together in embrace away from the hospital, the sensation of leaving you behind vanished.

JoAnn

A mother journaling through grief

After breaking his neck, Adam Worley admitted that the lesson of responsible driving was driven into his brain as securely as the bolts of the metal rigging screwed into his skull by the doctors.

I was able to stuff away my tears before greeting the Worleys in that horrible "Family Room." While I hugged and consoled Jeri, I apprehensively looked behind her at the white walls until I was reassured that they wouldn't close in on me. I wondered how this could be the same room in which I had waited in for word on your death. It appeared to be much smaller in my memories. Thank you for the daisy, Honey.

Last night, Danny asked if drowning hurts; I assured him it didn't. Then he told me he was still missing you, Billy. So we gazed out our bedroom window and talked to you, as we had during the first few days after your death. When noticing the sky fill with peculiar shaped clouds, we both thought the same thought, but Danny said it first.

"Billy's tooshie! Billy's tooshie is in the sky!" We laughed and I took pictures of a stretch of clouds that looked like a hundred pink angel butts "shining" down on us. And when the thunder struck and the rain fell, our imaginations brought more giggles.

We're having more laughs at your expense, Billy. I believe we're both getting better.

Chapter 43

DICK

*Yo*ur mother was leaning against the wall by the door of Danny's room, still apprehensive of the new sitter we had hired that night. She refused to leave until she was comfortable, even though we were already running late for a lunch reservation.

"It's 11:30, Babe. Let's get going," I spoke, but evidently not softly enough.

"Shhh….they're talking!" I shrugged, gathered my patience and walked away. Your mother continued to eavesdrop on the conversation.

"That's a great snake, Danny. I'm making a dog," the sitter said.

As your mother positioned her ear closer to doorway, she imagined them both sitting at Danny's miniature desk, creating art from the clay that she had provided.

"Do you know that I have a brother?" Danny's muffled voice proclaimed. "….but he's not here. You can't see him. He's in Heaven." There was a pregnant pause while your mother had to restrain herself from racing through the doorway to hug your brother.

"Are you sad?" the sitter asked with compassion. Your mother held her breath.

"I was, but I'm not anymore….hey, I'm going to make a car, you can make a house for the snake and the cat!"

With a smile on her face, your mother walked away from your room to retrieve her windbreaker from the closet as I waited at the screen door. No other words could have made her happier.

While holding onto the guardrail of the boat, I planted my feet on the gunnels. The waves forcefully rocked the hull as I precariously unsnapped the canvas cover from the sides. *It's going to be a rough ride today*, I thought. Despite the wind, the autumn leaves were at their peak of color and I didn't want to miss that weekend's boat cruise. Waiting merely another week would find the leaves gone from their branches.

Your mother walked up the dock carrying a small cooler for beverages, and I studied her as she neared me. Her face had aged over the last few years, but I still found it attractive. And her slender figure was still intact. Yes, she was different from the girl I married, but I had learned to accept that. Along with her new serious nature came deeper and compassionate feelings. She wasn't as lighthearted or as fun as before, but with your death she had matured into a woman whom I could admire.

After placing the cooler into the boat, she jumped onto the bow to release the lines. As we pulled away from the dock, I saw Danny waving through the screen door of the house with his sitter. So I waved back, thinking about the depth of love I had for that kid and what a fragile place I'd be in if anything ever happened to him.

As we cruised through Cook's Bay, every so often, I glanced at my wife's profile and felt blessed. We didn't need another child; Danny and she were enough for me.

"Calling the *Incognito* from *Worls Aweigh*." I picked up the VHF microphone to speak with my friend. Though it wasn't easy, Ed had moved on since his and Jeri's divorce. Your mother and I still separately spent time with the two, though their divorce had become civil, which made things easier for all of us. At that time, Ed was in a fairly new relationship with a girl with whom we were still getting acquainted. He had invited her on the boat with him that day.

"Come in, *Worls Aweigh*. This is the *Incognito*, switch to 7. Over." I turned the frequency knob.

"*Worls Aweigh*, are you there? Over."

"Hey, Dick, we're at the Park Tavern, and there are plenty of slips available. What's your location? Over."

"We're headed into Excelsior Bay right now. See you soon, Buddy. Over." Approaching the slow wake markers, I pulled the throttle back.

There were three docks at the Park Tavern, and the *Worls Aweigh* was slipped on the far left. While I moved the *Incognito* toward the right dock, your mother grabbed the lines and climbed onto the bow. With the strong wind coming from the port side, I needed to over compensate the helm's wheel that way. Despite the wind, we were going to make it on the first try. Your mother looped the end of the line into the cleat on the bow, as the boat rocked precariously toward the dock. Weaving the line under the bow railings, she positioned herself for a jump over the railings to the dock below.

When your mother had done this on our first boating date, I had cringed at the sight of her risky feat. But eventually I learned, over the years, that she could easily accomplish it. So on this day like many others, when the boat hit the dock and I saw her jump, I made my way to the stern to tie the aft line to the dock post. At that moment, a strong gust of wind blew the boat to the starboard side, and I looked up just in time to see your mother flying head first through the air toward the dock.

Panic overcame me while I hurriedly turned back to the helm and attempted to maneuver the boat toward the dock. When the hull hit the wooden planks, Ed was there at the stern to steady the boat as I jumped off.

"I've got the boat, Dick. Check on JoAnn!" Ed said as he struggled against the wind's pull on the heavy load. I looked down the dock to see your mother lying on her side and her eyes slowly opening into a squint.

Blood was seeping from her bruised nose, and her lips were red and blue, interspersed with splinters from the dock's boards. I ran to her side.

"Are you okay, Babe?" Her eyes opened wide. "Talk to me, Hon. Are you okay? Can you move?" She moaned and ran her tongue over her teeth.

"Yeah, I think I'm okay. Man, my nose hurts....are my teeth still there? I can't feel them." She grimaced in efforts to reveal her teeth. They seemed to be intact.

"Yes, your teeth are still there. Can you move your arms and legs? I think we need to get you to a hospital for an X-Ray on your nose. How does your head feel? Are you dizzy?" As I surveyed the length of her body for any other damage, she moved her legs and arms—all seemed intact. My hands gave her support under her arm, and she placed her feet beneath her to stand up. As she struggled to stand, I noticed that, from her left knee down, her jeans and dock shoe were soaked with water. I looked at the water over the dock's ledge and mentally estimated the distance. *Five feet, no less*, I thought as we made our way down the dock to catch a cab to the hospital.

JoAnn

A MOTHER JOURNALING THROUGH GRIEF

Danny and you were in the water playing with other children as I watched from the beach a few doors down from our house. The umbrella stroller was at the water's edge, and Danny lifted you into the seat and strapped you in. You both smiled at each other while Danny climbed into the double seat next to you, as he had done many times before. I felt that warm maternal completeness watching the two brothers; the older one taking care of the little idolizing one. The two of you were together again.

Then Danny climbed out of the stroller and turned from you to play with the other children on the beach. I watched in horror as the stroller gradually started to move on its own toward the water. I ran towards the shoreline yelling, "Someone save Billy!" Knowing there was no way to stop the outcome, all the adults on the beach shook their heads and stared at me with pity. My legs moved in a slow, thick motion, I was unable to propel my body to get to you. I could only watch and scream as your stroller sank into the cold dark water with you still strapped in. Then I woke up.

I know it was you who saved me, Billy. What else could explain it? I remember flying through the air, and then everything went black. The next thing I knew, I was completely on the dock with one soaked leg and saw Dick running toward me. Had my little angel saved me from the water that took him?

Grandma Jen bought me a piano last week. It's been 23 years since I've played, but it's slowly coming back to me—just like riding a bike. I love to sit at those black and white keys, pounding out my frustrations or caressing them with my memories of you. My mother must have known that I would release my emotions at that keyboard. Since your death, she has also reminded my sisters to keep in touch with me on a weekly basis. Even though I can't tell my mother my deepest thoughts, she has become my therapist by proxy.

Chapter 44

DICK

Though modest, it was the most beautiful home I had ever seen. It had three tiers of floors and window-lined walls, which led to an opened ceiling. It was small in dimension but still gave me a feeling of space. Everything inside the house was decorated in creamy white tones, yet I knew nothing could soil there. The entire lakeside wall of the house was an enormous window pane, containing no glass barrier to the outside. It was okay, because I knew it didn't snow or rain there. And it didn't seem to matter if someone saw in; the house was open to all.

From every corner of the room, I could see the expansive wooded yard and a cleared pathway through the middle of its lush greenway, allowing access to the dazzling, aqua lake beyond. Sitting in front of the window pane facing outward toward the tranquil scene was a white, bentwood rocking chair. I assumed a small child lived there with me.

Then I awoke, noticing that I had fallen asleep on the couch again. When trying to remember the details that got me to this place from the bar, I could merely conjure up pieces. Only short clips came to mind—like those from the preview of a movie, falling short of revealing the plot. This wasn't the first time I had lost recall of the night before. This lapse of memory concerned me a bit, but not enough to give up my emotional escape at the municipal bar with my friends.

A familiar pain simultaneously shot through my temples and lower back as my feet hit the floor. I glanced at the clock above the television, it was already ten o'clock. Danny must have gone off to school already, and your mother must have been running errands on her day off.

Okay, it's Tuesday, I thought and remembered that I had an appointment with a potential lease customer in an hour. We also had conferences for Danny that evening. Looking through the slits of my eyelids, I made my way into the kitchen to ingest three ibuprofen tablets.

A familiar disgust consumed me. *What a mess I am; no wonder my wife is pushing away from me.*

As the shower's water flowed over me, I shook my head to clear the fog from my brain. I thought of our boat ride just the day before. *Why was she asking about the price of homes on the lake? Was she planning on leaving me?* I had always felt secure in our relationship, but I wasn't feeling that way anymore. *When was the last time we had said "I love you" to each other?*

I've got to try harder. I just don't know if I have the energy, I thought as the warm water washed away the smoke fumes from the bar.

~ ~ ~ ~ ~

Your mother and I navigated through the sea of knee-high humans and their parents. The drone of excited chatter moved in a wave of unified voices through the school cafeteria. I was unable to distinguish one voice among the many, but your mother could clearly hear the ghosts of that place from a different time.

"I'm so sorry, if there's anything I can do…"

"Be assured, God doesn't give us anything we can't handle…"

"Feel blessed, you still have another child…"

"Sometimes people learn too late about the dangers of living on a lake…"

She took those voices from your funeral and discarded them for the moment. This time was for Danny, not her grief.

Danny was in the first grade at the local Catholic school that fall of '94, and we were attending his first school conference. He still asked questions on your death, Billy, but his eyes seemed to sparkle more brightly in direct correlation to the return of your mother's recovery. Although she was not the same person as before your death, she was familiar to Danny once again. And even though your mother knew her eldest son was going to be fine, she still needed reassurance from a third party, his teacher.

I, on the other hand, was confident that my son would come away with a glowing review. Danny had also grown intellectually in the past year, especially in math. He was multiplying and dividing, when most children his age were learning to add. Most of all, he seemed happy and socially active with many friends. Isn't that the world's standard of emotional well-being? As I waited in the hallway and anticipated our allotted time with Danny's teacher, I was clueless that I would soon be blindsided by the hidden turmoil inside my son's mind and how I had contributed to it.

Your mother was acting like her old self again, chatting with his classmates' mothers, making new friends. Sometimes she had the tendency to say inappropriate things that embarrassed me, mostly by bragging about our son. Yup, she was acting like her old self again. But I was a patient man, so I tuned her out and started studying the first grade art on the walls.

The students had cut out multi-colored, construction paper cats, composed poems on them, and hung them in a line with tape. I read them silently.

My cat's name is Maddie. She is a fatty. Matt
Cats are nice. They catch mice. Anthony

I have a cat. She wears a hat. Christine

Finding them innocently entertaining, I moved from one to another. My smile abruptly faded and my movements stopped as I read the words from the orange-colored cat.

My cat stunk. He was drunk. Danny

My body went numb. My son. My life. *I am so sorry, Bud.* I looked around to see if anyone noticed my show of emotions. Realizing that no one was looking, I tore the orange cat from the wall and buried it in the deep, secret corner of my pants pocket.

After the conference, your mother expressed her relief that there were no concerns from Danny's teacher about his behavior in class. She was equally disappointed that there were no raving reviews about his intelligence. I don't remember any of the teacher's words that day.

In response to Danny's little orange cat, I cut back on my visits to the bars. Yet that alone did not bring me home after work. When the Ojibwa Indian Reservation opened the Mystic Lake Casino near our home, I was still able to find an alternative entertainment venue that pacified my obsessive-compulsive nature. Because the casino served no alcohol, I was able to replace one behavior with the other.

So every night at the blackjack table, I tried to recoup the income I was losing from my business. Besides, the pit bosses and my fellow gamblers treated me like royalty in direct proportion to the money I laid on the table. When I was seated next to my comrades of the cards, I was not the dad who let his son die or the husband who was unable to bring in a suitable income.

JoAnn

A MOTHER JOURNALING THROUGH GRIEF

He was gone, too. Danny had died in a car accident. The familiar pain consumed me, and I tried to scream but no sound came out. Danny, gone, all my children gone…. No more "trick or treating," no more Santa Claus, no more playgrounds, no more childhood games. It was one of those terrifying, vivid nightmares—consciousness could not have been more authentic. I awoke this morning wide-eyed and drenched in sweat, clenching my pillow. The hollow void gnawed at the pit of my stomach until I discovered Danny asleep next to me in bed.

My heart leaped for joy as I put my arm around his shoulder and nestled next to him. But when I did, he subconsciously moved away, turning his back to my face. It was then I acknowledged that my dream had somehow been a reality. With the discovery of the mature, independent child lying next to me, I had, in actuality, lost my other little boy. He is indeed growing up.

I'll have to accept that he can't be everything to me and allow myself to liberate my oldest son as he claims his independence. How incredibly hard it is for me to let go once more.

Your dad isn't drinking like he use to but, instead, goes to the casino every night, occasionally not coming home until early morning. Sometimes he boasts of winning thousands and sometimes he secretly omits his losses from the night before. He must be laying a lot of money on the table to win in such quantities— and lose in such quantities. I see the credit card debt each month.

I've tried talking to him to no avail, and it infuriates me that he's too stubborn to see what he's doing. Such a smart man, yet so out of touch with his addiction. It should worry me more than it does; women have left their husbands for less. But, for me, I don't care if he gambles it all away. Going broke is a better alternative than him coming home drunk at night. It's better for Danny. And with the Billy puzzle piece missing, the stability of our family jigsaw seems to have weakened. After being reduced from four to three, I'm terrified at the prospect of it dwindling down to two. We have to stay together at all costs.

Chapter 45

DICK

The occurrence of your mother's fortieth birthday that February of '95 forced her to admit her childbearing years were over. I felt that I had been meeting her halfway by agreeing to forego the birth control, even though I was unwilling to try clinical methods or adopt. To my relief, the subject of having a baby was dropped. She had accepted that life wasn't fair; she knew that well. Yet, she blamed God and, especially me for her small family. Though she stopped badgering me, her resentment silently grew and occasionally displayed itself in angry outbursts directed solely at me.

On April 19, 1995, the Car Bomber in Oklahoma City destroyed 100 families' lives. Children and adults were blown apart, and the country mourned the brutal method in which their lives had been taken. Even though your mother was able to imagine the grief of those families, she was unable to shed a tear for them. Maybe there is a limit to the pain one person can feel and she had used her allotment. Or maybe she had become hardened to others' grief, because she had habitually needed to block her own out.

When people spoke of the terrible incident, she would lower her head and shake her head like the rest. She played along, continuing to hide a deep, unmentionable emotion as the whole world became acquainted with the faces, lives, and deaths of those children through newspapers and magazines; and you, Billy, remained anonymous.

She didn't, in any way, believe that your death was worse than those children or that their parents were suffering any less. She merely wanted to have the same footage, to have the world know you like those children. Those bereaved families would have never guessed that there was someone out there who actually envied them.

At that time, there was nothing else in my life but gambling. So consumed with the chips and the cards, I started to even scare myself. Going against all I had ever believed in, I borrowed money from business acquaintances and friends. My intentions were always to pay them back with interest. There was no doubt in my mind that they would be reimbursed, because I felt that I was proficiently skilled at blackjack. But the reality of my disease was that I would keep putting money on the table until there was none left to lay down. By the time you would have started your first day of kindergarten, Billy, I was precariously gambling with being sued by a dealership from which I had borrowed money.

That fall, we got rid of our $6,000 play gym, or so we called it. This was the cost of storing our boat at a marina over the winter for eight years versus storing it in our yard where the play gym stood. As the spikes were pried from the ground, I remembered how you and Danny had always sat at each side of the trolley seat facing each other. Your mother had devised a rope barrier on your side, Billy, to keep you from falling out. She would stand at the side and push it back and forth, with Danny yelling "Higher!" and you yelling "Mo!" Then you and he would smile at each other, sharing the laughter of your mutual adventures. I was surprised at the difficulty I had taping a "free" sign to its poles and the emotions that arose while watching a stranger dismantle the gym and load it into his truck.

Before the snow came that December, the sickle of death struck our family again. Having traveled there already, your mother was surprised by her new emotions of loss. Inanely, she had thought your death would be like an inoculation; the grief virus should have created antibodies to make her immune to future exposures. But the aspects of this new grief had only recalled another. Her grief lasted a full five days on behalf of this family member. And our beloved was cremated for one hundred dollars—quite pricey for a guinea pig.

Having denied Danny a viewing of your body, Billy, she decided to give him a conclusion to our little mammal's death. I believe your mother needed it more than he did. So against my objections, she respectfully cremated our squeaky friend, and his ashes were prepared in a little plastic urn without the hair of a cat or tooth of a dog—or so she was told. She and Danny spread Sammy's remains at your tree, Billy, and imagined by doing so that you would acquire your first pet in Heaven.

JoAnn
A MOTHER JOURNALING THROUGH GRIEF

Many of my bible-inspired acquaintances have told me that our loved ones who die are not angels, but spirits who sit higher in hierarchy than our winged guardians. It's so fashionable to believe in angels protecting us, though I'm not sure I can grasp that idea of invisible creatures among us. It gives me the willies to think of them looking over my shoulder, breathing down my back. On the other hand, I have come to believe in angels disguised as mere humans. There have been many in my life since your death, Billy. And, I guess, I've been one to other bereaved parents.

But if there is such a thing as guardian angels, Billy, yours must have taken a well-deserved break on the day of your death after the exhausting schedule of safeguarding you throughout eighteen months.

Chapter 46

DICK

I t was January 16, 1996. She was sitting in front of the classroom with her bottom overlapping the seat of a tiny wooden chair. As she read from the illustrated book, the children on the floor gazed up at her in total rapture.

Knowing that the children in your kindergarten class would never get the chance to meet you, your mother made a visit to your classroom on what would have been your sixth birthday. You were going to grow up with them, even if only through her presence on your birthdays.

She was barely able to see the words while reading about a baby bat that fell from his mother's nest. But your little classmates didn't notice her watering eyes or when her voice momentarily broke. And afterward, every hand rose in the air demanding answers to questions on loss, death, and the afterlife. There were so many she didn't have enough time to answer them all, Billy. And your mother was careful with her responses because most of their parents hadn't been given an occasion to address the subject of death with them yet.

Even though they were learning of death for the first time, and contrary to their adult counterparts, they seemed to accept the concept as merely another phase of living. Without personally experiencing a loss, the children seemed to have no more fear of death than they did of life, growing up, the first day of school, losing their first tooth, or having a terrible tummy ache. They hadn't yet seen the gruesome aspects of dying. It was as if death was merely another phenomenon of life that they needed to expect and accept, because they had no control over it.

The children in your class devoured the cookies and admired the little ceramic angel holding the number six in his hands your mother had brought as a present for the classroom. They asked her to come back the next year, and though she readily accepted the invitation, she silently hoped that she could control her tears by then.

~ ~ ~ ~ ~

In light of my gambling and your mother's extra hours of work, her stress level escalated, and she soon replaced her herbal tea with a few glasses of wine every night. Claiming that it was the only way she could relax, she would justify her routine as being healthier than prescription drugs; speaking of the grapes as a food source instead of a fermented toxin. Of course, I had no grounds to judge her. But in the end, this nightly practice proved ineffective when she developed a bout of the shingles that spring of '96.

Believing that her scab of denial healed the wound of her grief, the routine of her life before your death returned. The pace of her actions quickened and she started to take on more responsibilities. She stopped going to The Compassionate Friends meetings, feeling that she had no more need for support groups.

Though she tried to cling to her faith, your mother eventually found the wall I was hiding behind and joined me. She started to question everything she ever believed in before your death, Billy. And though she believed that there was a God, she didn't believe in prayer. She questioned if God had truly helped her through the endless days of her grief, or did she find the strength through a false security of imagined help?

She could have endured in this manner had she not left behind the lessons learned from your death, Billy. She could have functioned this way had the protective scab not been picked from her grief wound to start the flow of blood again. And a scab that has been torn off prematurely will bleed as profusely as the initial injury.

JoAnn

A mother journaling through grief

I couldn't understand what was happening as my body trembled with uncontrollable anxiety. The walls of the airplane moved in around me, and I felt as if I'd be crushed within the metal fuselage if I didn't flee. At the same time, I was terrified that if I broke free from the confinement of the aircraft, the blue sky outside its shell would close in on me in the same way.

My mind became a floating vortex of fear, and the thought of remaining in that mindset overtook my entire cognition. I was afraid of entering insanity to never come back. Then I would tear my hair out, rip the clothes from my body, and run screaming through the airplane aisles for all to see.

The terrifying horror that encompassed me was coming from my own unrestrained thoughts—my own mind had become the enemy. My thoughts couldn't reach beyond the frightening standstill of time and were, surreally, drifting in the moment. As my heart raced uncontrollably, I felt that everyone around me could hear its tumultuous pounding in my chest. The symptoms mimicked a heart attack, but I wasn't afraid of dying. That was preferred over living in that suffocating state of mind.

I'm having an attack every hour, and it stays with me for at least twenty minutes, though it seems much longer. Afterward, I'm so exhausted my eyelids fight to stay open. This is the only time I feel a reprieve from the threat of another attack, immediately after having one.

I'm afraid to leave the house, afraid to go into the next room. I'm afraid that by merely moving, the fear will pursue me. I'm afraid that if I write about it, it will emerge. I'm afraid to be alone with Danny for fear that I'll scare him. I'm afraid that I'm not stable enough to take care of him. What if I can't take care of my own child?

I thought I was immune from any emotion this strong, having already navigated through the alternating stages of depression, guilt, envy, and anger. But I never experienced fear in my grief journey; I had never in my life felt such intense terror.

Did my lingering doubts allow the doors of my mind to let in this primal animal of fear? Is God not real and have I only been brainwashed by man-made religions? What if there is no God at all and we'll fall into an infinite darkness of nonexistence in the event of our deaths? If there was no afterlife, I'll never see you again, Billy. If there is no reunion, there's no reason for life itself.

With the departure of faith, fear has taken over. I cringe inside the walls of my house when hearing the sirens from passing fire trucks. I hide in dread that they might someday need to come to our doorstep again. I'm vigilant at watching Danny board his school bus in the mornings, because the panic rises in my throat if I glance away for a moment only to find an empty space on the curb where he once stood. I can now admit that a death could happen to my family again; I'm not immune because of yours, Billy.

I'm afraid of my own death, if there's a chance that I won't see you in that dark nonexistence. And the notion of Danny dying grips me with horror. I can't trust life to be fair or for God to take care of my family anymore; he's already failed me. My mind must always be ready and alert, because only I can defend what's mine. It's all up to me, and that thought terrifies me. My family's disintegration brings about images of being trapped. Then the walls of the world seem to cave in on me.

At the onset of the attack, I feel like a deer startled in the headlights of an oncoming car—with my body frozen in place, my mind trying to escape. Sometimes I feel like a captured bird, jumping from limb to limb, startled by any movement of life; wide-eyed, alert, ready to fly at the first sign of danger.

But the confines of the airplane frighten me the most, because it's there where the attacks first occurred. I feel too weak to fight this monster of fear, but the more I retreat, the more potent he becomes. My comfort zone has become smaller as he invades any space I leave open. I find myself huddled in a ball on the couch afraid to move into the next room of my own home. I'm afraid of being trapped in my own insane mind. I'm afraid of the fear itself.

Chapter 47

*E*ven though the start of 1996 was uneventful, it exploded with action in July with a pipe bomb at the Atlanta Summer Olympics, killing one and injuring 110. Subsequently, the tremors were felt at our house when your mother's panic attacks arrived soon after the fifth anniversary of your death.

When she couldn't control the attacks in front of Danny, he reverted back to his symbolic gestures of five years before. As she sat trembling with fear at the kitchen table, he would tie her to the chair with ropes, attempting to stop the mother he knew from leaving his life again.

Then Danny developed a nervous tic of popping his lips—which either was in response to or the reason for your mother's continued panic attacks. I believed that one fed the other, but of course, she blamed herself. When she heard of the possibility of a Tourette's diagnosis, her fears escalated. Similarly, my thoughts became consumed with my perfect son being plagued with this socially-shunned affliction.

Through her, I found a name for my own anxiety, which had over-whelmed me in the church pews a few years before. Even though I understood what she was going through, I didn't seem to be helpful with what we referred to as her "attacks." It was like our grief all over again; she had to get through it on her own.

Trying in my own way to make things right again, my trips to the casino increased, as did the stacks of chips I laid on the tables. My only thoughts were on the money I could win to solve my family's problems, not on the risk I was taking. Though your mother was budgeting by cutting her own hair and clipping coupons, I bought the boat of my dreams with the money from the sale of our 28-foot cabin cruiser and my momentary winnings at the casino.

Spending $8,000 on the 32-foot Sea Ray, in desperate need of aesthetic repairs, was justified by me as an investment; I could refurbish and sell it for twice that amount. Most importantly, it could still be used for our enjoyment in the process of the redo. Besides, it was closer in size to my buddies' larger boats. It had always been like that, an untelevised Olympic competition of who had the bigger boat on Lake Minnetonka.

Dolly the sheep was born that summer of '96. When she was cloned from an adult cell a few months before, a protest escalated from the religious sector in fear that the procedure could be used on humans. But, I couldn't understand why faith-based people would believe that the human spirit might be diminished by the reproduction of some skin and bones. Having viewed your body as only a shell, I knew that Billy DNA could be reproduced a million times over, and we still wouldn't have you back. No matter how arrogant man may be, he must know he's incapable of cloning a soul.

That fall, your maternal Great-grandma Cencic, was getting less coherent with each day that she remained in the nursing home. During your short life, Billy, your mother had brought you and Danny to visit her each month, so Great-grandma had come to know you quite well. After observing your antics during each visit, she would repeatedly advise your mother that you should be on a leash. Evidently, she was a smart lady despite her memory loss. Also, your great-grandmother had an interesting history of answered prayers.

One desperate summer day in 1934, she had prayed to God to end her physically abusive husband's life. An iron ore miner's wife, she was granted release from her personal demon by a mine cave-in only hours later. I don't quite believe that God answers prayers in this macabre fashion, the proof being that she had, unsuccessfully, prayed for her own death for ten years while in the nursing home. Being well-versed in prayer, she was puzzled why God had taken you instead, Billy.

JoAnn
A MOTHER JOURNALING THROUGH GRIEF

When I saw my fear reflected in Danny's eyes, the need to recover pushed me forward. Even though I should monitor the extent of his tics at night, I wear ear plugs during sleep to block out the popping sound coming from his room. When I hear it, the panic rises to my throat until it chokes the breath from me. It's in the darkness of the night where I'm most prone to the fear—the fear of what Tourette's will do to him.

Futilely trying to hide my panic attacks from my mother, her maternal radar eventually overcame my avoidance of her calls. After being confined within the boundaries of my fear for a week, she prodded me to take that first monumental step out the doorway of my house. She knew that if I didn't leave the walls of my refuge, I'd be stuck in my own hell forever.

Facing the confines of the car, I successfully drove for an eternal fifteen minutes of deep breathing to a local mall to meet with her. There was a sense of pride when I finally arrived, as if accomplishing an amazing feat of astronomical proportions. Even though it was only one small battle in a lengthy war, I fought the fear for a moment and won. Since then, the fear retreats with each step I take forward.

Chapter 48

DICK

The tone of her voice spiraled with each sentence, while her eyes started to brim with tears. "What's the problem with including a picture of him? I took the picture; there isn't a copyright law against that is there? I give my permission, for heaven's sake!"

"Drop it, dear. It's okay." I whispered and placed a hand on her arm, while she immediately shook it off. After making that mistake once, I would never again dare to tell her to calm down during these outbursts. But feeling bad for the poor photographer who was the recipient of her wrath, I felt the need to say something.

"He's part of our family. He shouldn't be excluded." Her voice cracked, threatening to break into a sob. Danny and I stood, dressed in our best attire for a family photo for the church directory, shifting from foot to foot with unease and scanning the area for onlookers.

On the way to the church that day, we had reminisced about the chaos of the last church directory photo session five years before. Your mother's plan of matching outfits for our family was foiled when a spaghetti spill and milk regurgitation demanded that Danny and your outfits be changed at the last minute. And as for me, well, I absolutely refused to do the matching color thing. Despite the mismatched outfits, the last directory had included our family of four, Billy.

So in your absence, your mother had brought a life-size picture of you to include in the photo that day. But she could not convince the photographer that a photo should be within a photo. So, after a few tears and a lot of tension, we sat there trying our best to smile.

When we received our free 8 x 10 colored photo a few weeks later, we couldn't help but chuckle a bit at the comical image. In the picture, your mother's eyes were red and her teeth were exposed, trying, unsuccessfully, to mimic a smile—looking more like a grimace. Danny was in the middle of a tic so his mouth was opened in an O and his eyes were looking down at his mother. My lazy eye, which portrayed itself when stressed, was shut in a wink toward the camera. After opening the envelope and having a few laughs, we found even more enjoyment by tossing it into the trash.

~ ~ ~ ~ ~

During that time, when your mother and I fought, it was usually about finances. Not wanting my anger to control the situation and not being especially gifted in confrontation, I would give her the silent treatment afterwards. That winter her revenge was sweet, but not very nice.

The day after one of these arguments she brought home a kitten, even though she knew I was one of those people that joked about cats and microwaves in the same sentence. After she brought that wild animal into my house, I merely extended my silent treatment until I couldn't contain myself anymore.

It was Saturday date night and we were, once more, dining at our favorite table at The Mist, our favorite local restaurant. Gloria, our usual waitress, had just taken our order, and we were nursing our cocktails until the food came. The silence became more evident, almost awkward, in that venue. With a scotch and water in hand as my lifeline to courage, I finally spoke.

"Why did you do it? How could you have brought a cat home without my approval? I'm a part of this family, and we should have discussed it." Proud of my candor, yet thoroughly expecting a backlash, I braced myself for the rebuttal.

But instead of the instantaneous combustion I had anticipated, there was a slight rise of her head from the menu and a neutral gaze in my direction. It was the way she looked directly into my eyes that unnerved me the most.

She set down the menu and began her words slowly and calmly. "And when I wanted another child, you made the choice for us. Isn't that a more epic family decision?" She held my vision with her steely blue eyes until I had to turn away.

Needless to say, I never brought the subject up again. So the cat stayed, and I made a good show in front of your mom to ignore it. When I was alone with that little ball of fur, though, I couldn't help but pet him. Needless to say, I was a softy when it came to children and animals and so became quite attached to our tailless Manx feline, named Bob.

Bob often sat at that same screen door from which you left, Billy, begging to leave his confinement. And when he scratched and meowed at that sliding door, I had visions of you pushing on it with your little hands and yelling, "Out, out!"

He was a free spirit like you. The question was, do we give him a longer, mundane life by secluding him, or allow him to happily roam free for the short lifespan he will have as an outdoor cat? I know what you would have said, Billy. *Be free, Bob, be free.*

JoAnn
A mother journaling through grief

Like the days following your death, Billy, I couldn't envision the event of a recovery. I couldn't, at first, see an end to my panic attacks. So I've encountered this hurdle as I did my grief before it—one meager step at a time. I've devoured every book on the subject of panic attacks and, by their instruction, started taking anti-anxiety medication. My demons of terror need to be replaced with angels of hope again. I should be more like your Godmother Susie, Billy; she has no fear of life or death.

Like the sleeping pills after your death, Billy, the anxiety medication has enabled me to regroup. I vigilantly practice deep breathing daily, exercise routinely, and have even seen a counselor for a few sessions. The books I've read say that I am within the ranks of thousands who experience anxiety attacks; the books tell me that I'm normal. How could Dick have kept his attacks a secret? And why isn't the general public knowledgeable about this horror?

I like to believe that only abstract, creative thinkers are susceptible to these attacks. One can't have a rigid mentality to experience such uncontrollable wanderings of the mind. A person has to think in grays for thoughts to enter into the hells of unbridled imagination. And extreme imagination, I've found, can lead to a fearful reality. So I tell myself that I shouldn't feel ashamed when my attacks occur; I'm one of an elite, creative group.

When I returned to work a few weeks ago, my angels with metal wings disguised as mere humans visited me again. Half of the crew members I encountered had experienced panic attacks and the other half knew someone who had. Either this curse is prevalent among flight attendants, or God has shown his face in dire times of need again.

Every day, when arriving at the airport and dreading my reaction to the confines of the airplane, a new angel comes to my aid. I had forgotten those divine visits in the first year after your death, Billy, but they've returned like a sweetly-remembered friends.

So by direction from past experience, I'll humbly and desperately reach out to you again for assistance, Lord. I still feel the injustice of my son's death and occasionally still ask, "Why did this happen to me?" But at the same time, I'm able to look at my oldest son and question, "What did I do to deserve him?"

Chapter 49

A trip to the right doctor diminished our fears of Danny's tics. We learned that Tourette's syndrome, if that's what it was, can come in varying intensities, and Danny's case seemed to be mild. His tics could be permanently controlled through medication. When Danny told us he preferred the tics to the medication, we also learned that it had concerned us more than it ever did him. He said he was unaware of his habitual noises and could stop them at any time. And he did.

The doctors removed another cancerous tumor in Susie's thigh that spring of '97, at the same time torrential floods overcame the farmlands of the Red River Valley of North Dakota. This wasn't the first or last time flooding had occurred in this area, but, that year, the flood waters reached a record high. The damage devastated many families, but Susie bounced back from her surgery as usual.

Even though cherished material items were lost and many people were left without homes in those farming communities, your mother could not muster up compassion for them. Maybe this was because they cried for their losses while embracing their children, and they spoke of the incident as a "tragedy"—the same word we used to describe your death, Billy. Bereaved parents would love to embrace their children and forfeit their homes and all their belongings instead. So, you could say that your mother had become devoid of passion for anything short of a child's death.

By that June, DevCom Leasing was gone. I hadn't realized that my self-esteem was connected to my business until the moment I read the black and white bankruptcy notice in the morning paper. And it's odd that I didn't accredit my company's failure to my gambling addiction, time spent in the bars, or my inability to budget wisely, all of which had played their roles. I solely blamed the bankruptcy on my lack of business finesse, which was not at all the case. It must have been less intrusive to blame my lack of intelligence versus my lack of common sense or addictions.

With the loss of my company, my last shred of pride was gone. I had no choice but to admit I was a failure. To recoup some of the monies to repay my creditors, I was forced to sell my dream boat, along with our snowmobiles. Our new lease cars were replaced with used ones, and I was clipping coupons along with your mother.

Even though the credit card companies were ruthless, I understood their position. Many times before, I had been on the receiving end of a loan default at DevCom. The extent of disgust I had felt for my delinquent customers was diminished by my own self-loathing every time I erased a creditor's threatening message from the answering machine. What was worse, I had to keep Danny from answering our phones while hiding the truth and my embarrassment each time. Not being able to admit my failings to my son, I promised that I would explain everything to him someday. To my relief, he patiently accepted my answer.

With no credit or cash, I had no other option but to quit my trips to the casinos. It wasn't easy; I missed the attention from the pit bosses when they greeted me by name. And I craved, just once more, to feel the awe from my fellow gamblers as I lay down a $100 chip on the blackjack table and then proceed to double down. But mostly, I missed looking forward to something, anything, after your death, Billy. My addiction was stronger than I had known.

Despite my aversion to counselors and therapy groups, I attended one Gamblers Anonymous meeting. Being an independent kind of guy, I took their folder full of information and never went back. Among other things, I practiced driving to the casino thirty miles away from our home, only to prove to myself that I could refrain from entering its doors. I successfully made many trips there and back in that manner, never leaving my car. While educating myself on the addiction, I managed to fight it myself. Though I wouldn't recommend this method of treatment, it was the manner with which I was the most comfortable.

Despite the bankruptcy and loss of my business, I began to feel a slight sense of accomplishment after conquering my gambling habit. But like before, I replaced the old addiction with a new one—even though it was a much healthier compulsion. My friend Ed became my financier and I the mechanic in the refurbishing of old boats.

JOANN

A MOTHER JOURNALING THROUGH GRIEF

Even though your dad and I still have our disagreements, we're finally comfortable with each other's grief. Previously having grieved alone at the opposite ends of the spectrum, we have gradually migrated toward the middle, finding each other there. Now, your dad speaks of you more often and I feel comfortable speaking of you less. We're able to bend to the other's wishes without our own being trampled. We've finally lifted our heads above the waters of our own grief to look around.

Just yesterday, your dad asked me why I still write in this tattered notebook, Billy. So I thought about it. My initial incentive was to preserve your memories so everyone would come to know you. I wanted a shrine built in your name, even if it's in the form of paper and ink. But now my reasons have changed; I feel the need to see my grief in a tangible print. If it's in book form, I'll be able to remember it just by opening its cover…or I can choose to place it back on the shelf when I find the need to close its pages.

Chapter 50

DICK

"That was a great catch at first base, Hon. What was going on in the outfield when David threw his glove, Dick?" Your mother started with the first of many questions that were soon to follow. She scheduled her work around Danny's sports and always looked forward to being a part of our conversations after the games. Breathless, she was running to keep up with Danny and me, while dragging a bag of baseball bats through the dirt in her wake. She took one hand off the bag to return a wave back to Tim Palm, the first firefighter at the scene of your death.

"Hey, Tim, Eddie had a great game today...see you on Thursday. You and Kristi bring the treats!" Eddie was Tim's stepson and the same age as Danny. Your mother and I had come to know Tim and his family since the day he tried to save your life. This was one of the characteristics of a small town that I enjoyed, in this case, and disliked at other times. One gets to know all and their business.

That day, we were leaving the Little League field with another win under our belt. With the demise of DevCom, I had ample time to coach all of Danny's teams. I have to admit, though, the initial idea was never mine; it had all happened by accident. After one of Danny's basketball coaches did a no-show at a mid-season practice, I stepped in; I was the only dad who didn't have a job at 3:00 in the afternoon.

Besides horse showing, I had not been much of an athlete in high school. My pitching days were put to a halt in the seventh grade when a snow-blower took the top of my middle finger on my pitching hand. Nevertheless, I had some knowledge of all of Danny's sports and had ample time to do the research.

It had always been the little things that encouraged me, so that summer, I did a little web surfing and ordered a few used coaching books on baseball. What I didn't know could be found in print or online. My idle hours were spent learning the boys' skill levels, teaching them new ones, and placing them in the correct positions—wherever they could add the most to the team. Some were natural athletes, as Danny turned out to be. I tried not to show favoritism and played all the boys equally at their young age. Sometimes, by doing so, I would err against Danny's deserved playing time in the process.

Every boy had a talent, whether it was a batting average of .400, making a difficult catch at second, being able to run to first in four seconds, or supporting his teammates from the outfield. My goal was to find out where these kids should be played, because they could all contribute to the team, whether they were natural athletes or just mediocre ones. This was my obsession; I had found another addiction.

"Oh you know David. He gets pretty wrapped up in the game. He calmed down after I benched him," I said, while unlocking the hatch to the SUV and throwing the bag of catcher gear inside. Turning around to make sure we were out of sight from the team, with one motion, I reached in my breast pocket for a pack of Marlboros, popped a stick out, and absently lit it with expertise. Glancing at Danny as he loaded the balls and bats, I inhaled and reflected on the young man he had become.

After numerous swim lessons, Danny had finally become an accomplished swimmer. He only needed to conquer his fear of the dreaded "deep end" of the pool to move up three levels in one summer. He had night terrors on occasion, but never remembered them the next morning. When he walked in the middle of his sleep, he was always on some sort of mission. We were only able to urge him back to bed by entering his fantasy and concluding his story. These nighttime excursions didn't concern me, because they usually pertained to trivial topics such as Nintendo games or baseball tournaments.

"Great game today, Bud. Matt and you made a super out at first...." I waited for that first puff of nicotine to kick in before exhaling. "......We'll have to buy you a new first base mitt; yours is a little small for this level. But then you'll need to break it in, which takes some time and work."

"I don't need a new one. This one's fine," Danny turned to look at his mother, knowing we needed to discuss any new purchase with her. She smiled at Danny and nodded in assent to my suggestion. Besides working extra hours at the airline, she was giving piano lessons to a few neighbor children and working as a librarian at Danny's school. Even though the school job was minimum wage, it had its perks. With her teacher status, she was allowed in the teacher's lounge and became privy to the school gossip. To your brother's dismay, she could keep abreast of his progress, or lack thereof.

"Hey, what about that double play in the fourth? I thought we should have tried for the triple," Danny directed the discussion toward me. Even though your mother was knowledgeable about baseball from merely listening to our conversations, he still doubted her understanding of any sport. In truth, it was, most likely, her athletic ability and not mine that was genetically passed down to your brother, Billy.

After exhaling a puff of smoke outside the car, I climbed into the driver's seat. In turn, Danny took the passenger seat next to me, and your mother rode in the back, while straining to hear the game rundown from our conversation.

"Don't get greedy, Bud. There wasn't enough time, and we're not as strong at second...Say it's your birthday next month. What do you want from Mom and Dad?" After buckling my seatbelt, I rolled the window down a crack as your mother would always request. She and Danny, in turn, did the same.

Even though your mother was a smoker herself, she didn't partake in front of Danny. He was clueless to the fact that she often snuck outside the house for a cigarette fix or chain-smoked when we went out on our Saturday night dates. And hypocritically, she disapproved of my second-hand smoke when she wasn't able to smoke herself.

"We could buy you that mitt, Hon. If we go to that used-equipment place, you wouldn't have to break it in," your mother reasoned.

"I don't want a mitt. I like my old one...I know what I want for my birthday," Danny said as he sheepishly lowered his head to unlace his baseball cleats. His feet had grown to a size twelve and his height exceeded your mother's by an inch.

"No more computer games, Bud, you have enough, and you spend way too much time staring at that screen as it is." I inhaled and then exhaled out the crack of my window.

"I don't want another computer game, Dad." Then he paused and turned his attention toward me. "I want you to quit smoking for my birthday."

Looking straight into my eyes with anticipation, he waited for my response. There was a deafening silence, and my cigarette hung limply from my lips as I pondered his question. Even your mother seemed to be holding her breath with unusual silence in the backseat.

Since taking my first puff at the age of fourteen, I had never tried to quit, let alone entertained the thought. I enjoyed the habit too much. It had something to do with that first taste of tobacco in the morning with my coffee or that absent habitual motion of inhaling between sentences during a phone conversation—or it was the nicotine. Lately, though, it felt as if my body was purging itself of poison when clearing the mucus from my lungs every morning.

I turned my attention to the road ahead and could almost feel Danny's eyes staring at my profile, waiting for an answer. "Yes, Bud, I'll quit on your birthday." There. I said it. There was no turning back. While Danny let out a big whoop, I turned to him and smiled. I had quit gambling and excessive drinking, hadn't I? I could quit smoking. *Life without nicotine. Oh, God, help me.*

~ ~ ~ ~ ~

Even though Danny wasn't aware that your mother smoked, she secretly agreed to quit with me. So for Danny's tenth birthday on September 17th, we abstained from our cigarettes through five eternal hours of Circus Pizza entertainment with ten active boys. Needless to say, it was not an ideal day to quit smoking.

I always maintained that your mother was never addicted to the nicotine, because after that day, she could still imbibe in a cigarette on occasion without becoming immersed in the habit. I was envious of her ability to bum a smoke at the bars or restaurants and not want another the next day. Knowing that I could not take one puff without revisiting my addiction and being determined not to break this promise to my son, I never touched a cigarette again.

JoAnn

A MOTHER JOURNALING THROUGH GRIEF

The rain plummeted onto the windshield as I squinted through the moving wipers. I could only manage to see the car's bumper ahead of me. That familiar, paralyzing fear permeated from my gut to my head while the panic started to rise. It took me by surprise; I hadn't had a panic attack for almost a year.

Because I knew I couldn't get through it alone, I bartered with God in the small confines of my car. Though I don't believe in prayer, I tried to at least exchange a favor for His help. I promised Him that He could use me to help others. That's how I could pay Him back, if He would only show me some proof of His existence and take the fear away. Then I saw the canoe.

Passing me in the right lane was a rusted, dilapidated car, seeming as if it had little strength to haul such a large load. The car carried a canoe on its top, and on the canoe's side was its name depicted in worn neon letters. As the canoe named FAITH passed me, my panic subsided and the rain stopped. I was to discover that God was not going to forget our agreement.

When it was time to close the door of the aircraft after boarding that morning, the passenger service agent informed me that there was a woman in the gate area who appeared to be having a panic attack and couldn't bring herself to board the airplane. At the mere mention of the word, I felt my own anxiety rise. But then I remembered my prayers of that morning. Could I help her without creating my own attack?

*When the woman mustered up the courage to get on the airplane, I spoke with her, gave her a name for her episodes, and presented her with a couple of complimentary cocktails. I still carried a book on panic attacks in my suitcase, so the woman spent the flight sipping her scotch and poring over the information. Afterwards, she was extremely thankful. God, you used **me** this time.*

Since the threat of panic attacks has once again reared its ugly head, I've had no choice but to slow down my life again. It's important that I take control of my mind, not to let it wander or question. This is a quite different method than I used to survive your death, Billy, when I had to dwell on what pained me to avoid its entirety later.

To avoid my panic attacks, I have to take those negative wanderings, discard them in the nearest container, and tightly seal the lid so they'll never escape. I like to imagine that the container is God himself, because only He can restrain my fears for me. And the lid of the container is essential—it's my seal of faith in Him. As long as that cover remains in place, He can help me through this. But I'll have to keep a constant vigilance in preventing the Pandoras of my mind from prying the lid open again.

Chapter 51

DICK

The cool winter wind blew underneath the collar of my thin nylon jacket as I piled the plastic chairs in preparation for the forecasted snowfall. My warm breath lingered through the night's darkness, turning to condensation when meeting the frigid air.

I was lost in thought that evening of November 27, 1998, wondering how another summer had managed to pass by. Even though I had quit smoking more than a year before, at that moment, I craved a cigarette.

I grabbed the last remaining chair and sat. While staring at the reflective golden hues of the moon off the lake, I could hear the gentle rush of slapping waves against the rocks in syncopation with the howling wind. The ambience sent shivers through my body. Only by anticipating the Thanksgiving gatherings of the next day with our families, could I feel a warm affection replace the coldness.

I looked forward to the next day's Thanksgiving celebration, although the Devenys would be disheartened by the empty chair at the table. It would be our first Thanksgiving without your Godmother Susie.

Even though the cancer had never diminished her courageous spirit, it had finally conquered her body. She was gone from our sight and had arrived in yours on the other side of death, Billy. Though it was a comfort to know she was with you, I dearly missed her. And while it was difficult to watch my mother's grief mirror my own of seven years before, I tried to hold on to the valuable lesson Susie's dying brought us.

I had started a new automobile consulting business at home that year. Though no profit had been made over and above my expenses, I imagined that my orders would take an upswing within the next year. And the home office business still gave me time to coach Danny's basketball, baseball and football teams.

As promised, I revealed to Danny the reason for the bankruptcy and my avoidance of creditors' phone calls—finally admitting my addiction to gambling while advising him not to follow my lead. I wanted him to take my good qualities and leave the lessons that I had already dearly paid for.

Even though your mother still felt the need to maintain a physical bond with Danny, he had become a healthy, maturing, eleven-year-old boy through his transition. Because she understood that it was natural for a boy to pull away from his mother as a preteen, she was careful not to show her affection when in the presence of his peers. Though at times when he was not consciously vigilant, his fingers would naturally entwine with hers. And he still enjoyed the relaxing back rubs that your mother had initiated at your death, Billy.

My envy of others' financial fortunes gradually changed to an emotion close to apathy. Even though I imagined winning a lottery to relieve our debt, I could still recall how we had gotten caught up in the material things our monies could buy before your death. Although some people have succeeded in doing so, it's difficult to find the true riches in life when one's burdened with material wealth. I must be honest though, if burdened with that misfortune of fortune, I would have been willing to try again.

In the wake of a June thunderstorm that year, our 1973 vintage home was transformed from harvest gold to new gray siding, and the worn tiles the winds took were replaced by a solid, new roof. While I was in the basement of a golf club enjoying a drink with my brother-in-law until the storm passed, your mother and Danny were huddled under the floor boards, sitting on the gravel of our four-foot high crawlspace.

They probably would have chosen not to experience the terror while crouching underground and praying for their lives when the deafening winds ripped the protective shell from our home. And I would have opted to avoid the yard clean-up afterward. Yet we found ourselves blessed by the result of that random act of God with the insurance-paid restoration of our home. Similarly, I could have foregone my bankruptcy in '97, but I would have missed coaching, cooking, and being the main caregiver for my son. And I would have chosen to skip the years of my grief, Billy—but would hesitate to exchange the lessons I had learned from it.

There on the deck of my lake home, I was comfortable with the person I had become after your death transformed me, Billy. I didn't feel alone, as I should have, out there in the blackness with the waves' refrain lapping on the shore; I had my family and my memories of you to sustain me. I had forgiven Denise, and most of all, I had forgiven myself. Contentment was found in the absence of self-destructive emotions left behind.

I had come to believe that tragedies happened randomly without plan or as a result of our own actions. *My anger shouldn't be directed at God,* I thought, *but at the injustices of a world that we've all created. And, I know now, that "shit" doesn't only happen to me.*

Suddenly, I could almost feel God's arm around my shoulders and your spirit standing next to me—the passion within me thawed the cold chill I had felt only moments before. As His love flowed through my body and relief consumed me, ponderous worries were suddenly lifted from my heart. I felt the brine of a lone tear flowing down my cheek and my body shook, this time not from coldness but from revelation. A summation of all my blessings enchanted me.

I spoke to God, thanking Him for my blessings, the renewal of levity in my life, and His promise of our reunion, Billy. My gratefulness flowed forward as I momentarily broke down the unyielding wall of anger I had obstinately built for so many years. Then, before I could stop the thought from crossing my mind, a thanksgiving of shocking proportions entered my prayers.

I thanked God for your death, Billy.

Never again have I been able to feel that gratitude or explain the insanity of my gratefulness on that night. I can only conclude that the thankfulness within me was for the final results, not the occurrence of your untimely departure. Nevertheless, I found the ultimate emotion of thankfulness on that monumental Thanksgiving Eve. After placing the last summer chair onto the pile, I left the haunting of that private place and took with me the final phase of acceptance.

~ ~ ~ ~ ~

She hung old ornaments of a Christmas past alongside the newly pur-chased on the Scotch pine. They commingled, those old "sweet-bitter" memories and her new circumstances, into one symbolic collage. As she unwrapped the four smiling elves, she studied the letters written on the square wooden bodies. While gently placing them in sequence upon the hutch where our four family Christmas stockings hung, the definition of the word "hope" became clear to her.

Your stocking was green corduroy, cross-stitched with intricate multi-colored rocking horses and teddy bears. It harmoniously blended with the other three of our family's. I imagine how your Aunt Susie must have painstakingly, through her illness, moved her needle with contrasting thread through each small hole in the fabric, creating a matching master-piece to Danny's stocking. Yours was finally in its allotted space next to his.

At that time, I saw a new strength in your mother that had never been evident before. As I had always been quite opinionated, she had apatheti-cally kept a distance from confrontation, caring too much about what people thought of her. Over the past seven years, however, she had gradually become steadfast on current issues and her opinions. She was comfortable in the convictions she held and wasn't afraid to defend them. That must be what happens when one experiences extremely strong emotions in life. She couldn't be dispassionate or indifferent anymore. She felt more anger, an amplified injustice, a much deeper sadness. But along with that, she also felt a richer love and extended compassion, as if grief had sensitized her soul.

My wife had changed, which didn't scare me anymore. Even though that light-hearted person she had been before your death was gone, Billy, when she experienced enjoyment, it was a deeper, lasting enrichment. You see, Bud, life could never be the same as when your spirit ran, jumped, climbed, and fell across the earth. For those of us whose lives you touched, we could only temporarily sidestep over the space you occupied.

Your mother was still experiencing some anxiety in her life, but her newfound strength enabled her to ward off the panic attacks. She accepted their threat, as she accepted many other negative circumstances in her life, which made their existence less foreboding. She concluded that her panic attacks were bottled up tears unable to escape. In essence, she had forgotten to cry.

Stepping back to view the wholeness of our family's newly hung Christmas stockings, her thoughts stopped for a moment. The blare of trumpets and choir voices from the cassette tape player filled the adorned room, and your mother caught herself singing the words with them. As with the word hope, she reflected on their meaning—joy to the world.

Joy, she thought, *shouldn't be confused with happiness. Happiness is a naïve sentiment of great feeling but little depth. Joy is more profound. It doesn't come easily, and it can only be experienced after an intense pain subsides. It can only be felt in correlation to its opposite.*

That Christmas, your mother found herself singing the emotion of joy.

JoAnn

A mother journaling through grief

My visits to your grave are infrequent now, Honey. I only go when your dad wants to, which is on your death-day and Memorial Day. Instead, I find comfort in giving donations in your name to the entity across from your gravesite, St. Joseph's Home for Children. And in lieu of driving the long distance to St. Mary's Cemetery, I'll more often visit the maple tree I planted at your daycare closer to our home. The six-foot red maple has now grown to thirty, and I always subconsciously glance in its direction when driving by it daily.

The notion to visit your grave on your birthday has crossed my mind, but the reason to go escapes me now. I don't feel driven, as I did before, to place a gift at the foot of the cement stone on every Hallmark Holiday, including Groundhog Day.

"Groundhog Day." That was the first movie I could relate to after you died, Billy. You see, my grief was that formidable Groundhog Day. Now I understand the lessons of that movie: Don't look forward or back. Merely savor the pleasures of the moment, even if you're stuck in an eternal Groundhog Day. Or, I like to say, appreciate what you have because circumstances can get worse.

I still find it hard to live with the mindset of living in the present; I don't think many people have mastered the skill. Maybe very young children can live that way, because they have only a few memories and have limited ability to look into the future. The other people who must be successful at it are those like your Great-grandma Cencic—the elderly, who have lost their memory of the past and have no need to plan for the future.

After spending ten years in a nursing home, your Great-grandma Cencic left her suffering existence at 11:45 on Halloween night of 1997. We all wished that she would have held onto life only fifteen minutes longer for a more reverent death date of All Saints Day. After all, she had attended mass nearly every day of her mobile senior years, walking three miles from her apartment in downtown Minneapolis, despite her bunions. Yet knowing her history, it does seems more appropriate that she die on All Hallow's Eve, the night to thwart the demons of this world. After all, she had been effective at praying away her abusive husband. I like to imagine that your Great-grandma's eternal retribution for her answered prayer would be the assignment of holding the end of your leash in Heaven, Billy.

I still visit your classroom on your birthday, bringing treats, a book, and a little boy angel holding the age you would be had you lived. Your classmates seem to look forward to my visits. They thank me, because they think I'm giving them something valuable, when in fact their gift of acceptance is priceless. My eyes don't tear up as before in that room anymore. You see, I can't imagine you at their age. That magical age of eighteen months is now deemed "Billy's Age"—you'll always be a toddler to me.

The sliding door you so easily walked through that summer of '91 is starting to stick, as the one before it did. And the room where your crib once stood is still "Billy's Room." The other day I had to laugh at myself when opening the dresser drawer to find six full bottles of baby oil. I found humor in both—the futility of my efforts to bring you back through a baby contest and that the drawer hadn't been cleaned in eight years. The milk stains from your toppled bottles still mark the legs of our living room furniture. I tell people that I can't bear to wipe away those memories of you, in truth, I'm still the antithesis of Martha Stewart.

When I'm asked, "How are you?" I can respond, "Good!" without any pretense. Having once believed that grief would always be my companion, I'm now able to shove it aside. I know that I can dwell on it on a later date by merely watching your videos or opening this journal. In that way, I can chose to allow happiness back in my life or conjure up the roots of pain that formed me.

The morbid dreams of your ravaged body are gone, Billy; they've gradually abated and have surrendered their torture. Sometimes I miss those nightmares, because these days, my dreams of you are infrequent. Now when I hear those passing sirens in front of our house, I merely thank God that they're not for us. And that blood-stained tank top, which I wore when I held you last, has been discarded, along with many other defeating emotions.

Even the transitional seasons have become easier to face since I've stopped trying to hold the world's rotation for you. Instead of seeing a new day as leaving you behind, I see time's passing as a step closer to our reunion. Nevertheless, I would determinedly defy death to tear me away from your brother.

When Danny and I leave each other, I still say good-bye as if it could be our last. The fear of his death doesn't consume me anymore, but I vow never to be caught unprepared again. And Danny will never be an only child in name. I'll always claim to have two children. But I've accepted that I'll never have another child. Not because I don't deserve it, but because God doesn't owe me anything.

At times, I catch myself not thinking about you at all, Billy. But more surprisingly, this revelation comes without guilt. And even though the discomfort will always be there in the core of my heart, I'm able to continue living just in knowing the nightmare is past.

And when I walk through the sunshine beneath the silver clouds
I long to touch your golden curls, I want to cry out loud
Oh, let the Lord rock you gently in His loving arms, my dear
Until I see you again.
—Billy's Song

Chapter 52

DICK, 2002

*J*t was an unspoken occasion, but everyone knew why we were gathered. Your death date had become like this, Billy, an occasion to unite, instead of a remembrance of separation. This was a celebration of family, a time for the adults to catch up on conversation and for the cousins to reacquaint themselves since our last reunion.

New Year's Eve of 2000 had come and gone without the world ending or computers crashing, George W. Bush assumed the presidency, and Los Angeles Sparks' Lisa Leslie became the first woman to dunk a basketball. The impact of the terrorist attacks of 9/11 was still fresh in America's mind, even though it had been almost a year since those events. While the economy suffered after that monumental event, the world had moved on, Billy, just as it did after your death.

Because 9/11 took its toll on the airline business, your mother was taking another hefty pay cut. Our finances were meager and still the main focus of our arguments, yet it was times like these, at the lakeshore, which made us more determined to stay together. Our house was never sold, because we couldn't imagine leaving our lake home or the shores on which you played and died.

Even though I laughed with my guests, I could still feel the pain when glancing at the empty spot next to my father. My mother was never the same after Susie's death; her dwindling weight and advanced age finally took her that May. Even though the doctors said that the COPD finally overcame my mother's body, I knew it had been her daughter's death that had ravaged her spirit over the last four years. But like her daughter, that was not achieved without a fight.

Some of Danny's friends were there. I knew Matt, Josh, Joey, and Chris because I had coached them all. The girls were new to me, except for Kendra, the little girl who witnessed your helicopter ride at the soccer field. After meeting at school that year, Danny and Kendra became good friends, though neither was aware of Kendra's part in your story when she was only three years old. The intrigue of small-town living.

I couldn't help but smile at the dynamics between the genders. The boys were more animated than usual, and the girls were in constant giggle mode. *Yes, Danny was at that age*, I thought while watching him splash water at two of the girls, who both jumped back from the water's edge, screaming, though really enjoying the attention.

Danny had let go of the blame he felt in regard to your death, Billy. And most importantly, he still remembered your good-bye to him. But I would never know how your death had altered him. I couldn't help but remember his action figure battles, his who-is-stronger-than-who riddles, or his intent to be a stalwart garbage man when I witnessed his controlling nature. He had a tendency to be in charge of every situation, which often required patience from his overpowered peers. Yet, this was a facet of the survival techniques he had acquired when his life veered off-course, and he needed to hold on to those attributes for a later date.

Your Grandpa Joe took the empty seat next to Grandpa Frank on the bench under the maple tree, and even from a distance, I could see the camaraderie exchanged between them. A slow smile appeared on my father's face as he spoke, and then he laughed with his mouth wide enough to see the gold fillings in his back molars. *My dad must have told another one of his lame jokes,* I thought as Grandma Jen joined them all in laughter. In reality, people didn't find my father's jokes amusing, it was the intense enjoyment he found in telling them that made us all laugh.

That day, the water's temperature was much the same as the day you had died, yet it was not foreboding for me or the guests invited there. The sandy bottom appeared pure again. Your grandparents' chairs were positioned on the shady side of our yard under a large maple tree, while your aunts and uncles were crammed on our small deck and your cousins were dispersed in the water a few feet away. The older ones were engaged in a game of volleyball over a makeshift net I had extended between two dock posts in the shallow water. The younger ones were swimming on the other side of the dock in the warm mid-July water under the close surveillance of your Aunt Diane.

Your aunt and I, who had previously butted heads throughout our youth, had come to develop a closer relationship in the wake of our sister's and mother's deaths and through our mutual concern for Grandpa Frank's care. I had become a tad less stubborn in my conversations with her, because one of the lessons I had learned from death was an appreciation for the living.

I moved over to your mother's side and put my arm around her shoulder. Deep in conversation with her brother Tom, she instinctively nuzzled into me without skipping a beat in rebuttal to his viewpoint. Although she and Tom had a close relationship, her brother loved to play the game of devil's advocate with her as did I. Enjoying the show, I merely listened while trying not to smile. Life was not back to the way it was before your death, Billy—but it had comfortably become stable. While mingling in the sunshine with your mother at my side on that day of July 13th, I analyzed my life and found it pretty damn good.

Our families never overstayed their welcome, and when one left, the others would abruptly follow. So when they all said their good-byes in unison that day, there was enough time left for my family of three to make the road trip to your grave for the last time.

~ ~ ~ ~ ~

The boughs of the trees arched over the road, seeming to protect our passage as we navigated the familiar path. So different from the road on which we traveled from the hospital eleven years before.

"Look Dick, a gosling...we have to stop!" Your mother spoke at the same time I saw the injured baby goose in the center of the road ahead of us. It was evident that there was no hope for his life. While the gosling struggled for breath, a mother goose stood in the long grasses at the side of the road, stretching her neck in the air and honking at her fated child.

"It's dying, Babe. There's nothing we can do," I reasoned, while noticing the five other goslings safely grouped around their mother's flapping wings. Your mother nodded. You see, she knew all about that mother's desire to waddle into the oncoming traffic to comfort her suffering offspring. But your mother also understood the reason for that goose to turn around and leave the roadside—carrying her pain with her as she guided her other young goslings into the safety of the nearby bushes. That mother knew that her own life and those of her goslings would be wastefully ended if she ventured to the place where her agony led her. I drove around the gosling, taking care not to injure him further as your mother watched the image fade behind us through the side mirror.

So from the lesson of that goose, your mother turned her attention from the mirror, left the roadside of your death, and finally said good-bye. Not a farewell to you, Bud, but a farewell to the pain.

As we approached your gravesite, I immediately noticed the devoted elm tree was gone from your grave—leaving only an insignificant stump in its place. Its leaves and branches had gradually withered and emaciated with each pilgrimage there. We could accept its removal more graciously after watching its deterioration in opposite correlation to our recovery. While accepting the absence of that elm tree at the head of your grave, I also accepted the absence of my child from my life. I was able to cling to the ethereal qualities of my bond with you, Billy, because I had learned to base my beliefs on the intangibles. I guess you could call that faith.

Your mother stood by my side and bent over to place a pot of blooming daisies at our feet. Our arms held each other in a stronger bond than before, because we embraced the reality versus the denial of our child's death. Having worked so diligently through the odds of a statistically-fated, bereaved marriage, the journey had strengthened our marriage with defiance. Through it all, your mother and I had become more like each other. It's somewhat sad and somehow ironic why we had to part in this vein.

A tear trickled down my cheek, and I felt your mother's hand tighten around my waist. She knew that the tear wasn't for you, Billy, but for your Grandma Helen. You must know, Bud, that at that time, my mother's death had not thoroughly been grieved for yet. But even then, I knew my grief work for her would not be as difficult as the years following your death, Billy. Her death wasn't like yours; it was her time to die, it wasn't yours.

Noticing my tears, Danny joined us to fortify the totality of our family. His arms naturally wrapped around my upper back as he leaned his head on my shoulder. While we embraced by your gravesite, I remembered how those little three-year-old arms grew from their secure position around my knees, to my thighs, and how quickly they had elevated to their present position. And I thought, in that moment, that it was an odd setting for the wholeness of my family to awaken in me. Our trio's combined pilgrimage to your gravesite brought on a warm essence of completeness. Our mutual loss bound us together in embrace while we committed ourselves to your gravestone at our feet.

With my wife on one side and my eldest son on the other, the sun shone warmly upon our heads, and the birds, once more, sang in homage to the kind and gentle intentions of the world. We had taken on the challenge of living, not despite the tragedies but because of them. An inner growth had occurred only because we had allowed it

In the spot before the burial of your body, Billy, the secret of surviving the movie of life revealed itself. The film keeps rolling even though we only have knowledge of one scene. He alone has the whole storyline, so only He can make some kind of sense of it. I had to trust in that.

So I watched as your mother bent over the daisies in front of your headstone to pluck a withered, dying flower from its stem, allowing a new bud to grow. And we left your grave, Billy, knowing that even though one horrible summer had never ended and was followed by a long, dark winter—spring had somehow arrived.

JoAnn
A MOTHER JOURNALING THROUGH LIFE

I find it difficult to imagine the different course my life would have taken on that hot day in July had you not died, Billy. You see, my fantasies of your life up to the age of twelve are more obscure than the stark reality of the eleven years of your absence.

But you must know, Honey, that the lessons of your life will never leave my memory. They'll forever be inscribed in the final credits of my life's story. And I'll continue to hold onto your mischievous escapades that bring warmth and remembrance, without allowing myself to be stuck in the afterlife with you, Honey. While I live on this earth a while longer, I'm look forward to giving the overflow of my love to your brother.

I'll continue to hold onto my faith, and I'll never deny the One who helped me through hell and back. I often pour coffee as a Women's Guild member on the occasion of a funeral in the church's dining hall, as my colleagues did at yours, Billy. And the musical skills God gave me for therapeutic comfort, I'm giving back to Him as a pianist for our services. The same congregation I once found cold and rigid has become the roots of my faith and has helped sustain my faith convictions. But I don't embrace any religion in its entirety. It's the contradictions that baffle me.

I believe in the same generalities of many Christian religions. I believe that the bible is God-inspired and the finest written manual on how to survive life. I believe that God is the reason for our existence and that Jesus is not only our savior, but the symbol of the compassion we show for each other.

When I'm disgusted with a television evangelist, who takes money from the poor to pay for his private jet, I try to remember that when people live outside moral principles in the name of their God, it's a reflection on them, not Him. And for those who live within those ethical principles, but call Him by another name, we must worship the same entity. If the name of their god stands for the same loving compassion and principles as mine, He must be the same Supreme Being, because there is only one. I'm beginning to think that the differences in the world's religions are only evident through semantics.

Even though the details of our afterlife can only be guessed, I imagine that time is as nonexistent there as it is in our dreams. When we fall asleep and then awaken, we have no understanding of the lapsed time until we look at our clocks on the night stand. In our dreams, the visions may seem to last many hours, but may only be a moment of fantasy. Or is your world the reality, Honey, and am I only waiting to wake up? I like to imagine that's the reason why you're not missing me, Billy. When we meet again, it will seem to you as if it were only seconds before that we parted. Our love will transcend time and connect us to the same moment when our physical bond was broken.

When finally arriving where you are, I like to imagine finding a continuance of knowledge; knowledge of eternal subjects that are unfathomable to me now. Tiers of occupations in the "big conglomerate" above will be rated in pious tiers instead of financial levels. Those of us who have far to go in our spirituality may need to labor in a less-enriching position, much like an assembly-line job, until we achieve the inner love we failed to learn on earth.

I believe our homes will be comfortable, though some with less majesty than others. Some of us will need to build our faith brick by brick, having failed to do it on Earth. I like to picture Heaven this way. These are my own thoughts and not intended to be taken as fact—I haven't been there yet. Some might say that my beliefs could cause me to burn in Hell, if I believed in one.

I like to imagine that we'll have an opportunity to redeem ourselves in Heaven. How could a murderer be condemned to an infinite punishment if he was denied a teacher in love? Or, how could a deranged psychopath be committed to eternal death for his violence when his mind was altered by the birth God gave him? I tend to hold on to the conviction of a just and rewarding God. While resolving that life is not fair, I believe that the afterlife is.

But now I know that the specifics of your new daycare won't become known to me until I finish my drive through the rush hour of life and enter those celestial doors to pick you up after my work shift of life is over. Be assured, I will have many questions demanding to be answered once I get there.

I've learned to diligently wait for those precious moments with you, because, you see, bereaved parents are the most patient populace in this world. Our lives are measured by a time clock counting down the seconds to our anticipated reunion with our children.

So I'll linger in life here until the time comes when I actually feel your body's weight in my arms and my fingers touch your soft hair. I trust that I'll be able to rub my nose against your cheek to smell your distinctive aroma. And when I experience that face hug again, that will finally be the moment when the only good-byes are to the eternal longings and the only hellos are to an eternity without them.

That will be the time when the scars of your death will disappear. They'll be erased from my memory the second your body's in my arms, just in knowing that I'll never feel that emptiness again. After living through hell on this earth, I'll be able to relish in the elation of Heaven when I gaze into your sparkling eyes with a love I was so long denied giving. And I know you'll hear me when I speak to you, Honey. My words will finally find their audience when I receive a soft response from your eyes after I say them.

That's when I'll finally say good-bye to my comrade of grief and whisper to you with joyful ecstasy, "Hello, my little bluebird."

THE HOSPITAL
SEPT. 6, 2002

"The MRI is showing that it's an inoperable brain hemorrhage from the leukemia. I'm so sorry..." The doctor's voice was distant, but clear, as he spoke of me. I heard a gurgling, syncopated rasp in the background, and realized it was coming from me.

Trying to the best of my ability, I could not form a word with my lips. I was so tired, yet strived to stay awake long enough to tell them that I was all right. There was no pain anymore—my headache was gone.

Though I was unable to speak, I had no problem hearing their anguished sobs. I was also unable to move, yet could feel them both at my bedside, one at my right shoulder and the other at my right arm. Danny's hand was caressing my hand, and I tried to give him back a reassuring grip. *It's okay. I'll be fine. Please don't cry.* I wanted to tell him this. I wanted to hold my son, and comfort him, but could not.

"I love you. It's okay to leave. We'll be okay," Danny bravely vowed to me between his sobs. Feeling as if my head nodded in concurrence, I sighed and then let go.

Beyond the door
There's peace I'm sure
And I know there'll be no more
Tears in heaven.
—*Tears in Heaven*

ACT II

DICK

I'll stop my ramblings for now, Bud. As I've said before, this is your mother's story, not mine. I've relayed your mother's grief to you because I feel her pain more and, somehow, don't remember mine anymore. It's vanished along with my anger, my guilt, and my addictions. It's not merely buried, as it has been for so many years. It's gone, so completely gone.

I can honestly say I don't miss her, yet I love her more deeply than ever. And I'll always pray for the joy and happiness she deserves. And even though we're not together, somehow I feel closer to her. And, of course, I am always there whenever Danny needs me. I'm so proud of him and the man he has become. My impressionable son, who bravely survived through his brother's death, his own guilt, and the transformation of his parents. He has allowed himself to be molded into a strong, sensitive, and responsible young man because of it. I couldn't be prouder.

Oddly, I feel as if you already knew everything I've been telling you, Billy—so I've said enough. Now it's time to bask in the absence of pain; that wonderful void has been filled with pure elation. Now I want to relive those moments trapped in time. Has it been only seconds or hours since I swept you into my arms?

It was a scene that had often replayed itself in my imaginings. The movie reel started when I let go of Danny's hand and found you running toward me. I leaned forward with my arms outstretched, waiting for the familiar back pain that had always plagued me and felt none. I smiled at the image of my spirited son.

"Dahdee!" you squealed while running through a glowing aura of brightness and neared my embrace. Simultaneously, you collided into my chest and your little arms wrapped around my neck as I wholeheartedly received them.

"I've missed you, Bud," I whispered into your golden curls and tightly held you in my arms. The warmth of our bond engulfed us and seemed to permeate outward and around us. I could almost see it.

"I love you, Dahdee." The words didn't seem to come from your lips, but I heard them clearly.

How long have I been sharing my thoughts while rocking you? I can do anything here. I'm able to hold you in my lap in this white, bentwood rocker merely by wanting it. No more waiting for anything. I can't feel the anger I've harbored for so many years—it doesn't matter anymore, because the concept of time is leaving me with each sentence I relay to you. Have I been speaking or merely thinking? Oddly, that doesn't concern me either because I know you understand me completely.

My home is a beautiful cottage decorated with a collage of textured cream tones, but I know nothing can soil here. There is a large window to see out with no glass as a barrier to the outside. Yet, I don't worry about rain, wind or snow—somehow I feel safe. Through the frame of the window I see a lake with beautiful aqua hues; the surface is calm, the bottom is clean, and I know that you could never die there.

The hills beyond the lake are filled with colors that I can't name, and they're intricately clear to me without the aid of my driving glasses. I know that you can run and play there without ever falling or getting hurt. The hill seems to be in the distance though I know I can reach it in a moment, just by wanting to. And if I ventured there I would find that's not where its beauty ends. Nothing ends here. There is no bottom, no top, and no sides.

The colorful meadows at the base of the hills are vast, but I'm unable to guess their acreage. The concept of distance and size seems to escape me, but that doesn't concern me either. What would be the purpose of measuring where there are no boundaries? Nothing ends here. Everything is infinite.

The distant sound of laughing voices comingles with the water's gurgle and the whispering wind, and it soothes my senses. Your mother and I were wrong about the word *hope*, Billy. *Hope* isn't looking forward to a positive event, nor is it wishful thinking. It's a destination.

A comforting warmth intensifies as if coming toward me. Mother! Susie! They're so complete and young. And there are others with them; beautiful people who seem familiar, yet I have no names for them. Their love becomes more intense with each moment, and the whole of my thoughts are becoming as equally pure as their love.

The warmth surrounds us, Billy, coming from every direction, enveloping us within a blanket of softness. While I hold you inside this loving embrace, I feel complete, unadulterated happiness. No, it's joy… it's joy that overwhelms me!

And then there's the light, that glorious light…

JoAnn

A mother journaling through life

In my dream, I wrapped the familiar blue outfit around your body, noticing the multi-colored sailboats decorating the shirt. Your eyes were closed as I adjusted the garment around your torso and placed the pants that matched around your diapered bottom. Then your eyelids opened.

Your pupils were the color of the sky, sparkling like the stars. Your lips parted and your cheeks flexed into an animated grin with recognition and love.

You were eighteen months old. You were not brain-damaged, you were not decomposed—you were alive. You were finally back!

DANNY, BILLY'S BROTHER
2012

It's funny what a person remembers…and what a person forgets.

The first thing I can remember before the age of five is walking up our driveway toward the house with Denise, thinking that it was nothing more than a game. I knew that Billy was missing, but, for whatever reason, I remember being more excited than worried by the novel event. I casually followed in tow as we proceeded into the house and toward the back screen door, all the while contemplating the possible frivolous outcomes from a three-year-old perspective.

Then, the scream. I've forgotten the rest.

I guess it's pretty well-established that people lack the neurological faculties to remember events from when they are very young. In my case, I can't recall one day prior to July 13, 1991, and I can't recall a single thought or occasion within months after that scream. In essence, I've only preserved one retrospective, horrific series of moments from the first four years of my life.

Although there are numerous photographs and videos documenting Billy's and my time together and no doubt, my mother can attest to the bond we shared, I can't remember a single experience I shared with my brother apart from his death. It's a depressing thought. So the fact that I still miss him gives me some strange comfort now.

I have plenty memories of my father. But as time progresses and no matter how much I fight it, the memories start to fade. However, I can still vividly remember the last thing he said to me in the hospital before my family was diminished: "No regrets." It's a generic platitude to be sure. But as my father's final sentiment, it has taken on some meaning for me, and I think it's particularly relevant here.

I don't regret a single moment I spent with my brother or my dad, remembered or not. I don't regret how much they meant to me to leave such a painful void. I don't regret how our family broke down, healed, and in some ways, grew as a result of their deaths. And I don't regret a thing about the only part that's left.

In the end—though I may not remember much—I doubt I'll ever forget that.

Epilogue

JoAnn

A MOTHER'S CONVERSATIONS WITH HER FAMILY

2012

*T*he boughs of the willow tree hang over the sunset, sheltering while still allowing the beautiful image between their branches. Orange and pink blend together above the horizon, creating a pathway of sparkling stars on the blue, rippling water below. My iPod is spewing unforgotten songs, memories of a different time.

The lake that took you has become somewhat like an estranged friend to me, Billy. Gradually, but cautiously, we've made amends. I know now that the method of your death had nothing to do with my pain; it didn't matter how you left, just that you did. This isn't just the place where you died; it has become the last place you had lived. That's why I feel nearer to you here.

I often sit on the deck like this for hours; talking to you, feeling your presence, watching the movement in the crest of the water. While I feel a dark respect for its power over your life, at the same time, I feel peace at the shores of your spirit. I can still find you here, blending the lessons of your life into mine.

I watch as the mallard swims under the dock with her three ducklings. She's been around since her babies were fuzzy little downy balls—to her dismay and her ducklings' demise. There were seven of them this spring; it must have been that muskrat that lives in the channel.

Food dishes and drink glasses remain on the patio table, left over from a social gathering of friends only moments before. A feeling of camaraderie is still fresh in the air as I take the last sip from my wine glass and automatically pour more from the bottle in front of me. This is my last glass, no more tonight.

Even though I have many friends, I'm alone in the house now. Sometimes I feel as if a time machine has moved me back to my youth, and I find myself single again. Did that other life with my family really happen, or did I dream it? While things have drastically changed, sometimes I feel as though I've ventured miles to find myself right back where I started, only with the physical wear and tear to prove it. At other times I feel as if I had died too, then reincarnated and dumped back on Earth—leaving me to find out who I really am. But most of the time, I feel the strength that I've gained through the journey and how it has formed me. I've come a long way from hell and survived it.

I often think of the of people who were involved in the final scene of your life, Billy. There were so many who expended every effort to save you; but through your death, they have a common tie. Many of them thought they should have saved you, like I did. But I hope they have come to understand, as I have, that the future can't be foreseen so it can't always be prevented.

As I've come to reacquaint myself with these people involved in your last day, Billy, I'm finding that each is known by others as a compassionate, giving person in the present and has made a positive impact on the world. Did they all have those traits before your death, and that's why they tried to save you? Or were they transformed as soon as you ventured into the water, as I was? I imagine it was both, Billy. When your body hit the water, the impact you made didn't stop in that spot beside our neighbor's dock. The rippled current of your actions continued its motion far beyond and through the lives of all involved. Like the children of the

Oklahoma City bombing, I have to conclude that, even though your life didn't touch one thousand souls, your death did.

I miss your father still, Billy, despite and because of all we had been through. The accomplishments of his life are at a forefront of my thoughts, instead of his failures. He would be surprised that his real eulogy is the merits of his fatherhood and youth coaching and not of business or financial gain. I loved him more than I ever knew. Though, it's comforting to know that your dad is watching you. It's only fair for him to raise a teenager, too. I'm amused by that thought.

The overhead light above me goes out and leaves only the moon's glow on the deck. I wonder if I have extra light bulbs inside. Before your dad's death, I didn't even know there were lights outside the house to change. I guess I also needed your dad more than I knew. The moon is bright enough tonight, I'll change it tomorrow.

"*Wooo…wooo,*" the faithful loon croons to me again.

Hello, Dick. A tear gathers in the corner of my eye, and I remember the coffee mugs you bought two weeks before you died—before we knew you were sick. The leukemia hit hard and fast; Tuesday we went to the doctor. By Friday you were gone. The mugs you bought us two weeks before were decorated with two loons swimming side by side. After all, loons, in the wild, mate for life.

Was it the benzene that car manufacturers use in new cars that caused a perfectly healthy forty-nine-year-old to die of a mutation of the cells? Would your platelets have survived had you not personally delivered all your new lease cars, Dear? And had we stayed home that day, would Billy have lived?

You have to admit, Dick, that I finally managed to acclimate myself to our family of three. And after you left, I could even pretend that Danny and I were complete. Now with only two small felines and me at home, it's more difficult to remember the feeling of family—two brothers laughing together, a small hand in mine, or a husband's arms around my shoulder. I even miss the teasing from you and Danny, that male camaraderie a mother could never understand. But I won't ask why of God anymore. I've learned that my questions won't be answered yet. It's just a waste of my time.

Even though I would still be offended if someone else stated that Billy's death was "meant to be," as time goes by, I find myself entertaining the notion. And maybe our marriage was not intended to have fulfilled our infinite dreams, but was meant to create memories we can cling to now. Were you and I not meant to grow old together, Dick? Maybe we weren't destined to conceive a second child, so God merely lent Billy to us for a little while. I guess I've let go of my anger at God for letting Billy die, and I've let go of blaming you for denying me that third child. Because, maybe, our second was the big miracle.

With my wine glass in hand, I leave the deck to walk among the newly planted bushes, flowers, and trees in our yard. I still hesitate on the possessive pronouns, Dear, even though it's been eight years since you left and the landscaping has been reinvented by my own muscle, a shovel, and a wheelbarrow; a revisiting of my mining days. But I've found more pleasure in working with the soil, versus the red clay of the Iron Range.

I've surrounded myself with foliage. I want tall trees, lush bushes, and colorful flowers everywhere, so only the lake, the greenery, and the sunset are visible from the deck. Even though I entertain many friends here, my gardens and my lake shore are my refuge. This is where I can talk to you both, and God.

It was exceptionally difficult for me when Danny left home for his freshman year of college six years ago. When I hugged him at the door of his dorm and then drove off, the tearing of my heart was familiar. And it took me a few months to be able to walk by his empty room at home without tears. But it was time for him to leave me; it was his choosing. Besides, he came back home each summer to earn some cash for college by working as a captain with Al & Alma's charter boat company. And now he's starting his second year of law school. He's everything you wanted him to be, Dear.

I'm sure you know that the aftermath of your death hasn't been as hard for me as Billy's. But it has no reflection on my love for you; you know how deep a parent's love is. And maybe you know, now, what a wonderful father you turned out to be.

Even when you had no job, I tried to convince you that caring for Danny with unconditional love was the most important thing a person could accomplish in this life. Your money is gone, but Danny will forever fulfill your legacy.

I can admit now that I wasn't the perfect wife, and I wish I would have told you how important you were to me. But because of the last words you spoke to Danny and me, I'll feel no guilt. "No regrets." Thanks to you, I haven't dwelled on the what-ifs of your death, as I did with Billy's.

I approach the south deck garden and, with my calloused fingers, pinch off a couple of dying lilies that have completed their bloom life. This is what I call your rose garden, Dick, even though there are no roses growing here. I remember the fall of 2002 when I removed the sod to create this garden in your memory. That was when the loon first appeared. Because you had always given me four long-stemmed roses on my birthday and Valentine's Day to represent the members of our family, I chose to plant red rose bushes in your garden. Ironically, I couldn't keep the rose bushes alive, so I replaced them with these colorful perennials, which are easier to maintain. After all, and to coin a song's lyrics, you never promised me a rose garden, Dick. The Russian sage, lilies and cone flowers will do.

"Wooo...woo," the loon's cry carries over the water.

Many people have asked if my faith has been enriched since your death, Dick, and my answer is always decisive. You see, even though God and I still have our personal conflicts, my attitude toward Him is never indifferent. What I do know is that when you're searching upward, you need to look through the clouds to see the light. At times, I'll curse God as I never did before, but often feel a rich gratitude in my heart when I praise Him as frequently. And even though I may show anger toward Him on occasion, we always stay in touch. Sounds like an intimate relationship to me.

I feel the coolness of the wine trickle down my throat as I take my last sip. Even though the glass is half-full, I empty the white liquid over the stone wall into the lake water and return to my chair on the deck. Wrapping my cardigan sweater around my torso to fend out the night air, I notice how the cooler weather is returning, starving the delicate yellow leaves of the trees. I contemplate their majestic limbs, allowing their once-young sprouts to fall to the earth. The fallen leaves rot on the ground and replenish the tree's roots, using their energy to create new sprouts for the next spring.

Even though the bench under the tree is empty, I can almost see Grandpa Joe and Grandpa Frank sitting there, sharing their wisdom, solving the world's problems, and laughing at a lame joke. This is how I like to picture them now that they are gone, too.

Since your death, Dick, I've learned to adapt to circumstances over which I have no control. Life is a continual onslaught of acceptances. And, Billy, as every bereaved parent must eventually do, I've learned to accept the most unacceptable. By doing so, my longing for the reversal of your death is gone. I accept that your death could have been prevented by me, yet this knowledge doesn't consume me; even if it was partially my fault, it was not my intent. And I accept that my prayers will, most often, not be answered, or at least not to my liking.

But the one thing that I can't accept is that God has no control over this world. Because I have heard too many loon calls, been graced with too many daisies, been touched by too many little angels, and I've seen too many bluebirds.

Afterword-Disclaimer

ames and dates may have been changed. All events are true as experienced by or relayed to the author. All viewpoints narrated by the character "Dick" were relayed to, experienced by, or surmised by the author. Statements made after the chapters by other persons were either approved of and used with permission, or written by those mentioned. The only event faithfully imagined by the author is Act II, on pages 348 through 350.

The Deveny Family Photo Gallery

Billy's baptism (July,1990) - The author, Billy, Danny, and Dick Deveny

Billy and Danny
(August, 1990)

Danny and Billy at the lakeshore
(October, 1990)

The outfit from Grandma Helen
was too big in October, 1990. It
fit perfectly for Billy's burial.

Billy (December, 1990)

Billy (January, 1991)

Billy saying, "Well, guys, you did
what you could." (January, 1991)

Billy's 1st
birthday
(January 16,
1991)

Billy (March, 1991)

Billy sporting the bandage from his
St. Paddy's day burn (March, 1991)

Billy, showing bruise
from swing (May, 1991)

Billy (April, 1991)

Danny, Billy, and Dick (May, 1991)

Billy
(June, 1991)

Billy (June, 1991)

Billy (July, 1991) sitting in the screen door through which he escaped, with the lake in the background.

Billy (July, 1991)

Danny and Billy (July, 1991)

Danny, JoAnn, and Billy
(July 4, 1991)

Danny and Billy, horsing around.
The day Billy died (July 13,1991)

Danny and Dick, basketball coach
(January, 2000)

The Devenys—March, 2002 (above)
August, 2002 (below)

Dick, coaching baseball
(August 2002)

Danny's birthday
(September 17, 2012)

Danny and JoAnn (Thanksgiving, 2009)

Lyrics to Billy's Song

Song and text by Jennifer Kuzma Adamczeski & JoAnn Kuzma Deveny

Refrain:
Somewhere a child has risen
Someday I will rise
To meet you gladly,
My precious Billy, my precious Billy.

Verses:
I see your smile in the sunrise and the twinkle in your eye
When I wake up in the morning, when I count the stars at night
Your laughter follows me in the whistling of the wind
And your song stays in my heart

The darkness of that summer day was hidden in sunlight,
When you smiled at me the last time, and we both sang your goodnight
You didn't want to leave me, I thought you never would
A voice said, "Let it be," I wish I could.

Your costume was a pumpkin in the picture on our wall
Now it's in a box of memories, lying crumpled in a ball.
Why do monsters come from graveyards,
With death's goblins everywhere,
When my baby is sleeping there?

A turkey's in the oven, the table's spread for all to see
The yams are ripe for eating, I feel love surrounding me.
Lord, why can't I be thankful—my faith, please be restored
When my family's no longer four?

I feel the wonder of the season and the gift God gave to me
The Babe within the manger, who died to set you free,
The angels sing their carols to you in your home above,
All I can give you is a gift of love.

It makes me smile to see you dancing, joy glowing from your face
When I gaze into the flicker of the candles on your cake.
You came to me a miracle; you left me so much more.
Happy Birthday, my little boy.

Oh, little Valentine, sweet Valentine, please mend my broken heart,
Wrap your arms around me dear, as though we weren't apart.
Cupid pull your arrow back and let my message fly
To my angel in the sky.

The tears still warm my cheeks remembering the happiness I lost,
Just like the Mother Mary as her Son died on the cross.
Easter brought you gifts of bunnies and gave you life that never ends,
And I'll rise to hold you again.

When I walk through the sunshine underneath the silvery clouds
I long to touch your golden curls, I want to cry out loud
Oh let the Lord hold you gently in His loving arms my dear,
Until I see you again.

Bridge:
Oh, the joy that you brought us, the love that you gave
The light of your presence
Will shine in your name
Will shine every day

Acknowledgments and Thanks to:

- The Water Patrol Officers: Ken Schilling (the sheriff), as well as Jamie Demarais, Rich Kitzmiller, and Debra Rankl, the female sheriff who stayed at my side

- Dr. Randy Pilgrim (the doctor) and Nurse Beth Warner

- Jim Ross (911 dispatcher)

- Kevin Berg (the fisherman), Troy Anderson, Paul Berg, Ray Berg (Cayman's master), and Todd Erickson

- Officer Ron Bostrom (in memoriam) and the Mound Police Department.

- Tim Palm (firefighter), Jeff Anderson (firefighter), Kevin Sipprell, Phil Fisk, Jim Casey, and the Mound Volunteer Fire Department

- Rev. Greg Bodine (the man with Jesus Eyes)

- Waconia Hospital Paramedics

- Father Mike Tegeder and Nore Chandler Siers, his pastoral minister.

- Mary Adrian-Larson, Jeannette Clifford, Sandy Dougherty, Rita Gurney, Linda Wigner, Sue Weidenbach, Tamara, and Ellen (alias), a few of my many angels with metal wings

- The caregivers: Teresa Bockes, Odessa, Beth and Jessica VanPoll, and especially Denise, for making Billy's earthly experiences loving ones

- All our friends for their support, especially Sheryl Galonski, Shirley Meinecke, Rick Meinecke, Jeri Ostenson, Ed Worley, and Jim Fox

- The Kuzma and Deveny families, all whose persistence of concern and financial help sustained Danny, Dick, and me throughout the years to the present

- "My buddy" Liz Eggers, one of the few people who knew Billy and his antics well and never let me forget

- Those who helped me in the process of writing and proofreading my book: Marla Erickson, Kathy and Joe Grafft, and of course, my publisher, Kira Henschel

- My husband Dick (in memoriam), who hopefully understands that I had to put "words in his mouth" to make our story more universally appealing

- My son Danny, who has allowed his private life to be exposed to help others persevere through a similar nightmare

- Marge Heegaard, Danny's art therapist

- To all the nameless, but fondly remembered, souls unmentioned, who held my hand or toppled a boulder out of the way throughout my grief journey

Resources and References

- The Compassionate Friends, bereaved parent's support group. www.*compassionatefriends.org*

- FDA Phobia website. 18% of U.S. population experiences anxiety attacks

- Guggenheim, Judy & Bill. The ADC Project, PO Box 536365, Orlando, Florida 32853, for research statistics on after-death communication with children.

- Joncas, Michael. Composer, *On Eagle's Wings,* words based on Psalm 91.

- Kubler-Ross, Elizabeth (1926-2004). *On Death and Dying,* 1969.

- Marshall, Peter. Quote "Those we love are with the Lord and the Lord has promised to be with us…"

- Niebuhr, Reinhold. *Serenity Prayer.* 1943

- Parents Anonymous, a nonprofit organization for the prevention of child abuse, www.parentsanonymous.org

- Rubin, Ramis & Danny (screenplay). Ramis, Harold (director). *Groundhog Day,* 1993.

- St. Joseph's Home For Children; 1121 East 46th Street, Minneapolis, MN 55407. Nonprofit home for neglected and/or abused children, a program of Catholic Charities. www.osjspm.org

- US Department of Commerce. Statistical Abstract of the U.S.,107th ed. (Washington D.C.: U.S. Government Printing Office, 1987), 63, for statistics on divorce and separation after parental grief.

- Wilder, Thorton (1897-1975). Quote, "There is a land of the living and a land of the dead and the bridge is love."

Discussion Questions

- How was Dick's, JoAnn's and Danny's grief different from each other? How did their grief portray the differences between genders?

- What distinguished Danny's childhood grief from Dick's and JoAnn's? What are the traits of childhood grief that differ from an adult?

- What contributed the most to the different ways they grieved? (e.g., family and friend support, denial, addictions, openness with feelings, symbolism, upbringing, social expectations...)

- In your opinion, how did Dick and JoAnn's faith grow/diminish/change by Billy's death?

- Do you think that the spiritual communications/signs were real or just hopeful wishes? If they were signs, in your opinion, do you think they were sent from God or the deceased?

- What was the last emotion that JoAnn and Danny had to let go of in order to move on?

- How do you think Dick and JoAnn could have avoided their marital difficulties after Billy's death?

About the Author

JoAnn Kuzma Deveny grew up in Hibbing, Minnesota and graduated with a Liberal Arts degree from the University of Minnesota.

JoAnn has appeared on Fox National News, the WCCO Morning Show, the KQRS Morning Show, and other media events commenting on her humorous air travel book, *99 Ways to Make a Flight Attendant Fly—Off the Handle!* She has appeared in featured articles in *US News & World Report*, *Parenting Magazine*, and additional publications.

JoAnn still resides in her lake home in Mound, Minnesota and continues her flying career. On weekends, she is a piano and organ accompanist at her local churches.

~ ~ ~ ~ ~

Please visit JoAnn's website at www.whenbluebirdsfly.com or email info@whenbluebirdsfly.com.

She would appreciate hearing from you. JoAnn is also available to speak to your book club or organization as her schedule allows and would be happy to do book signings or talks to benefit worthy causes.